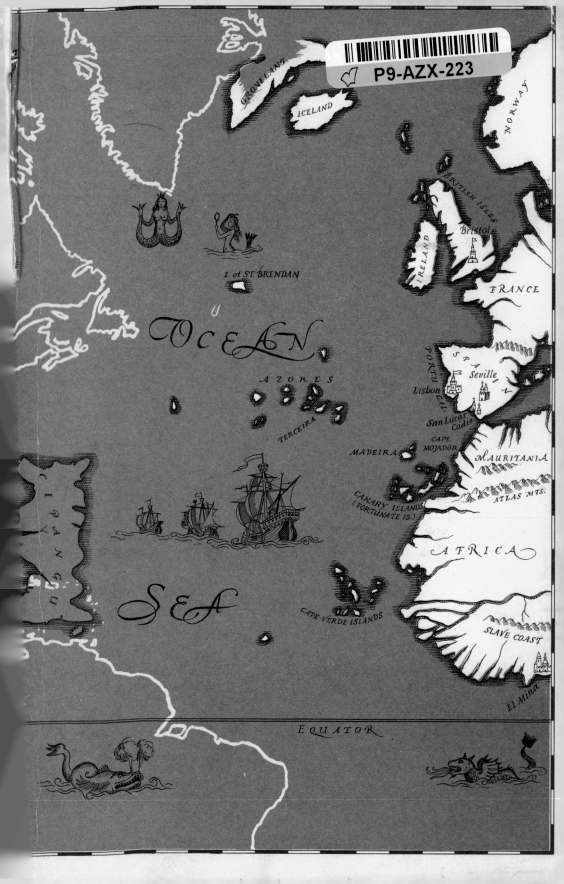

GROENLAND

ICELAND

NORWAY

BRITISH ISLES

IRELAND

Bristol

FRANCE

I. of ST. BRENDAN

OCEAN

PORTUGAL

SPAIN

Seville

Lisbon

San Lúcar
Cadiz

AZORES

TERCEIRA

MADEIRA

CAPE
MOJADOR

MAURITANIA

ATLAS MTS.

CANARY ISLANDS
(FORTUNATE IS.)

CIPANGU

AFRICA

SEA

CAPE VERDE ISLANDS

SLAVE COAST

El Mina

EQUATOR

Mainstream of America Series ★

EDITED BY LEWIS GANNETT

NEW FOUND WORLD

BOOKS BY HAROLD LAMB

"The subject and matter herein contained is the fourth part of the world, which more commonly than properly is called *America:* but by the chiefest authors *The new world. New,* in regard of the new and late discovery thereof made by Christopher Colon alias Columbus, a Genovois by nation, in the yere of grace 1492. And *World* in respect of the huge extension thereof which to this day is not throughly discovered . . . especially toward the North and Northwest."

RICHARD HAKLUYT, A.D. 1600.

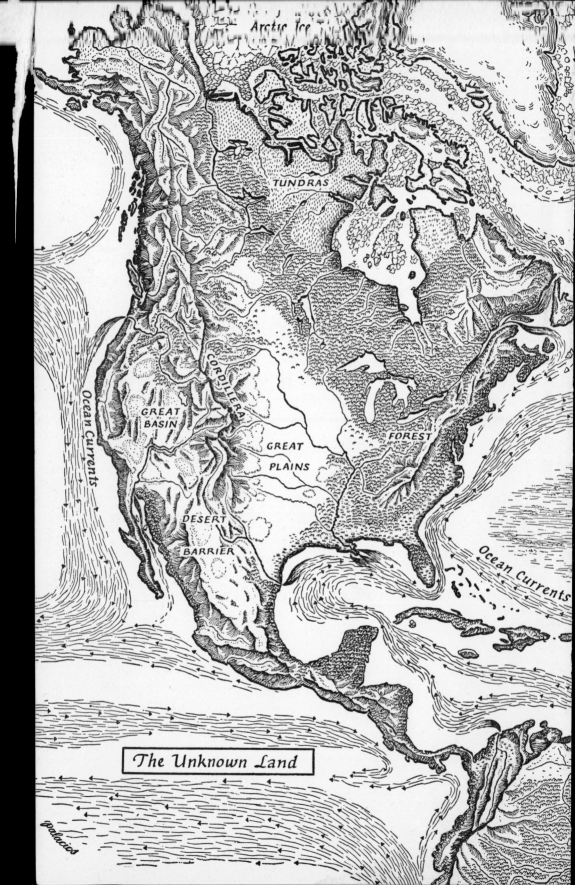

The Unknown Land

NEW FOUND WORLD

How North America
Was Discovered
& Explored

By HAROLD LAMB

DOUBLEDAY & COMPANY, INC., Garden City, N.Y., 1956

Foreword

THIS book ends with the year 1600, in which Richard Hakluyt
wrote his evaluation of *America*. It is primarily concerned with
the portion of the new-found world comprising the modern United
States and Canada.

Even 107 years after the Genoese "alias Columbus" set foot
on its remote islands a chronicler like Richard Hakluyt was filled
with the wonder of this unknown fourth part of the earth opening
up to the voyages of discovery. In his day what we call South
America held the center of the stage of public interest. For a long
time after that it held, for good reason, the chief interest of historical
narrators from Gómara to William H. Prescott.

The North American continent had within it no Aztec treasure
or Incan civilization. Its approaches were stormswept and forest-
screened; its people were ignorant and usually inclined to fight
for their liberty. It did not quickly yield up mines of precious metals.
Its first discoverers came upon no exciting glimpse of the great
South Sea; nor did they manage to find a passage through it. The
men themselves who first searched its coasts were usually adventurers more intent on keeping alive than on writing journals of their
voyages. For this reason their story remains obscured; it appeared
to be one of failure rather than success.

Yet it has become the heritage of our nation.

Contents

NEW FOUND
WORLD

I. The Unknown Land

The Outlying Island

THE sun set in a clear sky on October eleventh. The three vessels changed course a little, pointing their bows due west. A fair, strong breeze drove them on until moonrise. Lookouts on the foredecks had good visibility ahead and they kept a sharp watch because the Captain General had warned them of the danger of running ashore during the night. He had also promised to reward with a silk shirt and 10,000 maravedís of coin the man who first sighted land.

The crews of the three small vessels, however, were less fearful of sighting white water on a lee shore ahead than of not coming upon land at all. For a month they had voyaged toward the setting sun across the ocean that seemed to have no end except in the mind of the foreign Captain General. Yet they hoped and prayed zealously that the long voyage would end soon—having seen birds flying steadily across the moon toward invisible land ahead. That very day the men on *Niña* had picked up a floating branch with green leaves, while those on *Pinta* who watched the water had gathered quite a collection of driftwood, including one piece that seemed to be a board and another shaped by tools. All these must have drifted out from land not too far away.

The Captain General said so. He even offered to turn back, as so many of them besought him to do, to their port of Palos—if they did not come upon land in the next two or three days.

Through the early night the strong breeze held; the three caravels sped on beneath the rising moon. *Pinta,* which had gathered in so many vestiges of land, led the other caravels. *Pinta's* captain, Martín Alonso Pinzón, had ordered her largest cannon to be loaded and primed in readiness to be fired as the signal of discovery.

Discovery came in the early hours of the morning, with the moon high behind them. The foredeck lookout saw a white blur ahead, above the vague line of the horizon, and then another near it. These might be patches of sandy shore. The canny Basque sea- man scanned them in silence a moment, for others had shouted at phantoms of land, and the Captain General had declared that the next watcher to raise a false alarm would lose all reward. . . . A dark line now appeared along the whitish heights, joining them together above the sea. *Pinta's* lookout called his captain. Martín Alonso scanned the shape on the water ahead of them for a moment and ordered a match touched to the heavy lombard. It flashed and roared, rousing all the sleepers of the three ships in the quiet of that early morning of the twelfth of October in the year 1492 of Salvation.

When the smoke of the signal gun drifted clear, the largest caravel, *Santa María,* hauled alongside and the Captain General, Christopher Columbus of Genoa, called merrily "Señor Martín Alonso, you have found the land!" Thereupon he ordered the sails taken in except for the main courses, and the three ships kept care- fully away from the moonlit shore until sunrise revealed it to be a small island with refreshing green tree growth above the gleam of coral sand.

By daylight they easily circled the southern tip of the island. They sighted a break in the outer coral reef and felt their way in to anchorage in quiet water. Being thus on the lee shore of the island, they had no trouble lowering the clumsy small boats and rowing to the shelving sand beach where groups of strange naked people ran about excitedly, making signs and sounds of welcome. Those sea- men who had been fearful as late as the evening before kneeled down and kissed the hard ground gratefully: now they hailed the tall, moody Genoese with the red hair as Admiral and Viceroy, because he had found the land beyond the Ocean Sea, which he had predicted would lie there on their course, and over which his discovery gave him the title of Admiral, and the right to govern for the Crown.

The Admiral himself, with the Señores, the brothers Pinzón, accompanying him, brought ashore that Friday morning the bright banners of the Crown, each having a green cross with the letter *F* at the end of one arm and the letter *Y* at the other. These letters stood for the names of the sovereigns who had sent him upon the voyage, the harsh Ferdinand of Aragon and the well-wishing Isabella of Castile—now no more than thirty-three days' of sailing from distant Christendom. The Admiral had himself rowed around the small island, which he claimed for these his sovereigns. It was little more than a dozen miles in length, hard with coral growth, and beset with salt lakes. No more than a sentinel post, he deemed it, of the marvels that must lie beyond it.

To him and the seamen of the three ships that weekend gave almost fantastic joy. The caravels snug at anchor, the fair trade wind stirring the hardwood trees green as a garden of Castile in the spring, the gentle inhabitants, graceful as animals, painted in bright colors, plunging from their tree-trunk canoes to swim about the boats of the navigators, the women especially, who responded to the first embrace of a ship-weary Castilian—all this transformed the small island into a dreamlike haven. The seamen could get all the food they wanted, with parrots for souvenirs, for a few hawk's bells and glass beads. Simple souls they thought the strange people to be. "Gentle," the Admiral described them, writing his report to the sovereigns, "and capable of making good servants." With a thought for the future he added, "Fifty armed men could subdue them, and make them do all you wish."

It did not trouble him as yet that these inhabitants of the isle he called San Salvador appeared to be *different* from others and unaware of civilization. As a seafarer, he and the brothers Pinzón and shrewd Juan de la Cosa had come upon tiny backward islands before, of dumb shepherd folk or savage black folk, fit to be made slaves.

After daybreak Sunday the Castilians in their joy sang *Salve Regina, Mater Misercordiae.* Then the Admiral and the captains and Escobedo the secretary agreed to sail on to reach the great and rich island of *Cipangu.* This was, in their belief, the true outpost of the continent of Asia that they sought in their ships.

But Cipangu was not there.

The three caravels made their way into enchanted waters. Islands stood on the horizon, islands "the fairest that eyes have ever seen," wrote the Admiral, their discoverer, in his journal. The air here was milder, the sky clearer than on the coast of his homeland, Europe. Around his masts swarmed birds of magical coloring and sweetest sound. (But there were no animals except small dogs to be seen on the scented, emerald isles.)

Smiling men of that first island accompanied the ships as guides; eagerly these quiet natives pointed the way toward what the Admiral or his captains desired. Where were the islands thickest? *There*—to the south and east. Many? Yes, many, many. The largest? *On*—to the west. Did that great island have ships like these, with sails like those above, for the wind to drive? Yes, yes—on ahead toward the setting sun. And the caravels went on, to sight a coast where rivers flowed and mountains rose beyond, and the pine trees were tall as the masts of *Santa María.*

The tawny native guides understood no words of the navigators; they interpreted sign language according to their own ideas; and their chief desire was to please the masterly seamen by pointing out the way to the next island—which was the sum of the knowledge of the naked Arawaks of the islands. In the eyes of the Arawaks the robed Castilians armed with shining metal were men from heaven; their ships were houses that they moved over the sea by supernatural skill in raising mats upon bare roof poles. On their part the navigators believed the islanders to be gentle folk, happy to serve them—undoubtedly primitive Indians because they dwelt here beyond the coast of farthest India.

On both sides they were mistaken.

It seems incredible to us that the navigators of the three ships

—picked men, all the three crews—should not have suspected at once that in reaching the island fringe they had set foot upon *terra incognita*. The plant life was as strange as the human life. It simply did not occur to them to think any such thing. They had crossed the width of the Ocean Sea that separated Christian Europe from pagan and immensely wealthy Asia. The copies of two world maps in the Admiral's chest showed only open water between Palos and the unknown eastern coast of Asia. Moreover the only Christian who had sailed at all along that nebulous coast—Marco Polo had been dead for some two centuries—reported thousands of islands lying to seaward, the "isles of India." Some of these isles, said Messer Marco Polo, had wine-giving trees, spiceries, and harvests of pearls where "the people all go naked and wild as beasts." Well, something of all that was visible here.

And exactly here, by the Admiral's calculations, they should be sighting the largest of the isles of India, *Cipangu* (Japan). This Cipangu, according to Marco Polo, lay 1500 miles out on the high seas from the coast of Asia, and it had streets paved with gold two fingers thick, leading to "a palace entirely roofed with fine gold."

With that description very much in his mind, the Admiral wrote, on sighting the coast of Cuba, "Here I mean to sail around this island until I have speech with its king and obtain from him the gold I believe he has . . . but in any case, I am resolved to keep on to the mainland, and to present the letters of Your Highness to the Grand Khan, and to beg for a reply to bring home."

For not only did the guiding Arawaks devote themselves to pointing out what they fancied their Castilian heavenly masters sought, but the Castilians fancied their destination lay where the "Indians" pointed. Columbus hoped that the Arawak word *Cuban-acan* for middle-Cuba, might mean *El Gran Can* or the Grand Khan of Cathay. Inland, beyond the hills, might lie one of the fabulous palaces of Cathay where robed mandarins were carried in palanquins over stone bridges and princes gave out emeralds and rubies as souvenirs. So he sent his interpreter inland, Luis de Torres, who knew Hebrew and a little Arabic, with an experienced captain who knew how to greet kings in Africa.

These ambassadors returned without sighting a vestige of Cathay in the palm huts of a king's village where the folk inhaled through their noses the smoke of burning herbs (tobacco rolled into cigar form). They also ate beans from clay bowls, and slept in beds of woven cotton suspended in the air.

Perhaps after that the navigators of the three ships might have returned to Europe with no more than some scented woods and poorish cinnamon and the odd, friendly Arawak guides. They might have reported to the sovereigns, Ferdinand and Isabella, their failure to reach Cathay, if it had not been for two things: the determination of the Admiral and the sight of real gold. The lonely Genoese who led them refused to believe the evidence of his eyes, that these islands had little resemblance to those described by Marco Polo. In his mind's eye the coast of Cathay, with the teeming city of *Quinsay,* lay somewhere beyond the horizon; around the next point his mast-head lookouts would sight a sailing junk laden with the silks and ivories of the East. He had come upon these islands where he had calculated the isles of Cathay would lie. Their discovery could mean nothing but that. What man of his caravels would be idiot enough to imagine—as one or two already whispered to their fellows—that this was an unknown part of the earth, hidden away in some unaccountable manner until they set foot upon it? Such was the conviction of Christopher Columbus, now Admiral of the great Ocean Sea. During all his lifetime he would hold to it. And he was wrong.

Perhaps doubt assailed him already. Had he found a single object among these dreamlike islands that would prove he had sailed to Cathay, or the dominion of the Grand Khan? There was only the gold—tiny drops of it worn in the nostrils of some of his Arawaks. Stubbornly he questioned them by signs. If there was no such gold to be found on the greatest island, where did it come from? Again, as before, the natives tried to please the lord from heaven. By gestures and murmured words they assured him that what he sought could be found on the island to the eastward. Much of it? Yes, much indeed of it. Where? In *Cibao.*

To the navigators, listening greedily, the word *Cibao* sounded like Cipangu. And the Arawaks had told the truth. There, almost within sight on a lofty, fertile island the Castilians beheld thin, beaten plates of gold in the hands of chieftains and gold eyes and tongue upon a mask. "I believe they obtain little of it here," the Admiral wrote, "yet I hold that they are near to where it comes from, and much can be found."

An old man related by signs how the precious metal filled a land not far away. There people sifted it from the earth, melted it into bars, shaped it into statues and shields—thousands and thousands of them. "May our Lord in his goodness guide me to find this gold, I mean their mine of it," the Admiral wrote eagerly. To this island (Haiti) of little gold and much promise he gave a proud name *La Isla Española,* Hispaniola, as others came to call it. It seemed to resemble Spain. There, on a feast day, he displayed his banners and fired the lombards of his vessels in salute.

For they had found gold beyond the sea. They had evidence at last of the nearness of the treasures of Asia.

This glimpse of treasure to be had stirred rivalry among his captains. Martín Alonso, who had sighted land first, deserted the Genoese to sail first to the *Cibao* of gold; Juan de la Cosa, "the Biscayan," allowed his own vessel, *Santa María,* to pound herself to a wreck on a reef of coral rocks. Out of her timbers the Admiral had a small fort built on the bay behind the reef. There at Navidad he left the men of the crews who could not be crowded into the two smaller caravels. There, among the friendly natives, they were to await his return to Hispaniola, the region of gold where "the Lord had displayed so much favor to them."

With *Niña* and *Pinta* the Admiral departed to seek with his sure instinct the northerly current of the ocean and the winter winds that would speed him homeward. With him, as evidence of his discovery of farthest Asia, he carried bits of gold, scented woods, flame-colored parrots, and some of the "Indians."

But the men of the two ships would never see again their shipmates left in the wooden fort upon Hispaniola. Nor would they ever set foot on the continent of Asia.

Behind them lay an unknown continent.

The Area of Silence

It had not risen from the sea abruptly as a volcanic islet does. It had been there since the oceans themselves rose upon the earth. It stretched from the north polar icecap to its rocky tip in the south polar storms. This New World, as it would soon be called, was ancient as the threefold land mass of Europe-Africa-Asia, presently to be termed the Old World. Lying apart, behind the barriers of the two great oceans, the continent had developed life of its own beyond the knowledge of the human beings who appeared within the Eurasian continent and penetrated in due course to Africa.

This undreamed-of continent had one peculiarity. Human life came to it very late.

Exactly how late no one can say as yet. During the last of the ice age when the glaciers retreated, not more than 30,000 and not less than 10,000 years ago, there was still a land bridge to this remote continent. It stretched across the fifty-six miles where shallow Bering Strait now lies. Over it came and went hardy animals, among them the mammoth, musk ox, and giant elk. In the tracks of the animal herds followed dawn-age hunters able to make fire and endure on the fringe of the glacial deep freeze.

The land bridge itself was caused by the lowered sea level during the ice age. At least one animal crossed it, westbound—the small horse of that dawn age, which died out in the unknown continent yet survived in Asia.

Perhaps for a few millenniums a geological chance kept open the western (Siberian) and eastern (Alaskan) approaches to the land bridge into which fertile plant life drew the grazing animals and the beast herds drew the human hunters. There may have been a warm corridor of meadow and small-tree growth leading up, past the bitter ice of the more western plain, to this northeast corner of Siberia. The glaciers had a way of opening up at times when they melted away and advanced again. And on this side of the bridge, for an interval lasting until some 12,000 years ago, there were similar warm corridors with game-filled forests in Alaska. Moreover something seems to have happened to the hunting people of northeast Siberia about the end of the last glacial age. Most of them disappeared.

It is a logical guess that the missing hunters were over in the Alaskan game preserve by then, without the least realization or concern that they had changed ground from one continent to another. It is more than a guess that the people of this shadowy migration had middle Stone Age abilities and were rather of mixed race than Mongoloid. Non-migrants who turned back the other way to the Yenisei headwaters left traces that somewhat resemble objects that came to light on this side the ocean.

Actually the route of such a dawn-age journey is not so long as we might think. From the Altai Mountains, for instance, a great circle course leads across to Alaska and down into the valley of the Mackenzie River, where actual migrants left traces. Probably there were many such migrations; certainly some bands of Homo sapiens survived to follow the animals south into the new continent.

These enduring hunters came from no convenient "lost" continent of Mu in the Pacific, or a drowned Atlantis; nor did they arrive from anywhere else on imaginary fleets ages before the building of ocean-going vessels. They walked on their feet, following the herds that sustained them where rivers fed by melting ice tore out inland paths—perhaps up the Yukon and Mackenzie, perhaps along the Liard and Peace rivers. Probably most of them followed the coast where sea mammals and fish gave food. In time some appeared along the southern coast, separated by the snow and ice of the Great Basin from those who followed the east slope of the Cordilleras down to the great plains.

These vast plains stretching from the Rocky Mountains to the eastern rivers and woodland became the crossroads, the dispersal area, of the earliest migrations. From the plains the questing human bands disappeared into the wilderness—east toward far lakes, southeast toward the Father of Waters, south toward warmer valleys.

Few of them, however, retraced their steps toward the northern snow and ice.

When the vast ice sheets melted, and the oceans rose, the land bridge to Asia vanished some 9000 years ago, and the approaches to it also began to change. On the Siberian side dense taiga and stunted forest filled the once fertile, warm corridor and life became harder, the climate colder. On the Alaskan side the giant beasts died off, for reasons unknown; the game preserve became a cemetery. The dawn-age migrants were in the new continent, America, to stay.

Already its peculiarity was shaping the humans who came to it so late. Man in America was dwarfed by the wilderness and the animal life around him; as the millenniums passed he remained the one everlasting minority, and, to survive, he had to adapt himself to the environment immediately around him. As that environment varied throughout the immensity of the continent, he varied to conform to it. His search for game and plant life led him to the farthest corners, south of the retreating ice sheets.

As the glaciers melted, heavier rains fell, through centuries, and the saturated humans survived in caves or huts by swollen rivers and lakes. Then came greater warmth, followed by the slow drying out of the plains that drove many of the human groups to seek greener valleys. Some of them showed ingenuity in making fine flaked-flint weapon points, and leverage spear throwers. The throwers might have been carried over from Asia in forgotten times, but the peculiar ("Folsom") flint points were a native American product.

The hunters who used them did not, of course, expect to kill a giant bison of that time by throwing even a leverage spear with a beautiful flint point. Instead they formed into teams to drive a bison herd over a conveniently hidden cliff or into a lake-morass where they could slay the injured beasts with their spears. As the larger ice-age animals died out or drifted back to the north, the humans increased their skill as hunters. Families collected into villages.

But the hunting villagers did not coalesce into greater communities; their chieftains followed new game trails to fresh corners of the wilderness. Small subsistence villages, whether in cliff caves or hide lodges, remained the unit of social life in North America. As time went on the people spoke in different dialects and became strangers to the other bands on other hunting grounds.

When dominant groups appeared on the horizon of weaker bands, the weaklings moved on, often changing their rude culture as they shifted from grassland to woodland. Such refugee groups found safety in the farthest corners—the swamps of Florida or the sea-girdled Newfoundland. The first of the Eskimo folk (whose ancestors had hunted reindeer in Siberia) apparently gave up living on the caribou herds above the Great Lakes and withdrew to the sub-arctic shores where they learned to live in different fashion upon sea animals.

Perhaps the appearance of later migrants around the lakes forced the earliest Eskimo to move on into bleak, protecting cold. For, after the firstcomers, followed coppery-hued Mongoloids, a hardy, round-headed strain, whose remote descendants would be called the red men. Curiously enough, when the Castilian seafarers at long last intruded upon the inhabitants of the continent, they described the strange folk as the *yellow* men.

Through the prehistoric millenniums these human occupants of the vast continent effected little change in it. Forests dense beyond our imagining covered the eastern coast; grasslands endured in the great plains, kept clear by prairie fires and the grazing of great animal herds. The red men made no attempt to conquer the wilderness, being content merely to live upon it.

They remained, it seems, usually in small bands of a hundred or so. (It is estimated that they numbered a million or less on the northern continent at the coming of the Castilians.) Yet they held hunting grounds or clearings of their own—the more aggressive hunting groups holding the fertile inland rivers, the weaker members being driven to the periphery of the continent. This circumstance was to have an effect when invaders appeared from outside. Sandy, rock-ribbed seacoasts offered little food to hunters; a coral-island fringe attracted only refugees like the mild, grain-eating Arawaks, while only dislocated food gatherers roamed the inland frontier, the deserts of the Rio Grande where no game endured.

Isolated in this fashion from each other, the native folk had no sense of a larger humanity. They had a vague name for themselves, meaning "The People" or, more emphatically, "The Real People."

As yet they had not known human masters.

Meanwhile in the Old World civilization had arisen. It spread from the highlands of Central Asia as people migrated to the inland Caspian and Mediterranean seas. It domesticated some animals, taming the swift wild horse, moving swiftly upon animal-drawn wheeled carts, speeding to warfare with chariots. It raised food by cultivation, mined iron ore to make weapons. After that it sought safety in walled cities, and began to leave records of its progress in writing, stamped in clay, carved upon stones or traced on dried, pressed reeds.

But it hardly touched the unknown continent.

The way thither, the Siberia-Alaska land bridge, had vanished millenniums before when the vast ice sheets melted, raising the level of the oceans nearly 200 feet. The joining of the Arctic Ocean to the Pacific caused several things to happen. Ice floes that had been pent up in the polar region came down through the narrow strait. This gap between the land masses became a gamut of winds and storms. It ceased to be a thoroughfare. No mass of human beings could cross on the ice.

Yet small groups did cross the connecting strait. Three heights of the submerged isthmus remained above the surface as islands to guide them. There was also the route of the Aleutian chain with a favoring current. One odd people negotiated the strait in skin boats. The Innuits, latecoming Eskimos, kept aloof in their orbit from Siberia to Hudson Bay. In their arctic meanderings they extracted and carved the ivory of walruses in the Alaskan area, and found a trove of it in the tusks of the frozen carcasses of mammoths on the banks of the Siberian rivers. But what the Eskimos may have learned about the new continent they kept to themselves.

Some other tribal groups followed the Eskimo across. The Athapascan may have been one of these last arrivals. Perhaps they were fugitives from human enemies. We know there was a vortex of conflict during the centuries 1200–500 B.C. in northeastern Asia. At that time the Hunnic horse nomads made a battleground of the steppes and moved against the communities on the Chinese rivers. The Huns with their powerful bows conceivably drove weaker forest folk toward the Siberian jumping-off place.

Whatever force impelled them across, the last migrants emerge a little from the complete obscurity of the dawn ages. They had the aid of dogs, domesticated from the Siberian wolf, and the greater aid of the spliced Asiatic bow. They were dynamic folk with tribal organization, able to make rude baskets, nets out of twisted cord, canoes out of trees, and harpoons out of almost anything. They painted or tattooed themselves by ritual and their own fancy.

With them came certain skills, to make corded pottery or carve designs of coiled animals of the Asiatic steppes. Perhaps they had some memories of their homeland, of protective animal spirits. They invoked a lion spirit in a land where lions did not exist, and they remembered the killer whale as the bravest of sea animals long after they had left the ocean.

They left behind as well one heritage of their Asiatic kinsmen —domesticated animals such as the invaluable horse, sheep, and camel. In the new continent no beasts like those had been tamed. Dogs could help their human masters more in hunting than in drawing loads. Turkeys and wild ducks in captivity yielded no more than meat and feathers.

The last of the migrants entered a world without any Huns in it. Henceforth they were lost to the eyes of the Old World, and as they scattered they were lost to each other.

In that Old World as centuries passed—perhaps twenty centuries from the arrival of the Innuit to the landing of the Castilians —the aspect of the Eurasian continent changed. There the clever parasite, civilized man, altered the face of the earth with his works. An observer from the stratosphere could have seen the great wall raised by the Chinese to keep out Hunnic invaders; canals joined rivers together; mines spewed the slopes of hills with their dumps; walled cities strangled tranquil harbors; sailing vessels spotted the deep blue of the seas. Inland, explorers from China reached the outposts of Rome; empires touched cultures or fought for supremacy. Seaward, first Phoenician, then Arab merchant craft girdled the continent.

During those centuries, however, that part of the continent of North America from the arctic orbit of the Eskimos to the empty barrier of the Rio Grande, with its deserts, remained in oblivion. It became in fact the Unknown Land.

Intruders

Intruders reached it by chance in the year 1000 of Salvation. Like the Eskimos, they followed a circuit a little south of the Arctic Circle from the shore of one island to another; but they arrived from the east in round ships from the Old World, and they were barbaric Norsemen.

By then European seafarers were capable of crossing arms of the sea, guiding themselves by sun and star clusters, if the reason for doing so were urgent enough. Hermits crossed the open sea from outlying Ireland in open skin boats to seek refuge in the farther Iceland. An outcast Norseman sailed his family farther on to find a new home beyond the law—and settled down with his serfs and some cattle on a sheltered coast, which was the southwest coast, of the Green-Land. It was a short voyage, because the white heights of Greenland could be sighted almost as soon as the peaks of Iceland fell below the horizon behind him.

In this settlement of Brattahlid, the Norsemen of Erik the Red had no thought whatever of an unknown continent next door; they knew themselves to be rather far out from Christian Europe, with which they traded walrus hides and ivory tusks, white falcons and white bearskins. It so happened in the year 1000 that Leif, son of Erik, missed his landfall on his Greenland home and brought up upon a shore farther west. There the wandering Norsemen found tasty wineberries growing wild on vines; they cut themselves a new mast from a sizable tree—there being no such timber on the bare

Greenland shore—and they headed back, east and north toward home. On the way Leif picked up survivors from a wrecked vessel, and all his relatives agreed that he should be called rightly Leif the Lucky.

One of them, Thorfinn Karlsefni, no wiser than Leif and not so lucky, set out a few years later to backtrack the wanderer's voyage. With a steady round ship and women and cattle, Karlsefni was prepared to settle on the coast of "Vinland the good" if indeed it were good enough. These matter-of-fact migrants stumbled across a bare, cold island that they christened Flatstone-land; they skirted a wooded coast, calling it Markland, or Forest Land; they inspected long beaches, wonderful to them, encountered unexpected currents, and ended up for the winter in a shallow, sheltered bay, fertile enough. This they supposed to be Vinland, and it may have been an inlet of the Gulf of St. Lawrence. It was probably Hudson Bay.

Some of them, or others after them, might have explored farther south toward Cape Cod because they told of sweet grapes growing wild and grass that did not wither in winter.

But the actual cold in their winter huts was bleak, and the native men, arriving in a flotilla of canoes, too hard and hostile for the liking of the Norsemen.

Except for ability to navigate larger vessels Karlsefni's crew did not differ much from these Eskimos of the coast. According to their story, made into sagas later, the natives were more frightened by a runaway bull than by Norse weapons; the Norsemen discovered that fragile arrows could wound more seriously than heavy iron swords. They called the natives Skraelings—the Scandinavian name for the Asiatic Lapp folk on the western coasts of the Old World. The survivors returned to Brattahlid with valuable timber, and two small Eskimo children picked up at Markland. Efforts to make the captive children talk intelligibly did not succeed.

With new generations the tales of the first crossings to Markland and Vinland became the sort of thing that old men remembered, and they were embroidered with action, magic, and mystery on the model of other Icelandic sagas. Yet the voyages themselves had taken place. The tough seafarers of Brattahlid had probed at

the coasts of the New World, around Labrador, without realizing
what lay beyond.

Their landfalls appeared casually in written records thereafter.
When Greenland became a bishopric, it included Vinland as well,
and at least one bishop in 1121 sailed out to visit the other coast of
his diocese, and apparently never returned. Timber was taken at
times from Markland, and at Bergen, the port of Norway itself, a
merchant vessel was noted as "coming from Markland."

It does not seem as if the Greenland colony took notice of more
than the coasts across from them. A stone found recently as far inland as Minnesota, beyond the great lakes, bears an odd inscription
resembling runes, as if a small band of wandering Gotlanders and
Norse had traced it, after losing ten of their fellows in combat with
natives. But the wording seems to say they were on an island, no
more than fourteen days from their ships. Certainly the survivors
never returned with an explanation. Scholars today are inclined to
disregard both stone and inscription. Brattahlid itself disappeared
without record after three centuries of isolation, leaving its small
stone churches and headstones for others to find. The human remnant of the colony must have merged into the hostile Eskimos.

In Christendom one chronicler, Adam of Bremen, a schoolmaster, described the discovery of Leif and Karlsefni only as "an
island discovered by many in that ocean, called Vinland." There
was nothing in the brief Latin words to arouse the interest of a
reader of the schoolmaster's manuscript. Anyone capable of reading
at all knew that the ocean was filled with scores of islands, some
having flaming volcanoes or interesting demons.

The few others who scanned the *Hauksbook,* the Icelandic
saga of Thorfinn Karlsefni, could not have been impressed by its
mention of vines and timber far off. There were plenty of vines and
wine also, and hardwood forests along the coasts of the Franks and
Saxons near at hand to the south. In fact kindred Norsemen had
invaded the island of England, to settle there. While others, seeking
farther for greater gains, had become masters of fertile shores in
the warm Middle Sea (the Mediterranean).

The Mediterranean world which had become the Christian

world of that day took no more thought of islands far off in the western sea, and still less of the Unknown Land beyond.

The Hidden Empires and the Great Families

About the time the Greenland colony disappeared from view in the northeast, something appeared in the southwest. A hunting tribe known as the Aztecs moved south from the barrier of the deserts and the Rio Grande. They migrated on, to a lake in the highlands of what is now Mexico and presently they found one of the hidden empires.

The New World had one outstanding peculiarity. Its northern continent was joined to the southern half only by a land bridge as narrow as Bering Strait. This isthmus, overgrown at its narrowest part with rain-fed jungle, was more of a barrier than a bridge. In forgotten times the earlier migrants had forced their way through the jungle neck—they were probably food gatherers rather than hunters—to an existence apart from the northern continent. Some fugitive groups found isolation in the swamps of the Amazon and the rocks of Tierra del Fuego. Those who gathered seed and roots from the luxuriant growth of the tropics learned to thrive upon agriculture. Up in temperate highlands, where grain could be harvested, the native corn was grown, and human societies formed around it.

In the secluded peninsula of Yucatan they advanced to city building, driving back the jungle growth to raise block dwellings and white stone temples. From one city the Maya evolved a league of cities, the Mayapán. They designed as well a human edifice of hieratic priests and dynastic nobles upon the base of the food-producing population. Around this creation of Mayan culture the neighboring Toltecs stretched their rule of empire from sea to sea. The Maya-Toltec empire was guarded from intrusion on the north by the desert zone, and to the south by the jungle mesh of the isthmus.

Below that isthmus the Chibcha society jealously guarded its secret of a different culture in the protection of mountains. Far down the western coast in the loftier Peruvian heights the Incas built their amazing strongholds, dedicated to their gods and their own protection. Remote from each other, the hidden empires advanced their culture to a stage comparable to the early Greek city states of the Old World. It was fragile as the brilliant feathers adorning the heads of their nobles, yet enduring as the stone glyphs that recorded their achievements.

Unlike the Greek, their civilization was autochthonous. The southern American empire builders had no convenient neighboring Cretans or mathematically minded Egyptians to teach them. Some interchange there must have been, of invention with seeds, fertilizers, fabrics, stonecraft, and metalcraft. But they built no Roman roads beyond their fastnesses, having no wheeled carts to use upon them; nor did trade caravans cross this continent where neither horse nor camel existed. Slaves and llamas served them for transport. They did not make use of money for trade.

These orderly societies were no sudden flowering in the wilderness, as they might appear to us to be. How many centuries had it taken primitive men to isolate and grow a dozen varieties of maize? Or to plan and build pyramid temples on sites already abandoned to the wilderness? The Mayan calendar, accurate as astronomical time, gives mute evidence of progress for at least sixteen centuries before the coming of the Europeans.

Efforts have been made for a long time to explain the mystifying Mayan or Incan culture by the arrival of idea men from the outer, civilized world—whether far-wandering Egyptians, voyagers in Chinese junks off their course, or Macedonian seamen seeking a new world to conquer after the death of Alexander. But the Pacific is wide, the winds westerly, and fleets of cultured seamen seldom set out for unknown destinations.

The history of navigation between the far Polynesian island groups and the South American coast is not yet written, although much debated. Surely some seaworthy Polynesian craft might have reached that coast. Polynesian navigators found and colonized the remote Hawaiian group in the thirteenth century—and *somebody* reached the fantastic Easter Island.

Or it might have been the other way round. A modern balsa raft with a sail has been navigated along the westerly current from the coast to the far islands; Incan traders or migrants could have followed the same route. Incan culture, if not their corn, might have touched the outermost islands of Asia. No one knows.

Certainly a change came with the advent of the Aztecs and the settlement of what we call Mexico City in A.D. 1325. By their fierce cunning the hunters from the north overran the stagnating Toltec realm. In the process they absorbed in spite of themselves the Mayan-Toltec culture; like conquering warriors elsewhere, they settled down to enjoy the luxuries of a civilization that provided their food. They gathered a harvest of their own, of gleaming gold and radiant textiles, guarded in a citadel built within a lake.

Like the Incan strongholds, this city of the Aztecs was hidden behind the ramparts of mountains and the screen of coastal jungle, far from the sea.

Little of the miraculous science of the empires penetrated the barriers to the north, to the Unknown Land. There tribal man remained another sort of creature. There the kindred of the Aztecs who had stayed on the plains continued to hunt their food and cook it in coiled baskets heated with stones from the fire.

Yet a few secrets of Mayan-Toltec wisdom did pass up beyond their guard posts and the desert zone. The secrets of maize seed, of making firm pottery, and weaving cotton on looms reached the northern continent ages before the coming of the white men. Groups of "Pueblo" (Town) folk built great cliff dwellings and open towns where the dry earth yielded little game and the gathered families had to cultivate and irrigate the ground for food. Centuries behind the Mayas in culture, the Pueblo dwellers formed the beginning of societies. They were, however, a mixed people, migrants from the plains, living only as great families, unable to coalesce or repel strong invaders.

Yet they developed a tranquil way of life, suited to their land.

They painted with sand, danced with pine branches in hand, cherished the turquoise with its blue of the evening sky, and communed with invisible earth spirits in the kivas built deep within the ground. Their laws, religion, and the education of children they kept in their minds without the aid of writing. No Athens arose in the mesas above the headwaters of the Rio Grande, but the invisible tie of humanity united the Pueblo dwellers.

Farther north where the families of the plains followed buffalo, elk, and antelope herds the advent of corn appeared miraculous. From seed it sprang to life, multiplying in life-giving ears. These people made invocation to the Corn Spirit, with the spirits of the sky that they had feared from immemorial time.

One family of the northern plains, the Pawnee, mastered some rudiments of astronomy. They learned to calculate the passage of time by observing the movement of star clusters in the night sky. They had no instruments, nor could they write down their discoveries; they retained it in memory. Others, less knowledgeable, called the Pawnees "The Great People."

The notion that all the primitive folk of the Unknown Land were nomadic wanderers is not true. Where they could cultivate river land they clung to settlements of clay or bark and they fought to the utmost to defend both homes and fields. (The Pueblo families were forced by drought to abandon their cliffside apartments to seek water on the upper Rio Grande.) Only far inland on the prairies did the tribal folk wander habitually. There a group of families could halt for the night where a single buffalo had been killed. From it they took the horns for implements, the sinews for cords, the hoofs for glue; the meat they boiled, seasoned with guts in a makeshift caldron of the green hide. The neck hair could be woven into garments or tents.

No, the great majority of these tribal folk had not risen above a rude New Stone Age culture; they had no contact with any other, and little with the other humans. One family group, the Athapascan, last of the Siberian migrants advancing to settlements on the great lakes, were driven north to seek safety in tundra and forested waterways. These Athapascans reverted to the northern way of living, or rather getting around—by snowshoe, sled, or bark canoe when the ice melted from the streams. Others found their way to the Pueblo peoples. Still other aboriginal tribes sought refuge in California from the advance of the more aggressive hunters of the northwest. On this sheltered southern coast simple food could be gathered easily and they had no need to contrive better ways of living. These refugees of the southern Pacific coast increased greatly in population, but never raised themselves above primitive life.

Still, traces remain of collective efforts toward rude culture elsewhere. Along the central rivers an obscure people tried to settle upon earth mounds so huge that the labor of raising them rivaled the building of the stone pyramids in Egypt. Like the pyramids, these mounds had definite design, religious more than practical. The mound dwellers shaped a pottery of their own and ornamented themselves with pearls from the southern rivers. Then, for unknown reasons, they left their earthworks.

Only the Iroquois, clustered around the eastern lakes, held together strongly. They built long, communal houses, starting to join themselves together in a league for protection and further conquest. Like the pueblos of the southwest, the mounds of the midway rivers, and the stargazing of the Pawnee, the long house of the Iroquois marked a significant stage in aboriginal society.

A few centuries more and the Iroquois might have tapped the Mayan lore. Or the scattered Algonkins might have collected along the central rivers, to bring other groups under one developing rule as the Toltecs had done in Mexico. The strength of the Unknown Land lay embryonic upon the inland waters, not on the coasts that fronted the wastes of the seas.

What that native strength might have achieved and to what culture it would have risen will never be known. The first efforts toward growth of societies were interrupted. The native people of the Unknown Land never achieved their destiny. They became the Indians.

The invaders from the Old World were responsible for that.

They came back the next year in November, but not with three ships and three crews of reckless seafarers. This time the Admiral guided an armada of seventeen vessels, great transports and dancing pinnaces, loaded with some 1200 Europeans, including 200 gentlemen. They brought with them horses, cattle and fowl, seed, and the fittings of a church. This time they came to stay.

The Admiral led them to their new home as easily as a shepherd turns his flock home. All these varied vessels full of land seekers making their first ocean crossing he brought safely down to the Canary Island take-off and across the waste of water south of the Sargasso belt of calms. The northeast trade winds pushed them along. "In twenty-one days," an observer related, "they passed from land to land, the wind was so full and fresh with them."

Again at dawn the pilots pointed to land, this time the dark summit of a mountain. And the Admiral summoned all men to the afterdecks to sing *Salve Regina*.

He had found a sure way across the ocean.

Breaking the Ocean Barrier

Why had he come, and what force impelled the twelve hundred to follow him?

Since the beginning of human destiny the western Ocean Sea had barred the way out from Europe. Wind-tormented, vast and gray, it lay along the western horizon. Ancient men had a saying, "Beyond all things, Ocean; beyond Ocean, nothing."

Its storms that flooded over the coasts, the mystery of its tides appeared supernatural. Within its pulsing depths must lie some wonder to be revealed. Homer imagined "the Elysian field and the end of the earth . . . where life is easiest." This myth of a blessed abode beneath the sunset persisted for millenniums, in the hidden Fortunate Isles.

The practical Phoenicians probed the western sea, and Carthaginians pushed their colonies down the shoulder of Africa. Arab navigators, following long afterward, struck upon the Hawk Islands, or Azores. But these Phoenicians and Arabs—as well as some venturesome Greeks—turned right or left at the Mediterranean exit to seek tin, ambergris, silver, or gold along the outer coasts. What they found they were careful to keep to themselves; in doing so they added more interesting particulars to the myth of a forbidden sea. Out there, they said, lay indeed the "Sea of Green Darkness." Nay, more, at one place no wind reached the stagnant water, covered with slimy plants in which monsters wallowed (a tall tale of the Sargasso area). Furthermore, they said, beneath the equator lay a zone of furnace heat where no humans could survive.

Home-abiding Europeans who hugged the shores in going from port to port knew a little of the heat of the Sahara Desert belt not so far away. It was both logical and exciting to believe that farther south, beyond the Sahara, the heat burned venturesome travelers to a crisp. Townspeople usually liked to believe in monsters beyond the horizon. (The legend of primeval sea serpents arising from the depths died out very gradually, if indeed it is dead today.) But the same citizens of the land often disbelieved the true stories of far-wandering navigators, like Pytheas of Marseilles who described a sea of ice near the arctic and mists so dense they seemed to be a blending of water and air.

The popular notion that the habitable world was flat had little to do with it. By that notion a ship reaching the edge of the earth would fall off. Experienced seafarers, however, kept on going as long as open water showed ahead. Astute scientists for at least twenty centuries had known, or reasoned, that their earth was a sphere, if not "a whirling orb." Strabo, a careful geographer of the lifetime of Christ, wrote decisively: "If it were not for the immensity of the Atlantic, you could sail from Iberia [Spain] to India by keeping to the same parallel." That is, due west. Seneca, a Spaniard of the generation after Christ, added "This sea is navigable if the wind is favorable."

So Christopher Columbus never had to argue before the courts of Portugal and Spain that the earth was round, not flat. The scientists who listened to him knew that well enough. All around those

courts stood statues of dead kings holding a scepter in one hand
and the *orb of the earth* in the other. Arab experts had been making
globes of the earth for a long time. Up in Nuremberg, enterprising
Martin Behaim (the Bohemian) had just finished a fine globe
showing Asia right across the sea from Spain.

Nor did the medieval Christian Church, contrary to opinion
often expressed today, lay down the dictum that the earth must be
flat. True, ignorant clerics argued hotly enough that their habitable
world must be flat because the Scriptures spoke of "the four corners
of the earth"—and how could human beings ever stand *up* on the
sides or bottom of a sphere? Thinkers like Roger Bacon and Alber-
tus Magnus knew better. Asked by a skeptic how water could remain
in place on a sphere the great Albert answered simply, "Because it
does so."

The trouble, in medieval times, was that most of the philoso-
phers kept to their studies away from the sea, while all seafaring
men kept near the coasts on business—hiring out their vessels, going
after loot, or following the fishing banks, even as far as Iceland.
Those daring Norsemen, Erik and Leif, had been exiles looking for
a new coast.

Lacking such need of a refuge, other seamen avoided the open
Atlantic, afraid of its immensity—as Strabo put it. There was certain
risk in heading blindly west in small open vessels with square sails
that could not head into the wind. And what was the profit in
trying it?

Christopher Columbus believed that it could be done. And he
was given the means to do it, including the three decked caravels,
which could head close to the wind. He united, in his person, as it
were, the philosopher and superb seaman. Moreover he was willing
to go ahead blindly because he believed without question that it was
God's will.

And, undoubtedly, the need arose in his lifetime for *somebody*
to try to break the barrier of the ocean.

By that latter half of the fifteenth century the peoples of Western Europe were in extreme need. In order to understand what had

befallen them it is necessary to glance back at the changes wrought by centuries.

Once the enclosed Mediterranean Sea had been the center of the Western world's activities. It became the thoroughfare of the Roman Empire, which never managed to extend far from it. Yet always the vast hinterland of the continent exerted a pull to the eastward. There civilization had gone far in creating wealth and luxuries unknown to the barbaric peninsula of Western Europe. The great Constantine yielded to the continental pull in moving his reign from Rome, in the mid-Mediterranean, to his city in the eastern end, Constantinople. There, under the later Byzantine emperors, Constantinople tapped the trade of the eastern twin sea, the Euxine (Black Sea), and Africa as well. The Mediterranean ceased to be the center of Western rule even before barbaric peoples like the mis-called Vandals intruded upon its shores. Then came the conquest of the dynamic Islamic peoples, and the Christian nations lost the mastery of their one inland sea.

It was the darkest age for Europe, not for Islamic Asia. Enlightened city centers arose under the Kalifates, from Córdoba in Spain and Cairo in Africa, eastward to Damascus, Baghdad, Bokhara. And thither passed the trade routes to the wealth of Asia. In its new poverty—except for embattled Constantinople—and its new faith, Christendom tended to imagine a dream world in the forbidden East. There, beyond the horizon, lay the sanctuary of Christ. There grew the Tree of Life, there flowed the waters of salvation. At the end of land there in the farthest East rose the Mount of Paradise, guarded by everlasting flames, or perhaps out somewhere on an island. (Medieval geographers were never quite sure how to depict Paradise, but they always put it in, with the figures of Adam and Eve and the serpent coiling up the tree.)

Out of Asia came the precious things of earth, ivory and gold, jewels from "Solomon's mines," incense of Araby, with silk of mysterious Cathay (China) and such merely useful things as glass, paper, astrolabes, enamel, and spices. Inevitably, in wish fulfillment, arose the rumor of a fabulous Christian monarch ruling somewhere in the heart of Asia. Prester John was, a mysterious letter proclaimed, part priest, being *Presbyter* John. Out there, near Paradise, he reigned over seventy-two kings, and the wise Magi counseled him, giant ants dug up gold for him, fish salvaged jewels from the rivers for his treasury, pebbles gave out light, and a refreshing Fountain of Youth gave everlasting life. As for wisdom, a mirror in his palace revealed to him every day all that went on elsewhere.

The letter was an odd forgery, and Prester John a myth; yet the myth fulfilled the innermost wishes of home-dwelling Christian folk. Call it a delirium of the myths, but for centuries adventurous Europeans would seek to find somewhere the mysteries of Prester John. When little trace of him appeared along the routes of Asia, he was sought in hidden Africa, in Ethiopia, near to Solomon's treasures.

There was a brief opening of the eastern routes when the migration of the crusaders to the Holy Land set in, and the overwhelming Mongols created their serviceable post road across the continent to "Cathay." Toward the end of the thirteenth century Christian pilgrims could sail to the Holy Land, and merchants like the Polo brothers could be transported safely to China and back.

Then came the catastrophic closing of the routes, the loss of the Holy Land to the Moslems, the breakdown of Mongol control of the central continent, the ravages of the Black Death plague in Europe itself. In the early fifteenth century the young and aggressive Othmanli Turks ferried themselves across the Dardanelles into Europe. That did it. The Moslems of Andalus-Africa held fast to the other entrance strait at Gibraltar (Jebal at-Tarik, or Tarik's Height). The Mediterranean became a sealed-up sea.

The much-publicized capture of Constantinople in 1453 by the advancing Turks was no more than an incident in the containment of Christian Europe. What mattered was that the Turks now held the crossroads of Eurasian navigation and trade. They and the Persians tapped the arterials of the land routes to far Asia, while Arab merchants, having solved the mystery of the monsoon trade winds, went by sea direct to India, and Berber caravans drew out the resources of Africa.

Pent-up for the first time in their peninsula, the small Christian states fell to a dog-eat-dog conflict, in Hundred Years' War and sieges led by a Joan of Arc. Deprived of their Black Sea and Egyptian terminals, the galleys of Genoa the Proud and the Serene Republic of Venice fought each other for the last chance, the privilege of carrying trade from Moslem ports. Venice won a hollow victory. Curiously enough in one of those battles the world trader, Messer Marco Polo, was captured. In prison at Genoa, he whiled away his time by dictating his *Book of the Marvels and Wonders of the Kingdoms of the East.* In their dark frustration few Europeans heeded his tale at first, but presently they did so.

Despite their depression a ferment was rising in the Christians. Pent-up physically, they groped for new inward resources, in making things of their own. If the Sepulcher of Christ were indeed lost beyond the sea, pious Christians could adore a woman who braved the plague, St. Catherine of Siena. They evolved printing, which placed the Bible in ordinary homes, the true *Biblia Pauperum.*

With the printing press, ocean-going ships, and gunpowder, the medieval age was ending, the modern beginning. No one, however, was aware of that at the time.

But these first printed books of 1450-70 reflected the mysticism of the people rather than their hopes. The *Art of Dying Well,* the *Apocalypse*—when the trumpets of Judgment would summon humans to the end of earthly life—reminded readers that salvation would come only after they entered their graves. This mysticism colored their concept of the forbidden outer world. With the Judgment Day clearly drawing nearer they looked for miracles to transpire. One poor but determined prince of Portugal, Henry, who would be named "the Navigator," spent the funds of his religious brotherhood in fitting out vessels to seek, not a trade route around Africa, but some trace of the marvelous River of Gold, and a way to Prester John of Asia, who might relieve the sufferings of Christians, if not redeem their Sepulcher at Jerusalem.

In the universities of that day students turned from practical science to meditation upon a dream world. In their new printed books appeared the writings of the great lost days of Greece and Rome; the letters of Cicero were published before the *Physics* of Aristotle; the travels of the faker Sir John Mandeville, who told of miracles and monsters, became a "best-seller" rather than the realistic reporting of Marco Polo.

The Genoese navigator, Christopher Columbus, had been an eager reader while out of a job, like many other sea captains of the Italian ports. And he had read the prophetic book of Esdras, the mystical *Imago Mundi* of Pierre d'Ailly, Cardinal of Cambrai (more popular than the merely scientific *Cosmography* of Claudius Ptolemy of Alexandria, foremost geographer in the Roman age). And he had got his commission at last from the medieval and devout court of Spain very largely owing to the championship of the religious Isabella. He got it, not because he could demonstrate the scientific feasibility of such a voyage, but because unmistakably—at least in Isabella's eyes—he believed in miracles. He got it in spite of his exorbitant demand for viceroyal rank and royal percentage of profit if he succeeded.

In mid-Atlantic he had written to the "Most Christian Princes, King and Queen of the Spains and of the islands in the Sea" that he was seeking on their behalf "the lands of India and a prince who is called Grand Khan which means in our speech the King of Kings ... [to discover] ... the manner in which they may be converted to our Holy Faith."

Nothing could have been more mistaken.

India was not there across the Atlantic. The last of the actual grand khans of the far east had been driven back to their steppes long since. The few Nestorian Christians of "Tartary" clung to their churches far inland. The Ming emperors who reigned in the real China took no least thought for Christianity.

Columbus, however, had mentioned the islands in the sea.

The Fantastic Isles

Islands in the Atlantic appear unexpectedly. In that windy waste you come upon them suddenly, with a sense that they are intruders. The soft green summits of the Azores, the stained volcanic shoulders of Conception and the pillarlike Falklands—what are they doing there so far from other familiar land?

In the stress of the fifteenth century's end the eyes of Europeans on the coasts turned more and more toward the open sea. Some remembered ancient myths, and men who had never heard of Plato's *Atlantis* wondered if a happier land, *Antillia,* might not lie beyond the sunset. The way to the true Paradise in the east was hopelessly barred to them.

Then there was the tale of St. Brendan, or Brennain, who had ventured out from Ireland to sight a floating mountain of ice, and to moor his coracle upon the back of a whale. Surely the courageous Brendan had found his island of refuge beyond the sorrows of the Christian continent! As the Irish hermits had found their refuge on the Iceland.

Such remote isles were becoming important in wish fulfillment. Did not seven worthy bishops once escape from the Algarve of Portugal, at the coming of the Moslems, to some western isle where they shepherded their people into seven cities? This tale of the Seven Cities grew in the retelling.

Then there was the mysterious Brazil, or Brazl—"The Happy" —according to Irish priests who believed it might be found directly out from their own coasts. (The Brazil legend might have come from the persisting memory of an early North Atlantic passage from Ireland.)

Naturally enough pious fisherfolk, Catalans, Basques, or Portuguese, brought their dories in from the sea with exciting stories of mysterious land glimpsed in the flicker of lightning, or a far isle sighted at sunset which could not be found again. As early as the end of the thirteenth century two Genoese brothers headed their galleys to the west to seek the legendary islands. They did not return.

The concept of the farther, western isles was not confined to daydreaming monks in their cells or fishermen. It found its way into the medieval sea charts. Dogmatic Toscanelli (admired by Columbus) drew in *Brasil* just out from the Irish coast, with *Antilia* far west along the latitude of Gibraltar, and *St Brandan's Insel* opposite the known Cape Verde group. And commercial-minded Martin Behaim copied Toscanelli closely in drawing the Ocean Sea upon his new globe.

To scientists and would-be navigators alike this Atlantic ocean offered a real puzzle. As Columbus wrote from shipboard to his sovereigns, he was going upon a route "by which no one knows to this day for certain that anyone else has gone." The puzzle was to know what might lie upon this untraveled slice of the globe. From the familiar take-off points of Ireland or the Azores there must be quite a stretch of unexplored sea to the coast of Asia. Or was it sea? Some thinkers held it to be entirely water; others argued that some land must balance, as it were, so much sea. Had not the prophet Esdras proclaimed that habitable land covered six sevenths of the earth? In his day—A.D. 23—Strabo had pondered the riddle, remarking that it was a question whether "the spinning whorl of the earth was inhabited in its fourth quarter" also, and if so whether the men in the missing quarter were like his own kind. And Columbus assured his sovereigns that he intended "to make a new chart . . . on which I shall put the whole sea and lands of the Ocean Sea in their proper places, with proper bearings."

The best opinion, then, was that he would find more islands in the sea before reaching Asia, and this he did. The question remained what kind of land they were, inhabited by what sort of men, and whether they were in any way related to the long-sought Antillia, or the isles of the Seven Cities. The one thing no one anticipated was that an unknown continent barred the way and that beyond it lay another, greater ocean.

What Prince Henry Found

The quest for more and better islands in the Atlantic was by no means altogether a pursuit of myth. Real islands offered refuge and some riches. Madeira yielded wine grapes, and settlers in the mild Azores raised sugar. In 1456 the fertile Cape Verde Islands were rediscovered by the Portuguese. That was because of the driving impulse of one man, the prince without a throne, Henry "the Navigator" of Portugal.

Stark necessity led him to probe the southern Atlantic. Of all the hard-pressed peoples on the Atlantic seaboard the Portuguese were in the worst plight, being cut off on the land side by growing Aragon and Castile, while the nearby Mediterranean was made hazardous to them by Moorish sea power. They had to get out by the open sea or not at all. They had the courage to do this, being descendants of many crusaders and Moorish adventurers; they had skill, being in large part hardened voyagers after fish and the raw wool of the English coast.

Although called "the Navigator" afterwards Henry of Portugal probably never cruised out of sight of land himself. He set up a small school on the southern point at Sagres, to make his seamen into navigators. He abandoned the pursuit of the fisheries to explore, as one observer put it, "the secrets of the world." In so doing he drew on the lore of knowledgeable Jews and Arabs, like shrewd Jahuda Cresques, the cosmographer. In that way he tapped the secrets of early navigation, the trick of Phoenicians of taking bearings by the polestar, and of Arabs in making astrolabes (crude sextants that registered the height of objects above the level horizon) to do it. He sought, as a new-day crusader, to detour around the military power of Islamic countries, to reach the Río de Oro and the aid of Prester John. But he insisted on charting the route thereto.

To his outgoing captains he said, in effect, go south, map all the coast of Africa, mark your bearings, note all currents and prevailing winds. And then go farther south.

It took them twelve years to round the obstacle of Cape Bojador where the winds and current prevented a ship from returning, and the dread of the great stagnant sea lay ahead. "No ship," the legend had it, "that passes Bojador will be able to return." But one did. And south the Portuguese navigators drove, past the wastes of the dry Sahara belt, to green coasts. Those coasts revealed no River of Gold, but they yielded gold from some rivers—being christened by the navigators "the Gold Coast." They yielded another profit for desperate men, in tribes of black, untaught humans who could be caught, or bought, shipped back, and sold as slaves. That was the Slave Coast.

When the determined Henry died in 1460, his exploring ships had failed to contact Prester John, but had charted a navigable route to African trade. They had paid their way. The voyages went on, south and farther south—with Ca Da Mosto "Cadamosto" the Venetian and Diogo Cão, most daring of the Portuguese, leading. There came a year, 1487, when Bartholomeu Dias was driven far south by a storm, and, turning east to regain the African coast, found it was no longer there. He searched for it and discovered that he was on the east coast above the cape. Dias had rounded Africa and in so doing had found the sea route to India and the far east.

This great discovery decided the destiny of the small, stubborn Portuguese nation for the next century. It also sealed the fate of the Italian maritime cities locked up within the Mediterranean. When later Portuguese captains learned the route of the monsoon wind from the east African coast direct to India, they were able to tap at its source the vast wealth of "The Indies." The fleets of Venice, Genoa, and the one chartered by Florence were left to bargain for what they could take from the bazaars of the Nile and the Golden Horn.

The Mediterranean was ceasing to be the focal point of world trade. The Atlantic would be that.

Almost at once the Portuguese began to hide the knowledge of their new routes to Asia. One monarch, the determined John II, went so far as to imitate the secretive Phoenicians and Arabs of earlier explorations. Portuguese captains had banished forever the bogy of a ship-devouring leviathan far out on blue water, as well as the superstition that modern men could not survive in the burning heat of the equatorial belt. Under the very equator it seemed that men on shipboard could drink their wine and enjoy the breeze. But John bade his captains repeat the old tales of supernatural dangers. He even had several old round ships dismantled in full public view at the southern African gold port of El Mina, with the explanation that such ships could never beat their way back around Cape Bojador. Only the new Portuguese caravels, said the captains, could do that! The Portuguese kept silence also about their new navigation— how, for instance they were learning to take observations from the sun at noon in regions so far south that the guiding polestar had vanished beyond the horizon.

One secret the enterprising Portuguese kept so well that it remains a mystery today. Did they manage to reach the tip of Brazil in the west before Columbus sailed?

The northeast gales that sped the Genoese across from the Canaries to the Caribbean might have blown a Portuguese caravel the much shorter distance from the Cape Verde Islands (which the seamen of Lisbon frequented) down to the tip of South America. There is no proof that this happened, but fascinating vestiges of evidence make it seem possible.

A map of one Andrea Bianco, drawn in 1448, shows land sketched in west of Cape Verde—1500 miles west, according to the map's obscure inscription. The remark of an English geographer Robert Thorne generations later casually mentions the Portuguese in Brazil before 1494. A grant by John II gives a certain captain, Fernão Dulmo, privileges in an "island or continental land" of the Seven Cities in the west. Then, when Portuguese navigators did head west in earnest, they went to Brazil's tip as if on a known course.

Whether these Portuguese were the first to reach the new world in the south may never be ascertained; if they did they seem to have taken it for another island. In any case they did not reach the Unknown Land in the north.

One of the lessons learned by the scholars of Sagres aided mariners across the open seas. This secret could not be kept, because it was the design of their new ships. Rival captains could observe the innovations and rival shipyards build the new craft. Before then Mediterranean shipping—fragile, oared galleys or stout cargo round ships powered by the ancient square sail—could not live through Atlantic storms. (The Norsemen did get around the northern circuit in their open dragon ships and tublike cargo vessels, but the "Vikings" had their own way with a ship upon the sea—and they managed to keep a course without compass or instruments.)

The strong Arab lateen-rigged craft ventured out, being more maneuverable. Three generations of trial and error by the Portuguese of Sagres taught them what was needed to keep a vessel at sea for weeks. A fixed rudder, three masts, with a lateen rig on the mizzen to head into the wind, and a flying spritsail on the bowsprit to catch a stray wind—high prows and sterncastles to ward off raking seas. Dias, who rounded the cape, had a "caravel of the fleet" of this improved design, and Vasco da Gama would head for India with larger, more seaworthy *naus*.

So, thanks to the Portuguese, as the century ended there were vessels able to cross the Atlantic and instruments to guide them well enough.

Some long voyages were being made at need already. Fishing fleets cruised from the Tagus mouth to Iceland; Basque whale hunters voyaged hundreds of miles to their whaling grounds. The fleets exploring the outer seas, however, needed a government's aid to equip and supply them. Even Portuguese caravels of the fleet could manage to feed their large crews for little more than a month at sea. Even biscuit and salted beef or pork, eked out with vinegar and oil, soon wormed and rotted in tropical heat. Wine and water spoiled in the casks. Fleets advanced by stages, from one supply port to the next. The Portuguese possessed the cape route around Africa, not because Dias had discovered the cape, but because the monarch of Lisbon was master of the fortified bases like El Mina that lined the route. A questing caravel of rival Castile could not reach the cape because it could not supply itself from the chain of Portuguese bases.

More than that, crews had to be conditioned to the new, long voyages with the hazards of storm and the certainty of sickness aboard ship, and the necessity of keeping alive on strange coasts for months when they got there. While bettering their vessels and crews the Portuguese were also mapping the winds, currents, and harbors of the new routes. Captains like Dias came back to Sagres with charts entered up, as well as laden holds. No longer did Lisbon depend on famous Italian navigators who might give away her secrets. The Portuguese held fast to their monopoly of the outer seas.

The Genoese map maker, Christopher Columbus, had voyaged with them Africa-wards. He had used his eyes in their top-secret port of El Mina (The Mine). In one year gold dust to the value of 170,000 doubloons passed through El Mina terminal. Naturally Columbus had put before the court of Lisbon his single-minded enterprise of sailing west across the Atlantic to reach the same Asia they were seeking around Africa to the east.

Now Columbus was an able seaman; he could sense the pull of invisible currents and nurse a small boat through a northeasterly storm. (So he brought back *Niña,* no more than fifty feet on the waterline.)

The Portuguese had listened to him with attention. But the listeners were the young John II, "who spent his hours of rest in study of the outer world," and the new *Junta,* or Sea Council, which had in it skilled mathematicians, pupils of Rabbi Abraham Zacuto. Without hesitation they refused to give the Genoese a Portuguese fleet.

Superstition had nothing to do with this important refusal. A secretary, noting down the arguments of the redheaded navigator in search of ships, described him as "boastful" and full of fancies. ". . . because he read much in Marco Polo who spoke of the mighty isle Cipangu, he conceived that over this Western Ocean he could sail to Cipangu and other unknown lands."

The Portuguese mathematicians were right and Columbus
wrong. By their more careful estimation the coast of Asia lay distant
more than double the 3000-odd miles that the Genoese—and the
Junta was getting rid of Italian captains—vaguely believed it to be.
Even if this *Christovão Colomb* could take caravels safely that far
across the unknown part of the sea, how could he feed and water
his crews for such a time? The thing couldn't be done. And Columbus, as an experienced voyager, should have known that. The fact
that he argued for it made them instantly suspicious, and when he
invoked Marco Polo, it was too much for the Junta. A year or two
later this same John and the Junta readily granted their own captain Dulmo privileges to seek islands to the westward that might be
the Seven Cities. While they tracked down the eastern routes, the
Portuguese kept an eye cocked toward the unknown west.

Why had Columbus made such a colossal error in estimating
the distance from Lisbon to Asia? His own conviction led him to
it inevitably. While believing that God had willed ships to cross
the western ocean, his experience warned him that the crossing
must be made in a month or a little more (and he had trouble
enough, in the event, with his captains and crews in that length of
time). Therefore, in his devout mind, it followed that the distance
could not be too great.

He fed his enthusiasm with long nights' reading of "the an-
cients" who were being unearthed and published in the new books.
From them he collected every item that might show the one un-
known ocean to be narrow. Aristotle mentioned a "small sea." Good.
The greatest of geographers, Claudius Ptolemy (c. A.D. 90–168) in
Roman Alexandria, made out the land of Asia to be broad and vast.
Splendid—because then the sea connecting its end with Europe
must be narrow.

He sought for confirmation in Holy Writ, and found it, to his
satisfaction, in Esdras who was a dubious prophet in more ways than
one. He missed Strabo, who was too matter-of-fact to be popular in
awakening, credulous Europe. But he hit on Solinus, who had collected tales of wonders in ancient Spain in the third century after
Christ. Solinus (who also described dog-headed people and winged

serpents) wrote that the sea from Spain to India was navigable. If so, men could survive on the ships that crossed it.

Best of all a Frenchman, Pierre d'Ailly, a churchman and also a cosmographer, seemed to confirm Columbus's innermost thoughts. D'Ailly wrote in A.D. 1410: "Aristotle declares that the sea is small which divides the western end of Spain from the eastern point of India . . . of that other outer Spain which they call Africa now. Moreover Seneca, in his fifth book, on *Nature,* says that sea can be crossed *in a few days* with favorable winds."

If it could be done in a matter of days from Africa, it could be done in less from the outer Canaries, which Columbus had visited. Having marshaled in this way the authority of prophets, Roman geographers, and a French cardinal, Columbus proceeded, in his obsession, to doctor the figures of the scientists. Selecting the smallest figures hazarded by ancient scientific men for the size of the earth, he then whittled down their estimates by using the smallest measures. While Toscanelli placed the China coast some 5000 miles from Europe (less than half the actual distance) and Behaim charted it as 4400 miles away, Columbus came up with an estimate of 3550 miles. He knew that well-manned caravels, driven by steady trade winds, could survive that voyage.

Even if they failed at first to reach Cipangu of the gold roofs, they might fall in with other islands mentioned—even if not located —by the invaluable Marco Polo. There was *Malaiur* (Malaya) rich in spiceries, and Sumatra with its wine-giving trees, while Java the Less had eight crowned kings in eight kingdoms.

Cannily, in his first letter on shipboard to his sovereigns, the Genoese mentioned those possible "islands in the sea."

So it happened that Christopher Columbus broke the barrier of the Atlantic. And it befell that he did it, not for the scientific, exploring Portuguese but for the devout and less experienced sovereigns of Aragon and Castile, who sought to follow the Portuguese by sea into the outer continents.

It was an irony never to be repeated in human history that he led them to the wrong continent. When he returned thither in 1493, he brought churchmen and would-be officials and colonists who sought to convert, rule, and despoil the outer islands of Asia.

The impact of the Europeans upon the islanders was as forcible as the collision of three thousand years of time.

The Pearl Fisheries and Paradise

The Arawak islanders very quickly ceased to adore the unruly mob of Castilian adventurers. To the native mind these superior men from the sea were filled with the most deadly fantasies—demanding treasure for invisible sovereigns, obedience to incomprehensible laws, and submission to the ritual of a church.

To the uncompromising Spanish mind the native "Indians" were soulless creatures, no true descendants of Father Adam, who would not serve, work, or follow upon the blessed way to salvation.

At first, when a questing ship reached a new island, the Arawaks would throng around it in their log canoes, eagerly offering fruit, feathers, and oysters; but when driven to dig precious metal in mines, they would resist passively but stubbornly. (Already the mariners of the first voyage left at Navidad had been exterminated by the natives.)

The conflict of survival began when the Spanish stock of food gave out. The twelve hundred fortune seekers had no means of feeding themselves in this wilderness of islands beyond the sea. They forced the Arawak villages to cultivate the native vegetables for them; to keep the Arawaks at labor, they drove them from their villages into guarded pueblos. Native spears took the lives of some invaders, and massacres of the natives followed in vengeance. Bands of desperate—because half starved—Castilian crossbowmen raided sheltered mountain villages for food in their unending search for gold ore. Ironically the gentle Arawak population of the islands dwindled to extermination while the shiftier, raiding cannibal tribes, the Caribs, survived, until this island-locked sea was given their name, the Caribbean.

This conflict, begun in the Caribbean, between the native American peoples and the intruding Europeans would continue for centuries.

The disillusionment of the Castilian adventurers was complete. They beheld no evidence at all, in the deceptive beauty of the New Found Islands, of the wealth of Asia. Where lay the land's end of the Golden Chersonese, the junk-crowded river of rich Quinsay, and the palace of the Grand Khan? During the first years of disillusionment, 1493–99, most of the sick and weary Castilians sought for a passage home; they swore by a new oath—"As I hope to return to Castile."

The whole enterprise of discovery to the west might have been abandoned then by the Spanish monarchs if it had not been for their pride, their eagerness to follow the Portuguese across the seas, and the ambition of the minor captains of the fleets.

The Admiral, discredited by his own imagination, was driven to defend his claim that he had led them to the island gate of the Great Khan. After gleaning a small harvest of gold nuggets from the Cibao he writes joyfully that they are close to Ophir, the mines of Solomon. Pathetically, questing along the southern coast of Cuba in his ceaseless round of the islands, he marvels at the beauty of it, naming it the Gardens of the Queen, for his most steadfast friend Isabella. And hoping that the network of isles may indeed be that described by Marco Polo. A wandering captain reports seeing white-robed figures fleeing away into the jungle; the Admiral proclaims that these fugitives must be servants of Prester John.

But he sails unheeding past a boatload of strange natives clad in bright cotton garments, having utensils and shields of copper. This is his first and only contact with the real civilization of the Toltec-Aztec, hidden beyond the forbidding coast of Yucatan. Sighting the mainland so late (in his third voyage, 1498) the solitary Genoese can think henceforth only of redemption from disgrace, of the chains put upon him by an official of the Throne, and the command of his sovereigns to sail only as a navigator, no longer as Viceroy of the lands of the Great Gulf of the Ocean Sea.

For as Viceroy he has failed; he has not kept order in the des-

perate plantation settlements; he has not shipped back to Seville the
"good gold" such as the Portuguese extracted from El Mina. Driven
to imitate the Portuguese in drawing revenues for the Crown from
slaves, he has failed to squeeze taxes from the subjected Arawaks—
enough to pay expenses. It is the paradox of this unbalanced man
that he failed in his later years as explorer—which he was superbly
fitted to be—because he had shown himself incapable of serving as
governor—which he had no qualification to be.

Here on the coast of the mainland at last, behind lovely Trini-
dad—he christened the island so, believing it at first sight to be a
point of the mainland of Asia and so a miracle of the Trinity on his
behalf—he sights from his masthead the loom of dark mountains
and passes the mouths of a river too huge to be fed by island streams.
He reaps a harvest of pearls in a great gulf (Paria) but he rejects the
small trove of pearls for a fantastic dream of great discovery.

In the mildness of the still air, in the majesty of the heights van-
ishing into the clouds, his tired mind perceives a vision. This may be
no Golden Chersonese or swarming port of Quinsay; it is, incredibly, more. He is gazing upon the secret of the earth, Paradise
itself.

Does not this site of heaven upon earth lie on a forbidden height,
at the outermost point of *Asia*? Did not the revered D'Ailly say that
it lay here, in the hidden place of the sun's rising, whence the four
greatest rivers flow?

When his compass moves erratically off this mouth of the real
Orinoco, Columbus has an explanation of the phenomenon. Paradise must rise into the sky, forming a mound like the shape of a
pear's end upon the otherwise round earth. Like a woman's breast.
So it must attract the compass needle to it. . . .

Even the devout Isabella does not believe that. And Columbus
would leave the scenes of his enterprise in the end almost unnoticed.
He would nurse a leaking chartered caravel through the storms of the
Atlantic safely to his home, discredited after accomplishing what no
seaman has done, before him or since.

In his methodical traversing of the Caribbean, Christopher
Columbus had not quested to the north of it, where the Gulf Stream

would have brought him up against Florida. He never discovered North America.

No one else could depart at first on exploration because the Genoese, by terms of his one-sided agreement with the sovereigns, held a monopoly of that. With the failure of wealth to arrive from the west, the sovereigns ended his monopoly. Straightaway the little discoverers hastened in to seek kingdoms of their own that the blind giant had failed to find. After the word of pearl fisheries in the Gulf of Paria got around, the search became a race, in 1499–1500.

Many of the little captains, however, had been his shipmates and when it came to picking routes of their own they tended to follow where the Genoese had led, especially toward the pearls. They had chafed under his moody authority and were certain they could make landfalls of their own on the elusive Asian coast, or at least bring back a treasure.

The impetuous Alonso de Ojeda, who had danced on a rafter end to amuse Isabella the Queen, teamed with Juan de la Cosa, "the wisest pilot of these seas," to make a haul of pearls and explore an odd coast of villages astride waterways, like a funny little Venice— *Venezuela.* One of their vessels bearing a mathematical landsman roved away on a course of its own, with unexpected consequences. Its passenger was Amerigo Vespucci, unknown at the time.

In a flurry of kidnaping, thefts and wrecks, and hurricanes the little fellows sought new pearl and gold coasts. (They did not have Columbus's habit of careening and scraping his vessels, or his knack of riding out a storm.) Niño, who had been pilot of lucky little *Niña,* sailed in a derelict craft and returned to Santo Domingo safely with his sailors wreathed in pearl necklaces; ambitious Vicente Yáñez Pinzón kept on south to probe for a landmark of Asia, and reached the Amazon and the bulge at the end of Brazil, before his ships were seized for his debts. Silent Diego de Lepe went further and examined the coast line more closely. A pen-pusher of Seville, one Bastidas, caught the fever of discovery and outfitted a fleet with Juan de la Cosa to pilot it.

Bastidas, the amateur, alone quested far north of the pearls in Paria. His worm-eaten ships sank under him, but the luck of the novice preserved him, to walk back to Santo Domingo with wealth enough to retire in luxury.

These little discoverers broke out of the Caribbean only to the south. They found the outline of a great continent. It was a mainland, soon to be known as "the Spanish Main." For discovery meant possession of this ever-expanding wilderness of flowering jungle rising to mountains, cut by rivers huge beyond belief. No one could know, as yet, how far it extended to the south.

Meanwhile the Unknown Land had been discovered far to the north by a seaman from Venice with eighteen men in a small bark.

II. Riddle of the New World

The First Reports Come In

THE news that a Genoese navigator had found land on the other side of the Atlantic caused no excitement at all in workaday Europe. The tidings that Ferdinand of Aragon had managed to drive the Moors from Granada in the same year made more stir in the streets of Christian cities.

Word of "the new-found islands," however, passed swiftly among those interested in such things. By irony of fate the Portuguese Junta, most interested of all, had the earliest accurate description, from Columbus himself, because he had been driven by a storm, in little *Niña,* straight into the mouth of the Tagus, and so to Lisbon. Naturally enough the curious King John and the once-skeptical Council of the Sea wanted to know what the boastful Genoese had actually discovered, and he told them frankly enough. A note taker at this dramatic interview wrote down the opinion of the Portuguese listeners, that the redheaded man of fancies had come back, actually, "from the discovery of the islands of *Antilha* by order of the King of Spain." That is, from the once-legendary *Antillia* far out upon the sea.

After that the Portuguese scientists may have rechecked their figures, but they held to the same conclusion as before. This Bible-spouting Columbus had not reached India, or Cathay, either, in his

voyage of thirty and three days. He had not done so for the simple
reason that it couldn't be done. But what he *had* done posed a problem for the Council of the Sea at Lisbon. He had made a practical
crossing to a new island base for the rival monarchs of Spain, on the
way to the real Indies, whither the Portuguese were working their
way in the other direction, around Africa. The alert King John—
called by Isabel, who admired him, "The Man"—and his experienced Junta went immediately to work on their new problem, with
momentous consequences, as presently appeared.

Other interested parties were the rulers of Italian cities de-
pendent upon trade and the routes thereto. These had their agents,
who acted also conveniently as spies, in the active ports of the Iberian
Peninsula. The agents hastened to send the tidings of discovery
home by letter, written with a mixture of scientific surprise and
humanistic appreciation. A letter of October 1493 to an archbishop
of Braga in Italy sums up: "While the Portuguese push themselves
day by day farther and farther below the Equator . . . the hidden
half of our earth comes to light . . . a certain *Cristoforus Colonus*
has followed the setting sun to land's end in the east, more than
five thousand miles away—in three and thirty days."

This writer did not question the brief voyage to the Far East,
although you can sense a question in his mind. Quickly enough the
Spanish court gave out a news bulletin, carefully phrased for political ends: *"A letter of Crisoforus Colom who has greatly benefitted
our age . . . concerning the Islands of India this side the Ganges,
recently discovered."* This was seized upon eagerly in Rome and
printed many times. A Latin version of it sped from the presses of
Paris to the seaports of the Atlantic, and Antwerp. Along the coasts
other navigators studied the news bulletins.

Ordinary folk were interested chiefly in the strange people of
the unknown isles. "Naked and simple," a bulletin assured them,
"and exceedingly timid." Another report explained that the men of
these far Indies wore only a "cotton leaf to cover their genitals."
While the women went about everywhere similarly covered, or uncovered. It all had a Garden of Eden touch, and Europeans of every
sort waited to hear more about the naked women.

Meanwhile some copy of the Columbus letter reached the obscure port of London on the river Thames. It so happened that merchants of Venice and other Italian cities kept agents in London around Lombard Street, because Italian galleys carried most of the cloves, silk, and porcelain of far Asia to the poverty-ridden folk of England. In due course of time news of the discovery penetrated to the wharfs of "Bristow" where fishing fleets fared out into the Atlantic, as far as Iceland.

It so happened that this news acted like a spur upon one man in "Bristow" (Bristol) who eked out a living by selling charts and ideas at that land's-end haunt of the fishermen.

And Cabot Sails

Giovanni Caboto, who took the English name of John Cabot, remains a shadowy figure. His appearance, his words, and writings seem to have escaped the scanty records of England at that time, which, however, make very clear the amazing thing he did.

Cabot had a wife and three growing boys on his hands and he seemed to be about at the end of his obscure career as a learned Venetian navigator. He had served in the thriving terminals of the Moslem near east where he had heard of the long-distance caravans that brought in precious spices and silks from the far east. Like Columbus, he had speculated about this Oriental trade, and in so doing had made one mistake. He imagined that the transcontinental caravans must have started from the far northeastern point of cloudy Asia (actually Siberia). Naturally he argued that by sailing west from Europe a fortunate navigator might reach this rich source of the caravan trade.

He had not been fortunate. He seemed to wear poor clothing, and the wealthy Italian observers of Lombard Street describe him as a man of lower class, with a keen mind, who made maps and a globe of the earth. Certainly he had prevailed upon the solid Bristol merchants to send out at least two yearly fleets westward in search of legendary lands like "Brazil" and the Seven Cities. The fleets had found nothing of the kind.

Then came the devastating news that a rival Genoese—Cabot was born in Genoa—had found such lands for the King of Aragon. And very probably tuna fishermen came back from the Bay of Biscay with tales of taunts from Basque and Portuguese rivals—that *their* foreigner, Columbus, had steered a true course to the stepping-stones to Asia and the wealth of the Great Khan. Nothing could have been more galling to a homesick and hard-pressed Venetian trying to set himself up as an English navigator. John Cabot petitioned his adopted king direct. "To the Kyng our sovereigne lord. Please it your highness of your most noble and abundant grace to graunt unto John Cabotto citizen of Venes . . . [permission to sail, to discover on the King's behalf] whatsoever isles, regions, or provinces of the heathen, whatsoever they be, and in what part of the world soever they be, which before this time have been unknown to all Christians."

So Cabot begged for a discoverer's license to seek what he could find not already known to other Christians, i.e., to the Court of Spain. Now the tidings of Spanish discoveries in the west had stirred the interest of that thrifty Tudor, Henry VII, who readily gave his blessing to the eager Bristol mariners to set out "upon their own proper costs and charges." (By then Columbus had led back his second armada to the mysterious west, laden with the colonists of Spain.)

With himself as sole captain and navigator, Cabot sailed in the small bark *Matthew* with eighteen mariners of Bristol early in May 1497. Raimondo di Soncino of Lombard Street wrote the Duke of Milan that "he committed himself to fortune." He had scant provisions, and no guide except the polestar after he rounded the north of Ireland and set out across the wind-swept North Atlantic.

Although the courageous Venetian tried to head due west, his small vessel was blown about for fifty-two days and must have been carried north when it reached the (unknown) Gulf Stream. Its lookout first sighted land ahead early in the morning of Saturday, June 24, 1497.

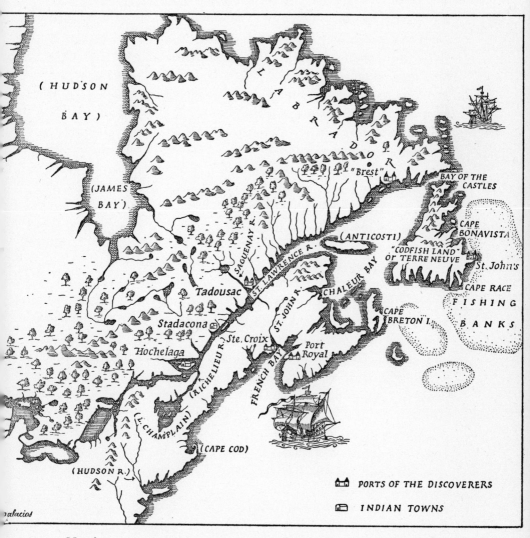

Labels on the map:

(HUDSON BAY)

(JAMES BAY)

LABRADOR

"Brest"

BAY OF THE CASTLES

CAPE BONAVISTA

(ANTICOSTI)

"CODFISH LAND" or TERRE NEUVE

St. John's

CAPE RACE

FISHING BANKS

SAGUENAY R.

ST. LAWRENCE R.

CHALEUR BAY

Tadousac

Stadacona

Hochelaga

ST. JOHN R.

CAPE BRETON I.

(RICHELIEU R.)

Ste. Croix

Port Royal

(L. CHAMPLAIN)

FRENCH BAY

(CAPE COD)

(HUDSON R.)

palacios

PORTS OF THE DISCOVERERS

INDIAN TOWNS

Northern entry of the continent. "Codfish Land" of the fishing fleets
and ports of the French explorers who sought a passage inland.

But what land? It might have been as far south as Cape Breton
Island, or as far north as the jutting cape of Labrador. Cabot's
course must have been near to 50°, but the place of his landfall is
as uncertain as the Norsemen's. All that coast line is peculiarly
deceptive. Capes that appear to mark the mainland turn out to be
island-ends; peninsulas jut out like islands; great bays lurk in hiding,
and wide entrances narrow to inlets. And mist often hangs like a
veil over the coast. The green of moss and firs seemed to Cabot's
eager eyes to be evidence of great fertility. And he rejoiced in the
mild midsummer climate of those northern latitudes.

We armchair navigators of today think of John Cabot and his
men as anchoring in a convenient bay and hurrying inland to meet
the people of the great continent they had, in fact, discovered. Nothing of the kind happened. The silent Venetian did land somewhere,
to plant as duty prescribed the standard of England—and some say
that of St. Mark as well—and claim the New Found Land for his
patron, the frugal Tudor. That done, he made haste to get away
while he could.

A small sailing vessel is in constant danger off a stormy, uncharted coast. Cabot had, with great courage, taken a gambler's
chance, as Soncino remarked. Now he had to get his ship home, to
save the lives of his people as well as his winnings. For perhaps a
week he coasted this northeast point of North America, taking on
wood and water, finding some animal snares set by unseen Eskimos,
and bone needles—and seeing the marks of axes on trees. Certain
now that human beings dwelt in this land, he headed home before
his food stores gave out and autumn storms set in.

But his Bristol men had sighted one marvel off the coast of what
is now Newfoundland. Water boiling with great fish, over undreamed-of banks. Codfish.

"That sea," Soncino wrote after interviewing them, "is so covered with fishes they can be caught not only in a net but also in a
basket with a stone in it so it may be plunged into water ... they say
they will bring thence such great quantity of fish that England will
have no further need of Iceland."

So the fishermen of *Matthew's* crew boasted. Unfortunately for himself John Cabot did some boasting on his own account. He had promised to find a way for Englishmen to the land of the Great Khan, and when he hastened from the wharves of the Severn to his patron the Tudor king, he claimed full success in his remarkable voyage.

Cabot claimed he had discovered more than the Castilians in the south. He had sighted a main and continent land out there. Yes, surely, for his vessel had coasted it for 300 leagues. (Impossible in that time.) Silk and valuable dyewood? Yes, the new land had them. And the route to his discovery was shorter than the route of the Genoese, Columbus, to his Hispaniola. (Not entirely true, in reality.)

"This Master John," Soncino commented to his duke, "being a foreigner and a poor man would not be believed if the crew, who are nearly all English and from Bristol, did not testify that what he says is true."

Henry Tudor believed Cabot, and was delighted to have found a way at so little cost to the country of the Grand Khan. In reward he gave out money recklessly—all of ten pounds sterling in gift to the daring Venetian, with a pension to follow, and loans to merchants who would sail back with him. "The King," Lorenzo Pasqualigo wrote to his brothers in Venice, "has given him money, that he may have a good time until then. . . . He is called Admiral, and great honor paid him, and he goes about dressed in silk with these English running after him like mad and indeed he can enlist as many of them as he pleases, and a number of our rogues as well."

Those rogues were Portuguese or Italian seamen looking for a ship bound to the western discoveries. Cabot did enlist at least one of them, a certain Juan Fernandes, a *llavrador,* or farmer, of the Azores. Fernandes had been up to Greenland before, and he wanted very much just then to explore what lay beyond Greenland. (Eventually his nickname was to stick to the coast of Cabot's landfall, the Labrador.) Perhaps during his few months of fame Cabot crossed over to the Algarve of Portugal to pick up news of the discoveries south of his landfall.

His Bristol fishermen loyally backed up their master's tale of finding the entrance to Cathay and added trimmings of their own. Had their voyage been a hard one? Well, it would be a simple matter, now they had their bearings. A matter of a mere fifteen days' sailing. Storms? Not a ghost of one, beyond Ireland.

Furthermore back in their old haunts with Breton, Norman, and Basque rival fleets these same fishermen told of the wonders they had seen out there. *"Yonder the sea was slimey with stockfish. We had only to dip baskets, to haul them in."*

Word of this wonder passed along the coast, and up the Seine and Tagus. Sun-darkened toilers, hauling their dories ashore with oxen, glanced out at the horizon with longing. Out there, fifteen days' sail, they could haul fish in *with baskets.*

The day came when after several years they could resist the thought no longer and they went out to seek the wonder of the great banks off the New Found Land.

Henry Tudor and the small merchants of England possessed little knowledge of the world outside their own narrow seas; from that world the Venetian galleys and Hansa luggers brought trade goods in to them. Now they anticipated fetching in their own vessels the spices, silks, and jewels of Asia by way of "the new isle" or "New Found Land." With that expectation they watched John Cabot depart again from the river Severn with two large vessels and three merchant craft of Bristol in company. The fleet had provisions for a year, and plenty of cargo space to fill with the riches of Asia. Outward-bound, the ships carried trade goods of the kind described by Messer Marco Polo, to barter with the merchants of the Grand Khan. It was then late May of the year 1498.

"Master John has set his mind," Soncino reported, "on going on from the place he has already possessed, hugging the shore, further toward the east until he is opposite an island called by him *Cipango* somewhere under the Equator, where he thinks grow all the spices and also the precious stones . . . as long as it costs me nothing, I believe him."

With his departure into the Irish Sea, John Cabot disappears from the records. Whither he shaped his course thereafter and what happened to him in the western sea can only be conjectured.

For one thing, he seems to have taken along with him his son Sebastian, about twelve years old—one of the three sons for whom he tried to provide by his dangerous voyages. Sebastian was to seek fame for himself by denying the achievements of his father. Among the things he falsified was this voyage of 1498, which Sebastian claimed had been made by himself alone some ten years later. John Cabot, the true discoverer of northeastern America, died soon afterward in disgrace; Sebastian, his unworthy son, lived to a ripe old age and a fame achieved by consummate lies that have baffled historical geographers ever since.

Weighing the probabilities, we can reconstruct the second voyage somewhat like this:

After the Cabots set out, one vessel of the five, severely damaged in a storm, turned back to the Irish coast. The others apparently headed far north to Greenland. Perhaps Fernandes prevailed on John Cabot to search this coast of lofty headlands for reasons of his own, which will be manifest later. Certainly the anxious Venetian named it after his Portuguese companion—the Labrador. Then from Cape Farewell, they seem to have searched to the westward, along the haunts of the Norsemen, who had disappeared from the coast by then.

Their small fleet did penetrate to a high latitude in the north because the men noticed the length of summer daylight and the clearness of the nights, as well as the unexpected vagaries of the compass. They felt the set of the arctic current against them and sighted drifting icebergs. Now, according to Sebastian's dubious tale, they pushed ever farther north, seeking a passage around the New Found Land, along snow-covered coasts, in menacing ice floes until the crews mutinied and they had to turn back.

It is hard to believe that they actually made this excursion toward the Pole in that brief summer. (By Sebastian's account the crews mutinied in icy waters in early June, less than a month after their departure from Bristol!) John Cabot surely was desperately

anxious to satisfy the English king by reaching the riches of Cathay
—as he hoped—south of his first landfall, not to the north. Fernandes, the silent partner of the enterprise, might have given a true account of their voyaging, but for reasons of his own the Portuguese
made no public report.

In any case John Cabot very quickly arrived on the coast of his
first discovery, the Newfoundland of today. There they met again
the swarming codfish that actually hindered the navigation of the
vessels, and sighted again the "English Cape" (Cape Race). This
time they met with the inhabitants of the land. Explorers who came
after them found a gilt sword and Venetian-made earrings in the
hands of the Nascapi tribesmen there. They were amused by the
number of brown bears that waded along the streams to claw out
fish to eat.

They missed the entrance to the Gulf of St. Lawrence at the
strait of Belle Isle, mistaking it for a bay. But somebody gave a name
to an island, *Baccalaos,* or Codfish. After that this nebulous point of
a continent was widely known as Codfish Land.

Then John Cabot sailed south along modern New England,
seeking the landmarks of Asia and not finding them. How far south
he went no one knows.

Only one trace of his passage has survived. Two years later the
great Basque pilot, Juan de la Cosa, returned from coasting his
little Venice (Venezuela) and made a map of the discoveries he
knew. On that map the northern coast is drawn in crudely. On this
coast tiny English flags are painted two thirds of the way down to
Cuba—down to a projecting point where words are written, "Sea
discovered by the English."

Those who know best conjecture that this cape, described by
John Cabot, might have been either Cape Cod or Cape Hatteras.

Probably after he brought back his small fleet that autumn the
older Cabot had little to say to anyone. The ships unloaded the trade
goods meant for barter in Cathay, while the merchants of Bristol
wrote off their losses and swallowed their disappointment. Cabot
brought back only a few furs.

He had seen forests stretching unbroken for hundreds of

leagues; he had anchored in the mouths of giant rivers; he had caught the scent of a flowering land while miles at sea. It was a continent, almost without inhabitants.

But he had no spice, no silk for the merchants of Bristol.

Ironically John Cabot died in ignominy, like Christopher Columbus.

His Tudor king had lost good silver in the venture, and had gained nothing except some dried furs. Besides there was trouble in England with one Perkin Warbeck, and more trouble across the Channel. No more did Henry VII give serious thought to the "new found isle" as he called it. He allowed some trading ventures to depart toward Greenland, but no more voyages to discover Cathay. Not for sixty years, not until a young queen came to the throne (and Elizabeth was tutored by Italians), would the Tudor monarchs of England again seek their fortune in the western sea.

The Cabot voyages, however, immediately alerted the courts of the Iberian Peninsula. Undoubtedly Juan Fernandes played a part in bringing the news to Lisbon. Observe his movements after the autumn of 1498. Without explanation he appears in Viana (where John Cabot paid such a hurried visit), and then in the Azores—the observation point of Portugal in the North Atlantic—where this seemingly casual Fernandes gains a grant from his own king of Portugal to islands he might discover in the northwest. Thereafter he is back in Bristol again, persuading three hardheaded merchants to voyage out to the "new found isle." Were they persuaded to go after fish, seals, or gold? Henry allows them their voyage as a trading venture. They return without explanation but with, according to the English records, "three men brought out of an Iland forre beyonde Ireland, the which were clothed in Beestes skynnes and ate raw fflesh and were rude in their demeanure as Beestes."

Obviously the Tudor court was satisfied with this voyage, because one of the Fernandes family was granted a 10-pound pension for service as "Capitaigne into the new founde lande."

Something momentous was astir on the Ocean Sea unheeded by the drowsy islanders of England.

The Kings Gamble for Half the World

In the fair sailing weather of April 1500 new activity showed on the Atlantic, which had been so barren of ships only eight years before.

Out in the Azores our Fernandes was preparing to leave his home at Terceira for the venture with the innocent Bristol merchants. There an adventurous nobleman, Gaspar Corte-Real, made ready to embark on a voyage of his own, with a grant to any lands discovered in the Portuguese sphere of the new lands. At home in Spain after his voyage with Ojeda, the great pilot Juan de la Cosa worked over the first rude map of the startling discoveries—painting in the English flags to the north, sketching two ships flying the broad banner of Castile to the south. (No one could conceive as yet what might lie between the Great Gulf of Columbus and the odd Codfish land.)

Somewhere in the Atlantic just then a stray caravel was bringing the still-unknown Amerigo Vespucci back to Cádiz, followed by the survivors of Vicente Yáñez's shipwrecks. While the silent Diego de Lepe also fared homeward from the mouth of the Amazon. Farther south in the Atlantic a gentleman named Cabral navigated a large Portuguese fleet in very strange fashion—ostensibly bound for the Cape of Africa, he was heading across to the coast De Lepe had left (modern Brazil).

These comings and goings were entirely Castilian and Portuguese. The rival Iberian powers raced to discover, and accordingly claim, the best territories hidden to the west. In those summer months of 1500 the voyagers of Lisbon seemed to be leading in the race toward the Unknown Land. For a brief moment in history there was the likelihood that the future North America would be claimed as part of the new sea empire of Portugal. These years, 1500-01, may have decided that.

Just then Manuel, King of Portugal, and his Council of the Sea were on the verge of gaining an almost incredible heritage. It was no more or less than the richest slice of the earth. It was the heritage left them by a gamble of the hardheaded John, Manuel's predecessor on the throne, just before his death in 1495.

In 1493, after the first discovery of Columbus, the supreme authority of the Pope (Alexander VI) had divided the outer, unexplored world between the rival sea powers of the Iberian Peninsula. On one side of his famous Line of Demarcation, 100 leagues west of the Azores, the monarchs of Castile and Aragon were to possess all discoveries, while on the other side new lands would fall to the Portuguese.

So matters might have ended, or at least taken a different course, if it had not been for some amazing conjecturing by the forthright John of Lisbon and his advisers. They drew the preoccupied Spanish king and queen into diplomatic argument about the Line of Demarcation—after having questioned Columbus sharply on his arrival home. At the moment Ferdinand and Isabella and their scientists believed vaguely that the way to India and Cathay lay westward across the ocean where the dreaming Genoese seemed to have found it. Certainly Columbus himself believed it. The Portuguese, however, were not so sure. To their thinking a huge space on the earth remained unaccounted for, and the Castilian discovery of a few islands in the void did not change the size of the earth or the position of Asia in the least. John himself did not seem convinced that Asia lay as near at hand to the west as the excited Spaniards believed. By then those Spaniards were feverishly eager to gain for themselves new territories overseas to match the Portuguese domain of Africa.

In the Treaty of Tordesillas John's envoys persuaded the diplomats of Castile and Aragon to shift the papal line far to the west in the Atlantic, to 370 leagues out from the Cape Verde Islands. That, of course, conceded to his Spanish rivals a large stretch of the farther ocean, upon which they had their eyes fixed at the time. John knew pretty well what was in it. Water.

But since the line ran from pole to pole, by the Pope's edict, it also extended through the other, far half of the earth. It followed that the Portuguese gained title to much of that eastern half of the globe.

By what they knew of geography at that time the Portuguese seemed to believe the great prizes of Asia, from Africa to the Golden Chersonese, lay safely on their side of the new line in the east, as indeed they did. The Portuguese also made safe the known waters around Africa and the known routes *toward the east.*

By moving the line at Tordesillas nearly a thousand miles out into the Atlantic, the Portuguese pushed, as it were, the Spanish zone farther from Spain. They conceded to their rivals the unknown portion of the earth. What was to be found there? More islands for Columbus? The icebound *north* projection of Asia? Who could say, in 1494?

But certainly the Spaniards would have a long, long way to sail to their west across uncharted waters to reach the richest marts of Asia. Could the caravels flying the castles of Castile ever get there? And if they did, could they ever conceivably make their way back again to Spain? The Portuguese at Tordesillas hoped they could not.

The new line of Tordesillas also gave to the Portuguese the bulge of Brazil. Was this accident? Or did John and his cosmographers realize that land lay there within 370 leagues of the Cape Verde Islands?

Now the navigators of that day could determine latitude fairly closely. By observations of the sun and the stars they were assured of their north-south position. The best of them, however, had no means of determining longitude—their east-west position. The pull of unsuspected currents played havoc with a master's reckoning in strange seas. How far west was 370 leagues due west of the Cape Verde Islands?

The cosmographers at Seville could not say. They were, besides, rapidly becoming disillusioned about their islands in the Great Gulf, or Caribbean. The more alert Portuguese, however, determined to find out, if it strained their small resources to do so.

Then all Lisbon rejoiced at the return of Vasco da Gama. This supreme navigator had probed far into the east, to *Calicut* in India.

More, he had filled his holds with unbelievable wealth, cloves, ginger, damask cloth, great precious stones, and such. The men of Lisbon knew now where their profit lay—eastward to India, and on to the Moluccas—the veritable Spice Islands—and the kingdoms of Java. All this and more seemed to lie definitely on their side of the far line.

But then word come in of Cabot's find for the English in the mysterious northwest. Was not this unexpected *Terra Nova* or Cod-fish Land actually within the Portuguese zone? The men of Lisbon wanted very much to find out, and quickly.

For they suspected what the less skilled Castilians did not realize as yet—that Cabot's far point of land and the coasts ranged by the little discoverers of Castile might be part of the same great continent.

On one pretense or another secret searchers went forth from Portugal, Fernandes to observe the northern discovery, and Duarte Pacheco to scout the southern coasts. What might exist there worth having, and how much of it lay on the Portuguese side of the line?

Secret Search of the Portuguese

In Terceira, Fernandes had neighbors who were noble-born and wealthy planters, and patriotic—being sons of the former Captain General of the island. Their family, the Corte-Real, had explored the sea westward before then. (Rumor insisted that their father had reached land, and that the three Corte-Real brothers followed the course he had taken thither.)

In any case two of the brothers, Gaspar and Miguel Corte-Real, made three voyages from 1500 to 1502. Secrecy veils their routes and findings. Each brother took three ships and each sailed alone in one to his death. Gaspar touched Greenland, turned—as Fernandes seems to have done—southwest to the new lands. After sending back two of his vessels to report, he kept on around the New Found Land and was lost. But the surviving ships brought back "wild woodmen and white bears" and tales of reindeer and giant walruses of the sea.

Miguel went in search of his brother, perhaps questing into the Gulf of St. Lawrence, then turning north up the Labrador. When last seen Miguel's caravel was headed northeast with winter coming on. Did the venturesome nobleman of the Azores enter the unknown eastern strait (Hudson's) to be trapped there by ice?

They certainly died on a mission for their king, who, "in sore grief for them," attempted to send out a third, rescue fleet. Oddly enough map makers two generations later came to name the mysterious waterway to Asia by the northeast strait the "Strait of the Three Brothers."

The silent Corte-Reals gave the name Bonavista to the cape which still retains it. And for a long time after them the name *Corte-Real Land* appeared on maps, at least on Portuguese maps.

One such map makes claim to *Corte-Real Land* (Newfoundland-Labrador) as "discovered by order of the Most High and Excellent Prince, Dom Manoel, King of Portugall. It was found by Gaspar de Corte-Real, one of his noblemen, who sent back a vessel with men and women of that country."

This claim of the Portuguese to the northern lands where Cabot had planted the English flag was noted by the observant eyes of Italian envoys to the court of Lisbon. A Venetian, Pietro Pasqualigo, wrote home to the Signory in 1501 that the vanished Corte-Reals had believed the new territory to be a continent by reason of the large rivers flowing out of it.

"One caravel has brought back seven natives, men, women, and children from the land discovered. It was toward the north and west, 1800 miles away. These men resemble gypsies, having their faces marked [with paint] and being clad in animal skins, chiefly of otter. They are well formed in their limbs, having most gentle countenances but beast-like habits. No one here understands their speech.

"The crew of this caravel believes the above-mentioned land to be a mainland joined to the other that was discovered last year [i.e., the Caribbean coast]. It seems they could not land there because of great masses of snow, and the sea being frozen over. They also believe this land is connected with the *Antilles* [islands of the Spanish

Caribbean] which was discovered by the sovereigns of Spain, and with the Land of the Parrots recently found by this king's ship [Cabral's] on its way to Calicut. Because after ranging the coast of the said land for 600 miles and more they did not find it come to an end; also because—they say—they have observed there many very large rivers entering the sea. . . . This news has given the king here [Manuel] great pleasure since it seems to him this country is so near, he will be able to get from it a large amount of timber suitable for masts and ship-building, and plenty of men slaves to do the labor. . . . And his majesty is very desirous of enlarging his fleet for India, in order to conquer and discover more."

So by then, at the end of 1501, the Portuguese court was still uncertain whether the Cabot-Corte-Real finds were within the Portuguese zone (actually they lay to the west of the line in Spanish territory). But Manuel and his Junta evaluated Corte-Real Land as yielding merely fish, with timber and a possible crop of slaves to build new ships for the India voyage.

Meanwhile a courier caravel had come in to the Tagus from another secret searcher, Pedro Álvares Cabral.

Cabral had set out early in 1500 with a dozen vessels, and a remarkable group of pilots. Among them Bartholomeu Dias had mastered the African cape route, and Duarte Pacheco had crossed to the point of modern Brazil, to map it and take a quick look at its resources of natives, fruit, and timber. Since that nebulous bulge of the southern continent projected into the Portuguese zone, Cabral was sent to make a more careful survey. With such a large fleet he could not possibly hide his movements. So he claimed, truthfully enough, to be bound for India, whence Da Gama had returned.

On April 23, Pedro Álvares Cabral dropped anchor quietly off that same Brazil, but far below the bulge. He brought twelve armed caravels and *naus* (galleons) guided by the best pilots and cosmographers of Lisbon, laden with 600 men and provisions for a year and a half. Portuguese historians explained his intrusion near Spanish waters by saying he had swung out from Cape Verde in Africa to catch a wind for the Cape of Good Hope, and had landed by accident on the wrong continent instead. Modern historians have conjectured that a storm may have blown him far to the west, or his pilots made an error in navigation.

But Cabral, who voyaged thus officially the wrong way, had with him Pacheco, who knew the route to Brazil, and Dias, who had rounded the Cape of Good Hope. And the letters of his pilots mention no storm in the 660 leagues, as they estimate their passage; nor do they show surprise at landing in the New World instead of the Old. Nor does Cabral himself show any signs of anxiety.

At his landfall he sights a distant, lofty mountain and names it Pascal, since Easter was at hand; he runs up the low, wooded coast watching out for dyewood until he enters a safe harbor, calling it Pôrto Seguro. There the ostensibly lost Portuguese take on wood and water, and hold the first Mass of history in South America.

For a few days these alleged castaways linger, inspecting the brightly painted natives (without calling them "Indians") who sing and dance hospitably for them. They inspect the native parrots, breadroots, and sleeping hammocks; they set up a great wooden cross with the name and shield of arms of their king, Manuel. They describe all this in letters to Manuel, adding that as for the situation of this new land, which they call *Vera Cruz,* His Highness can see it himself on an old map drawn by one Pero Vaz Bisagudo. (So the Court already possessed a map of the point of the new land.) They conjecture whether it is a large island or part of a continent and decide that by its size it must be a continent. Whereupon Cabral sends a fast caravel back to the Tagus with news of his discovery. And after a nine-day sojourn he departs briskly for his official destination, the Cape of Good Hope and India.

Did all this happen by accident?

In their second crossing of the Atlantic the venturesome Portuguese did encounter a storm; they lost five ships with Bartholomeu Dias on one of them. Dias and the Corte-Reals were the first of many who would lose their lives on the new paths of discovery. It was the beginning of the *Historia Trágica Marítima*. Other navigators did not have the uncanny skill of the Genoese, Columbus, and the Venetian, Cabot, at bringing back their men alive from the far seas.

Manuel the Lucky promptly claimed Vera Cruz, or Santa Cruz Land, by right of this officially accidental discovery. But he kept the details secret. Strange plants, painted people, and dyewoods the frugal Portuguese found useful enough but not especially profitable. They waited anxiously for news from the east.

Then in midsummer of 1501 the capable Cabral brought in his surviving ships. They were fully laden with pepper, musk, camphor, India paper, and great jewels. He had voyaged for 15,000 miles and fought his way through Arab shipping and into Indian ports. It was the first victory of European gunpowder and sailing ships over the forces of far Asia, but it would not be the last.

The pattern of Portugal's sea empire was set. A new armada gathered with greater armed force—first of the yearly "spice fleets" —to conquer bases along the new trade route to India and beyond to the Golden Chersonese and Spice Islands.

So, after 1501, the ships of Portugal turned away from the Unknown Land.

The enthusiastic Portuguese hailed their king as Manuel the Lucky, "Lord of the conquest, navigation and commerce of India, Ethiopia [where Prester John might yet be found] Arabia and Persia."

When haughty Spanish envoys at the Court of Lisbon claimed title to the northern New Found Land as being on their side the line, little heed was paid by the Portuguese. They had no further interest in those nebulous, northern icebound shores.

For those few years of the first decade of the sixteenth century the entire east coast of the Unknown Land lay open to Castilian discovery, which failed to materialize.

The fishermen, however, went back. Their one objective was Codfish Land. After the turn of the century their fleets began to slip out of Dieppe and the muddy Tagus, to head for the banks where the Bristol men had hauled fish in by baskets. The Portuguese led the way.

It was more than fifteen days to the treasure of the New Found Land banks. But the men of the Algarve found the way. How did they navigate across an unknown sea? Why, easily enough, even without charts, astrolabes, or tables of the sun's declension. They may have picked up bearings from the Corte-Real crews. One vessel out of Dieppe, *La Pensée,* led the fishing fleet of Brest across to Cape Bonavista. They ran down the latitude of Brest itself (about 48° of north latitude). They watched the sun set beyond the line of bowsprit and mast—they watched the swing of the guides of the polestar against their masthead.

If they kept charts, these fishermen did not publish them, nor did they write journals for other eyes to see. We hear of them only by accident, by a tax on their catches levied in Viana, or by the stir in Rouen when they brought back seven Eskimo and a canoe. For they fell to bartering with the strange folk of the west when they dried their season's catches on shore. They bestowed polyglot names on their landmarks—such as the Flat Cape (*Capo Razo*), which we pronounce as Cape Race. *Baccalaos* itself is a Basque or Portuguese word. How else did Cape Breton get its name?

Some twenty years after John Cabot died in obscurity a gentleman of England penned a rude poem of the voyaging fishermen who alone had followed steadily in Cabot's wake.

> . . . Now Frenchmen and other have found the trade
> That yerely of fyshe there they lade
> Above an C. sayle.

So a hundred sail may have gone yearly to Codfish Land. This silent stubborn traffic was to have consequences in years to come.

The New World Is Not Asia

Just after the turn of the century the Spanish court at Valladolid began to realize the stubborn and almost unbelievable fact that it had stumbled across a hidden part of the world.

"While the Portugese," wrote Peter Martyr from Seville, "day by day push themselves farther and farther under the Equator, the hidden half of the globe is coming to light."

This young Peter Martyr had migrated from Anghiera in Italy to the new frontier of Spain in time to watch Christian banners carried to Moslem Granada and to hear the tales of the voyagers back from the far islands of the Atlantic. Of the two happenings the latter seemed to the quick-witted Italian cosmographer the more important "because never before did man, starting from the known world, penetrate to those unknown regions."

With enthusiasm Peter Martyr wrote letters home to his patrons in Rome and elsewhere relating what he heard at the wharfs, taverns, or Court. Almost at once he seems convinced that the explorers had hit upon a strange sort of people. "Certainly among them the land belongs to everyone, like sun or water. They know no difference between *meum* and *teum,* the source of all evils. They are satisfied with little; their land is so vast, little of it need be cultivated. No hedges or walls close in their dwelling places; no laws or judges govern their lives."

He is the first writer to imagine a "golden age" out there beyond the sunset; he gleans fresh words for his racy Latin—*hamak* for a hanging bed, *cannibals* for the eaters of human flesh, and *Novus Orbis* for the whole of it.

Now when he speaks of a New World, the realistic Peter Martyr means merely the newly discovered fringe of islands, as Columbus writes of the "other world" of the Great Gulf of the Ocean Sea. In the same way sight of great continental capes and rivers seems to reveal the coast of the Asiatic mainland. Or does it?

With each year Peter Martyr grows more doubtful that this *Novus Orbis* consists merely of islands off the far coast of Asia—"for the size of the globe seems to say otherwise."

He listens to the arguments at Court, and writes with hurrying pen to his friends. This discovery goes beyond the science of the ancients, beyond Aristotle himself, or even the infallible Ptolemy the Geographer. For young Peter Martyr studied that science in the medieval academies. Moreover he has a check on the boasts of the sea captains, because he is more adept than they at astronomy—and the stars do not alter with changes on the earth. "Melchior has told me that among the cannibals the days of December are as long as the nights. Nobody who came back from this second voyage is more readily to be believed than he. But our knowledge contradicts this . . . for nowhere on earth during the solstice does the night precisely equal the day. . . . It is certain that on this voyage the Spaniards never reached the equator, for they constantly beheld on the horizon the polar star which served them as guide."

Peter Martyr admires Columbus, but doubts that he ever sighted Paradise on the farthest coast out there from the masthead of his ship. No, the great Admiral "ended by convincing himself that this was a fact."

And Peter Martyr wonders about another fact related by the Genoese discoverer. "He declares that he has pushed his way so far from Hispaniola toward the west that he has reached the Golden Chersonese which is the furthest extremity of the known globe in the east. The Admiral thinks there is left for him to discover only the space covered by the sun for two hours of its four and twenty hours passage encircling the earth."

Now the skeptical Peter is certain of one thing. "The sun circles this globe of ours in twenty-four hours." He turns to his books of the ancient geographers. "It is known to us that the ancients only followed the sun during the half of its course since they knew only the portion of the globe stretching from our Spanish Cádiz [eastward] to the Golden Chersonese." This old world of Aristotle and Ptolemy, then, stretched for only twelve hours of the sun's passing. Could the Genoese Admiral have reached within two hours of it by "following the setting sun from Cádiz"?

He had not voyaged for ten hours of the sun. He had sailed only some 5000 miles.

Were the ancient geographers wrong? Was the Genoese entirely mistaken? Or did the earth contain a vast space, undetermined by European science, within its "hidden half"? Peter Martyr will not try to answer the question in those first years of discovery, but he adds cryptically, "Not without cause have cosmographers left the boundaries of India beyond the Ganges undetermined."

Unaware, Peter Martyr at Seville is observing the change from medieval learning to the consciousness of an enlarged world in which things would never be as they had been before.

It remained for a Florentine gentleman at sea in the west to give an answer to his question.

Amerigo Vespucci of Florence, kinsman of the powerful Medicis and friend of Botticelli, worked in Spain as confidential agent of the bankers while he pursued his own hobby of astronomy. His portraits, painted by great artists, reveal a sensitive man, yet muscular and determined. He had a way, as events show, of keeping his own counsel. His skill lay in the tough mathematics of astronomy. Laboring at that, he tried to solve the mystery of longitude—a fix of east-west position on the earth—by watching the conjunction of the moon with the planets.

To carry on his chosen study of the stars, Amerigo wanted to be taken out on the western sea. It was simple to arrange this, for a man of his position and skill. As supercargo, and probably as consulting navigator, he voyaged with Ojeda and Juan de la Cosa across to their "funny little Venice," where his ship strayed, to be lost for a while from the records. Because of what happened afterwards there has been much conjecture as to where Amerigo's vessel wandered; it could hardly have sighted the North American coast, because his knowledge in that early year seems to have been confined to the Caribbean and the coast by the Amazon. Except for his dutiful letters to the Medici and others he kept his observations to himself. Unobtrusively he met Gaspar Corte-Real, returning for the first time from Codfish Land, and probably learned the bearings of that mysterious point in the north.

Then in May 1501, Amerigo got started west again, this time with three Portuguese caravels. There is nothing very surprising in an interested Italian changing over from the Spanish to the Portuguese flag. Probably he was loyal only to his study of the stars and his own city of Florence. But this time his fleet had a government mission. The Portuguese Junta, if not Manuel himself, worried a little that year about Santa Cruz Land, recently visited secretly by their explorer Cabral and now openly claimed by Portugal. Did this point of a far nebulous continent really lie on their side the line? If so, for how far to the south? Did they own, as it were, the southern end of this continent—if such it were? Did the sea at the end— if indeed it ended—offer a possible route direct to distant Asia? And above all, what were the rival Spaniards doing about Santa Cruz Land, which the seamen called Land of the Parrots?

Obviously Amerigo Vespucci was skilled in taking accurate bearings at sea, which the Junta wanted badly. So it happened that his second and vital voyage went toward the south of Peter Martyr's *Novus Orbis.* "We went to make discovery," he wrote to Florence, "not to make a profit."

And it happened by luck or prearrangement that his three ships fell in, at the take-off point of Cape Verde, with two of Cabral's vessels returning well loaded with wealth from India. However it happened, it was the sheerest good fortune for the single-minded Amerigo. For here in the cane huts of the Verde station he could sit down with the Portuguese pilots who had already made the crossing to Brazil, and had voyaged the thousands of miles to India and back—"although they did not have navigators to take the latitude and longitude of that place." (His specialty.)

One of the India veterans, Gama da Guaspare, in particular could point out on a chart the far fabulous places which lay beyond India—here lay the great island of Ceylon, over there Sumatra. China? Well, they had lain alongside Chinese junks which had rounded the Golden Chersonese. The distance? Only the Holy Spirit knew—but a voyage of many weeks.

Amerigo's trained mind absorbed these distances and bearings greedily, for he wrote of Cabral's eastern voyage with great detail to Lorenzo di Pier Francesca de' Medici. He must have left Cape Verde with kindled imagination, if not with a new perception of the circuit of the earth. Could it be larger than the ancient geographers had estimated?

Then the scales of fortune turned, and Amerigo Vespucci had the worst luck that could befall a devout astronomer. For weeks a storm blinded the three vessels on their way from Africa to the new coast, and he could not get a good sight of sun by day or stars by night. Yet they touched land close to Cabral's turning point under the bulge of Brazil. Then, as they had been ordered, they quested south.

They pushed on, below the equator, beyond the limit of Portuguese territory, to the Spanish side of the line. They skirted a seemingly endless coast of impenetrable forest strange to them, broken by vast river channels. Eight hundred leagues, Amerigo claims, they went on a course southwest by one quarter west.

He had no medieval illusions about what he saw. It was the eastern coast of a vast continent. "A new world," he wrote later to Florence, "because none of it was known to our ancestors. . . . I have found a continent in its southern part more populous and full of animals than our Europe or Asia or Africa, and even more temperate and pleasant."

More than that came into the mind of this Florentine keeping his night watch at sea with astrolabe and quadrant in hand while others slept. He sighted stars new to him, among them the Southern Cross, which he said had the shape of a mandolin. His three ships slipped farther south on the shore current, "until the South Pole stood above my horizon at 50 degrees, which was my latitude from the equator." They passed the estuary of the great Plate, perhaps reaching San Julián, almost within sight of the Falklands. But they did not sight the tip of the continent, or the strait leading through it to the unknown east.

When they turned back, Amerigo Vespucci knew how far he had voyaged from Lisbon, and how far he was still from the real Indies in the east. He became convinced that the ancients had been wrong, and Ptolemy's map was wrong. The Atlantic, as they had called the ocean, was no narrow sea filled with oddments of islands between Europe and Asia.

No, between those quarters of the Old World lay this unknown continent, in itself a quarter of the world. Did it lead by land to Asia, or was it an altogether new world, isolated between *two* oceans?

Amerigo had no way of telling that. What he reported to the

Junta in 1502 and wrote to the Medici was not at first made known elsewhere.

The Continent Is Named America

Something very decisive happened soon after Amerigo Vespucci returned to the Old World. Tidings of the discoveries escaped for the first time from councils and courts, to be broadcast to the public. The man in the street heard that strange lands and peoples existed beyond his ken and he demanded more news of them.

Amerigo's letters had circulated from hand to hand, with those of Peter Martyr and others, after the manner of the time. Editors of printed books began to quest after them—to print them, or pepped-up versions of them, in the latest pocket-size editions or cheap illustrated pamphlets. A four-page flimsy with the eye-catching title *Mundus Novus* brought to the public the gist of Amerigo's remarks about a new world and the great southern continent. This excited the popular fancy because it linked up with the ancient and honorable myth of a vast south land mass below the belt of burning equatorial heat. It was copied out hastily in Italian, German, and more Latin.

Enlightened Florence was the home of the illustrated pamphlet as well as of Amerigo. There appeared for all to read in 1506 *The Four Voyages of Amerigo Vespucci*. This slim volume had purple patches that endeared it to home-fireside readers—the wonders of a whole new world, with the sexual behavior of the women, and even a mention of Paradise. Its high point was the detailed account of a Christian seaman clubbed to death by amorous naked women, butchered and barbecued and eaten before the eyes of his shipmates. Honest townsfolk of that day preferred marvels related by explorers to dry figures of the elevation of stars over the sea. They also had a way of believing, as they do today, more in familiar fables than in unaccustomed facts.

The *Four Voyages* became the most popular book of the discoveries; it was taken whole into the great *Paesi* Italian collection of voyages. And it started a controversy which has not ended today. It was full of contradictions, wrong names, impossible dates. How much of all this was truth? For centuries scholars have labored to extract Amerigo's real writings to the Medici—his original letters have all been lost—from the notions of translators and the flourishes of ghost writers. For centuries Vespucci's name has been under the cloud of the *Four Voyages*. The best belief today is that he made only two voyages, in 1499 and 1501; that he never commanded a fleet, but did make the celestial observations where he reported them. Remember that Vespucci did his work under seal of secrecy; he was never attacked in his lifetime.

Up in the Vosges, in the small town of St. Dié, with one stone church, a few young Germans formed a circle of scholars. They set up a printing press in their college and went to work enthusiastically to print something new and scientific about the enlarged world, which none of them had beheld.

Martin Waldseemüller, a skilled geographer, drew a large map of that outer world from the charts he could accumulate of the western discoveries. Mathias Ringmann, a scholar with a leaning toward poetry, aided him with the writing. Their labor might have remained in obscurity except for two circumstances: the map was remarkably good for its day, and a copy of *The Four Voyages of Amerigo Vespucci* arrived in St. Dié with most of the purple patches intact and a few errors added by a French ghost writer.

It delighted the enthusiasts of the Vosges Mountains. They added it, in Latin, to their new map. On April 25, 1507, their book, the *Cosmographiae Introductio* was published.

Within it the Waldseemüller-Ringmann observation upon the parts of the inhabited earth contained a thought of their own: "Another fourth part has been discovered by Americus Vespucius ... wherefore I do not see what hinders us from calling it America, that is, the land of Americus, after its sagacious discoverer—since both Europa and Asia have drawn their names from women."

So the name of America was put on the map. Waldseemüller

placed it on the southern continent, which had been known as Santa Cruz or the Land of Parrots.

The large folding map and the small book turned out to be a best-seller. It was reprinted again and again. Ringmann went off to teach in a university, and Waldseemüller edited the ancient Ptolemy, with more of his remarkable maps. In fact he changed his mind about Amerigo and a woman's name. Six years later he labeled the mysterious southern continent simply *Terra Incognita,* adding carefully that this land with its adjacent islands was discovered by Columbus of Genoa.

But the name America had a nice sound to it. Readers of the popular early *Cosmographiae Introductio* relished the romantic touch, and thought it matched well with Europa, Asia, and Africa. Because the name was repeated it began to appear elsewhere on later maps as *The New Land, or America,* and still later as *Brasil which some call America.*

Perhaps Amerigo Vespucci never saw his name so in print. Certainly he had nothing to do with putting it there. He worked in his accustomed silence as Pilot Major—of Spain. The accusation that he attempted to steal the fame of Columbus in those years is merely a thought of latter-day commentators. Columbus of Genoa was a broken man by the time the map with the name of America appeared. The year before his death he wrote his son that Vespucci "is a very honorable man, and has always desired to please me."

Vespucci did his last work, as Pilot Major, with maps. About the time Waldseemüller's Ptolemy came out at Strasbourg the middle-aged Peter Martyr visited Burgos in his quest of information of the New World.

"I addressed myself to the Bishop of Burgos," he wrote to the Pope, Leo X, "to whom all navigators make their reports. Seated in his room, we went over many reports, and we likewise studied the terrestrial globe on which the discoveries are marked. There, too, we went over many parchments which the explorers call navigators' charts. One of these maps had been drawn by the Portuguese, and they say Amerigo Vespucci of Florence helped in the making of it. He is very skilled in this art, and has himself voyaged many degrees beneath the equator. According to this chart we found the continent was larger than the caciques of Uraba told our countrymen."

Yes, Amerigo had found that out. In those years, however, the other continent, the Unknown Land, had neither name nor shape upon the maps.

And the Maps Go Underground

Something like a chain reaction was convulsing Europe during those first years of the sixteenth century. The impulse of the Renaissance penetrated even the Spanish-Portuguese peninsula with its flood of printed books and new concepts. Common folk there could read the Bible with their own eyes, and share the wit of the beloved Erasmus. To this escape from the medieval prison of thought there was added the growing certainty that a new part of the world was opening up beyond the sea.

Here was something undreamed of by the ancients, unnamed in their Biblical tale of Creation—unless it were indeed the fourth corner of the four corners of the earth.

The popular mind, devoted to miracles, seized eagerly on the wharfside tales of returning seamen who had wonders to relate for a goblet of wine; it fed avariciously on Peter Martyr's description of Garden of Eden people, animals that grew larger over there, and plants that sprang up from the soil a cubit in fifteen days. This happy conviction of the populace was not, however, shared by the scientists who had the duty of charting the New World. What was its true shape, size, and nature?

Never before had honest Christian map makers been faced with the problem of the earth opening up, as it were, beneath their eyes to disclose a new sixth, even a quarter of its sphere—surely not a *third!* Their earliest surviving maps reveal a remarkable confusion.

Peter Martyr related how "Thenceforth every Spaniard who thought he understood the science of measurements has drawn his own map."

Bartholomew, brother of the Admiral, sketched the upper coast of the southern continent—as *Mondo Novo*—circling up to a vague land mass he identifies as Asia, as far as a line of *Serici montes,* or mountains of China. He does not show the island of Cuba because the Admiral insisted until his death that this island was part of the mainland of Asia.

The indefatigable Basque, Juan de la Cosa, in the year 1500 painted an oxhide with Cuba correctly as the Isle of Isabella (although he had sworn with the others, at the Admiral's demand, that it was mainland). North of it he drew in only an imaginary coast line running almost due east, beset with the English flags of Cabot's discovery. He did not venture to say *what* it might be.

The map makers had no way of deciding what this Unknown Land might be. They did have the old-style *mappamundi* showing Asia projecting way over, almost to Iceland; they did cling to the old belief that anything new out there must be small, rather than large —islands rather than continents. There, up north, Codfish Land, Cortereal Land, and Cabot's coast all had been called parts of Asia. Well . . .

In the city of Ferrara its duke, Ercole d'Este, called upon his agent in Lisbon, one Alberto Cantino, to furnish him quickly with a clear map of all these new discoveries. In some way the agent got at the guarded Portuguese charts, and sent his lord in 1502 the famous Cantino map.

It marks the chaos of the birth of a continent. The tip of Greenland appears as Portuguese, "which cosmographers believe to be the end of Asia." (Fernandes had been there.) Cortereal Land becomes a chunky island, "Land of the King of Portugal." (Conveniently just across the dividing line.) Then, far back on the sea, there juts out a squarish mass with a point toward Isabella-Cuba. What is this, if not a part of Asia also?

This same apparition shows on Canerio's map (1503). Inland it fades into a mass of giant trees. It stands also on the 1507 map of the geographer of the Vosges, Waldseemüller, who fades it into mountains and sea with the inscription "Farther Unknown Land."

But something odd is happening to the embryo of a continent. It keeps the tip (Florida) pointed toward Cuba, and names are scrawled along the lateral coasts—names like River of Palms or Cape of the Sun. Names that a straying ship's captain would jot down for landmarks on an unknown coast. *Somebody* has been to the Unknown Land and talked about it.

Then in Seville in 1511 a map is printed with some of Peter Martyr's *Decades*. Here the vague coast above Cuba bears an odd title, "Part of the Island of Beimeni." So there is more to the island of Beimeni than this corner. An archipelago beneath it appears as "los Yucanas" (the Lucayas). And a legend on the back of the map states, "At the north there have been discovered marvellous countries and lands."

But what is Beimeni? An isle of wonder, according to the surviving natives at the one Spanish town of the New World, Santo Domingo, on Hispaniola. The wonder was a spring of water that restored the strength of youth to old men who bathed in it. A spring or a river? the Castilians demanded of the "Indians." It might be a river, but surely it was off there in the small islands, not on Hispaniola. On the Lucayas? Surely, surely—once a generation of native people bathed in the spring or river of Beimeni, and remained strong and young, unlike other generations. Where were these ageless Indians? Off yonder, not far, on the island the noble Castilians called San Juan.

Rumor of this wonder spread. It reached the ears of a veteran nobleman, Juan Ponce de León, who was then exploring the fertile and fairylike San Juan (Puerto Rico) for gold. The tale linked up with the old rumor of a "Brasil" isle of blessed long life somewhere in the Atlantic. Juan Ponce and his companions deemed it remarkable that the Indians should repeat a tale known, seemingly, only to Europeans. (The surviving natives tried desperately to escape being taken away as slaves, or forced to labor in the gold mines; they tried to send their implacable Christian masters elsewhere in pursuit of gold or other useless things craved by the strange supermen of the sea.)

Now by then Juan Ponce had heard also rumors of "marvellous lands" to the north. This undiscovered Beimeni, or Bimini, of the Indians might well be one of them.

The shadowy explorers of the tip of the Unknown Land might have drifted thither on the as yet unsuspected current of the Gulf Stream, or they might have been questing for slaves on new coasts. They left no official record for good reason.

The Spanish Court held a monopoly of navigation, claiming title to discovered land, and a fifth of profit in trade, if any. In Spain the *Casa de Contratación*—House of Trade—licensed strictly all overseas voyaging; it outfitted all vessels and inspected them on the return home. More, it set up a department under Amerigo Vespucci as Pilot Major, aided by Vicente Yáñez Pinzón and the experienced Juan de Solís, to make certain that shipmasters served the Crown, not themselves. Above all, the Pilot Major's new office demanded that voyagers' charts be turned in to it.

These charts then went under lock and key, to enable the Pilot Major and his Junta to prepare a secret master chart of "all the lands and isles of the Indies until then discovered and belonging to the Crown." The master chart, or *Padrón Real,* was kept under lock probably at Seville, with two keys, one being given to the Pilot Major, the other to the Cosmographer Major.

This was the Spanish counter to the efficient security measures of the Portuguese Junta, which erased new discoveries from the charts of returning Portuguese, kept its findings about Santa Cruz Land hidden, and sent more fleets racing eastward where Tristão da Cunha and Albuquerque were already at Ormuz, making a chain of fortified posts to the rich source of the spices, the Golden Chersonese. But those fleets from the small Portuguese ports sailed under patriotic captains, with an empire in view and immense profits already in hand. Spanish voyagers of stubborn Basque and Catalan strain often revolted against the Casa's control and slipped out of unofficial harbors to seek some profit for themselves. They also kept their charts to themselves.

So, while rumors flooded the ports of Europe, an illicit traffic sprang up in secret routes and charts. Much the same thing was happening at the western control point of Santo Domingo, where ships slipped away at night to voyage off the record.

The South Sea Appears

That restless war veteran, Juan Ponce of León, did not revolt when he fitted out two vessels in 1512, turned his back on official-dom, and started forth on his own. Since the second voyage of Columbus he had fought and conquered for the Crown, while clearing the surviving Arawaks out of eastern Hispaniola, and sub-duing the others of San Juan (Puerto Rico) to slavery and gold hunting for the Crown and his own pocket. For the Castilian "people of war" were often finding it easier to burn and mass-slay the natives than make them labor as peaceable slaves.

The year before his take-off stunning news from Europe acted like a goad on such Castilian frontiersmen as he. Manuel, King of Portugal, announced then to the Pope, and so to all Christians, that the Portuguese Viceroy, Affonso d'Albuquerque, had captured "the Golden Chersonese which the inhabitants call Malacha, a city of wonderful size . . . the most fertile land and most famous market for all spices, all incenses, and also gold, silver and precious stones."

The Portuguese in the east had mastered one of the great goals of Christian fortune seekers, while the Castilians still sweated in dirty plantations, growing roots and breeding pigs while driving savages to dig fragments of gold ore. And that year Ponce's island of San Juan was taken from him to be given to two governors of the Crown. Ponce immediately sought and obtained a license from the Crown itself to discover and develop the promising isle of "Beniny," which was Bimini ("Beimini") with the Fountain of Youth.

He set out with good men and the veteran pilot Antón de Alaminos on seaworthy ships, and skirted the chain of Lucayas (Bahamas) looking in at San Salvador, where the Castilians had first sighted land. He fell in with another roving vessel. Deciding that neither slaves nor fountain was to be found on these coral isles, Juan Ponce kept on going with the rover.

On a Sunday in March 1513 the three ships sighted a coast to the west. It was abloom with flowers, in "wild green growth, that stretched on unchanging." Since it was Easter, he named it for *Pascua Florida* (Feast of Flowers), going ashore for water, and to claim the island, as he took it to be, for the Spanish Crown. Actually he was close to the St. Johns River in Florida.

Heading south along the coast, the fortune seekers found that it did not change, and they began to wonder whether it was island or *terra firma*. Pelicans flapped around them, and a rushing current held back the ships even with all sails set in a fair breeze. Nor did anchors hold inshore against this current (the Gulf Stream).

Whenever the vessels put in to fill water casks or careen for repairs, the men of Florida thronged around, armed with bows, shields, and spears tipped with sharp fishbones. Apparently they had encountered Castilians before; they showed no awe, and used their weapons when disturbed. The experienced Juan Ponce tried to avoid conflict, but he got little trade and no slaves—only one old man to guide them along the shore and make them understand the language. These thronging men were not as fearful as the Arawaks, nor as shifty as the Caribs.

Rounding a southern cape of their Tierra Florida, the voyagers estimated it to lie at 28° 15' (a bad error in navigation) and began to be uncertain of their own position, because the current was pulling them back "with more force than the wind." Still hoping to find a trove of some kind, they headed westerly along other islands, with no better luck. Juan Ponce had not been able to fill his hold with slaves.

The summer was ending, and he turned back to search for his own island of San Juan. The record, as it survives, says that the mariners searched "all banks and streams" for life-giving water in vain. Juan Ponce himself does not seem to have set his heart on this, for he made no search inland, and at the end he allowed a lieutenant, Juan Pérez, to take one vessel to continue the search. He had not found Bimini, and the luxuriant coast of Tierra Florida yielded little to pay expenses. He did apply for a patent to colonize it, but the Casa and King in Spain saw nothing worth further effort in Tierra Florida, and sent the veteran Ponce to subdue Caribs instead.

Another voyager for the Crown touched down on Tierra Florida presently with more evil fortune. Hernández de Córdoba, with the same Antón de Alaminos as pilot, was driven after a storm upon the western tip of the peninsula. He sheered off after a savage fight with the natives, to die of his wounds later in Cuba. For nine years Florida was left to its alligator-eating inhabitants.

For that space of time the eyes of the viceroys and adventurers of Spain were drawn to the west and south, not to the north. For there in the west an explorer climbed the ridge of the isthmus and beheld, incredulous, the other ocean.

A new horizon opened, with word of the discovery: "A main sea, the Sea of the South, is found."

Until then the wilderness had defeated the Castilians. It was the one force greater than the driving spirit of the invaders from Spain. The strange personality of the Castilian had been laid upon the islands of the Caribbean; starving, it imported swine for meat, and gathered sugar cane to ship back to the home ports. Idealizing its conquest as the Christianization of a new world, it endured only by the encomiendas that gave to each Spaniard a number of natives who learned only to labor while being taught in theory to save their souls.

When the slaves died off, the Castilian brought others, Negroes from Africa, by Portuguese ships. The black slaves were stronger and more submissive; the plantations on the islands survived under their hands. Fresh food came from cassava, sweet potatoes, cocoa, and guava. Lacking women, the Castilians—by Court decree—took native wives. But on the mainland the wilderness withstood them.

They came to it as conquistadors who had expelled the Jews from Spain and subjected the Andalusians, and carried their banners across to the north of Africa, where Cardinal Jiménez dreamed of creating a Christian empire. The conquistadors in the west shared this sense of mission, enduring their suffering in this region of

deceptive beauty, being strangely at home in such an escape from
reality.

"The Pinzons, from Andalusia," Peter Martyr wrote, "fell to
their death while exploring the vast coast of the continent and the
banks of the marvellous Maragnon [Amazon] River . . . they fell
by the arrows of savages and were cut to bits to be served up in
dishes."

On the coast they called hopefully Golden Castile, Ojeda, the
witty acrobat of the Court, died in the wilderness, and that fine
pilot, Juan de la Cosa, ended his life in the jungle swollen by the
poison of an arrow. *Somewhere* ahead of them had waited their
destiny, appointed by God.

Their ships sank when the teredo worms ate through the wood
of the hulls; their strength drained away with yellow fever in the
jungle where the earth lay dark under growth that climbed towering trees toward the sun. Nicuesa, who had charmed listeners in
Spain with his lute playing, led an expedition into Golden Castile
(the Isthmus of Panama) and became a witless scarecrow of a man,
set adrift by starving followers in a derelict brigantine, never to be
heard of again.

Young men, wearying of the penurious island plantations,
drifted out to the mainland to attempt to win with their swords
some fortune from the Indian-infested wilderness. They escaped
from the laws of the Casa and the policing of Santo Domingo to
find some new horizon of personal glory. One of them, Vasco
Núñez de Balboa, who had come over with the notary Bastidas, to
find only poverty in the islands, escaped as a stowaway to the mainland, and gathered together the survivors left by Nicuesa and Bastidas on the coast of Golden Castile. Leading them away from the
fever marshes and poisoned arrows to food in the Gulf of Darien,
he heard from Indians the rumor of a sea beyond the isthmus. Vasco
Núñez and his outlaw band—with a swine keeper named Pizarro
among them—served the Indian caciques as mercenaries and followed the rumor into the wilderness with Indians as guides.

For twenty-five days the Balboa band cut its way through the
jungle to the heights, where a Quarequa native led Vasco Núñez

to a peak overlooking the Pacific. "Vasco looked longingly at it," Peter Martyr relates. "He ordered a halt and went alone to climb the peak. He raised his hands and saluted the South Sea—according to his story—giving thanks to God and all the Saints for reserving this glory for him, an ordinary man."

Down on the shore of the Pacific Balboa's men had no monument to set up; they could only carve the name of the King of Castile on trees with their knives, above a pyramid of piled stones.

They named it the Mar del Sur because at that spot, a little east of the present canal, it lay to the south of them.

And their discovery in 1513 turned the search of other Spaniards to the south, away from the unrewarding north.

The Search Goes South

With the opening of this new horizon, 1513–19, to Spanish eyes a sort of intoxication stirred Spanish minds. No more than a narrow isthmus separated the two oceans. And beyond this neck of land lay untold riches.

There was the Isle of Pearls. Pearls big as olives to be gathered by the pound. "The mouths of the Spaniards fairly watered," Peter Martyr reported to Rome, "as they talked about this great wealth."

There was new gold to be had. Vasco Núñez gathered in shining breastplates of men and bracelets of women from the caciques of the South Sea coast, friendly or subdued. The son of one such Indian chief watched the ragged Castilians weighing out the ornaments on their scales. This son of Comogre heard them quarreling about the sharing of the gold, and he caught their attention by striking the scales, scattering the gold. "What is this thing, Christians?" the Indian exclaimed. "Why do you value this? You destroy its worth by melting these necklaces into metal. We value such metal no more than a lump of clay until it is made into a jar or necklace. You thirst for it until you go from your country to seek

it. You bring calamity on other people to get it. If your thirst tor-
ments you so, I will show you a land where you can get it."

It turned out that this gold country lay beyond vaster mountains
and savage peoples, far to the south. (This was in fact the first evidence of the gold work of the Panama natives. Beyond it waited the
treasure of the Inca in Peru.)

At the same time news of fresh Portuguese discoveries in the
east fanned the excitement in Spain. The Portuguese had reached
the Moluccas, the Spice Islands, and were sailing toward the coast
of Cathay (China). Now for the first time it appeared that the
Castilians might come upon wealth in the New World to equal the
enormous trove of the Crown of Lisbon. Were not the findings of
Balboa's band "proof that Nature conceals vast treasures in this
country? What it will prove to be when the mysterious depths of
the country are penetrated, no man can say."

Even the usually noncommittal Peter Martyr was moved to
hopeful speculation. "Spain need no longer excavate the earth down
to infernal depths to draw out her wealth. She will find riches in the
sun-dried banks of rivers by merely sifting the earth. Pearls will be
gathered in with little effort."

Such speculation was heightened by some odd pseudoscientific
reasoning. In the east precious stones and incense came from the
equatorial zone. Then did not the direct burning heat of the sun
under the equator fuse these diamonds and emeralds out of stone,
and create balm and incense from plants? And would not similar
products of the sun's heat be found to the south under the equator
within Santa Cruz Land that some called America?

"To the south is fortune to be sought," exclaimed Peter Martyr.
"To the south, I say!"

Vasco Núñez de Balboa, who had cut a road through the
wilderness of the isthmus and had found a way of mutual existence
with the Indian people, was made Adelantado (Advancer) of the
South Sea. He was building a fleet out of green trees to search that
sea, when he was tried on a faked charge of treason by the new
Governor of Golden Castile, and hanged. The Governor proceeded
to carry on the search for his own profit, but without the redheaded

Vasco's uncanny knack of getting things done. (And Incan Peru would be entered in later years, not by the fairly humane Balboa, but by the brutal soldier-adventurer Pizarro.)

The office of the Pilot Major of the Casa de Contratación at Seville reacted at once to the discovery of Balboa's sea and the capture of the Moluccas by the hated rivals of Lisbon. It started a search to the south.

Its secret master map, the Padrón Real, must have shown an unbroken coast line of the new continent from Yucatan down around the bulge of Portuguese Brazil (Santa Cruz Land). Where did the continent end? There at the end would be the salt water route around it—and the direct way from the ports of Spain to the Spice Islands of the east. By this route the caravels of Spain could pass from the Atlantic into the new South Sea.

Like cosmographers everywhere in those years, the experts of the Pilot's office held to the illusion that the earth was smaller than it was. By sailing due west *now* they could accomplish what Columbus had failed to do—reach the treasures of Asia by a shorter route, and snatch them from the Portuguese. For the Moluccas, if not the Golden Chersonese, might well lie across the globe on the Spanish side of the line.

The Pilot Major, Juan de Solís, sailed himself with fast vessels along Vespucci's track down from the bulge of Brazil. He made his first try to the west at the deceptive broad estuary of the Plate, which he named the Fresh Water Sea. It led him up, into the hinterland, to his death among savage natives, who ate him within sight of his crews. These failed to show the unquenchable courage of most Spaniards, and sailed home with a cargo of red wood.

Then along their track came a ghostly Portuguese craft. Whatever it found was never reported—if the vessel survived its secret search.

(For the record of history preserves for us little more than the accounts of successful discovery. The failures are not written down. We know little of the many early navigators who set out in desperation or illusion to feel their way into strange waters, guiding themselves by strange constellations while the hulls of the ships rotted and scurvy, thirst, or starvation decimated their crews, and they kept on in the face of disaster.)

The finest of these navigators came after Solís. Ferdinand Magellan hardly looked into the Plate estuary. He kept on to the south with five ill-found vessels officered by mutinous Spaniards and manned by sweepings of the wharves. A Portuguese, born Fernão Magalhães, he had voyaged under his own flag in the far east at the capture of Malacha, and perhaps at the Moluccas; he had sold himself (1518–19) to the King of Spain under the delusion that the Moluccas were near Balboa's port of Panama.

Magellan drove ships and men south, to find the strait that bears his name. He entered the southern Pacific. But the unknown ocean stretched to incredible length; he brought the remnant of his fleet across it to the Philippines, to die there as a mercenary, fighting for an island king in order to get supplies.

One rotting vessel survived to anchor again after three years at the mole of Seville, with eighteen white men and four Malays still alive. They had made the first circumnavigation of the globe. The scarecrows on *Victoria* had kept tally of the days, and they protested angrily when the cosmographers of Seville assured them they must have dropped a day somewhere. The survivors of the voyage had kept a true count; they had followed the sun for the twenty-four hours of its course around the earth, and one day was gone forever from their tally.

By their voyage the true width of the Pacific was made known to the Casa and the King. Only by desperate hazard could a ship pass Magellan's strait and the waste of the far ocean to the Spice Islands, and the ports of Cathay.

The planners of the Casa turned after that to seek a way through the middle of their New World. Surely some strait must sever the neck of Balboa's isthmus. "They panted," an observer related, "to find their strait."

Miracle of the North

Balboa had not found it. Avila, the governor who hanged him, could not find it. The brittle and entirely cruel Avila built a mule track across the isthmus, instead, to the new port of Panama. The daring Hernández de Córdoba could not find it before he was blown by the storm across to Florida and his death.

Then, if the strait did not exist upon the isthmus, it might lie in the still-unknown north. So the planners of the Casa conjectured, and ordered search to be made in the northern region.

On their guarded map, the Padrón Real, the amazing outline of their new southern continent was taking shape in these years from 1517–21. Far down, near the other pole, the continent ended; its coast rose wavering to the Fresh Water Sea of Solís, rose to the bulge of Santa Cruz-Brazil-America claimed by the hated Portuguese, around Cape Augustine, curving in to their Pearl Coast and little Venice, to Darien on the gulf, to the neck of the isthmus marked by the new ports of Nombre de Dios and Panama, up to the small bulge of Cape Gracias a Dios, and to the vague projection of Yucatan. But in all that immensity of thousands of leagues no passage for the salt water of the sea had been revealed. Only the unbroken line of forest or jungle, backed sometimes by the bastions of verdant hills, stood there like a rampart. Surely it was against nature and the will of God that narrow land should make a barrier from pole to pole between the two oceans. Somewhere the waters of the seas *must* flow together. How else could the mysterious ocean current flow to the east around the barrier of the tip of Florida that Juan Ponce had examined? And if Florida were truly an island, the passage might lie north of it.

The cosmographers and councilors of Seville remembered that the oldest surviving pilot, Antón de Alaminos, had talked of a new passage to be found for the ships of Spain. . . .

When they ordered the search for the passage to be made, how-ever, other forces interfered with it.

First came the weakening of the law. The new King was a boy named Charles from Flanders, who understood little of the very complex Spain. "He directs nothing," Peter Martyr wrote tersely, "but is himself directed." The power of *El Rey, el Ley* of the Ferdi-nand and Isabella rule stretched thin now across the Atlantic. It was said that the Council of the Indies in Seville became the gather-ing of the adventurers in Santo Domingo. More than that, the governors of the new islands looked for profit of their own from the new beachheads on the mainland. To this end they made use of the fleets in the Caribbean which no longer came from Spain on mis-sions of the sovereigns. Then, too, the adventurers like Balboa, who held the beachheads in the wilderness with their swords and wits, took every opportunity to avoid the authority of the governors like Avila.

In this near-lawlessness the force of the rumors began to be felt. As Balboa's men had heard the first reports of the gold beyond Panama, Córdoba's band in their northern search had heard of, or seen, wonders in Yucatan (the first report of the Aztec civilization). Up in the northern hinterland, they said, corn grew in fields worked by people wearing colored cotton garments, living in great houses of stone, worshiping giant idols. It was like Grand Cairo, in Egypt!

So when the governor of (newly conquered) Cuba sent his cousin Juan de Grijalva to search for the missing strait, he also urged Grijalva to investigate this rumor of wealth and well-being inland. There had been so many rumors from the Indians that led the Christians nowhere. So the careful Grijalva—who desired to escape the fate of Córdoba—rounded Yucatan (1517-18) and searched gin-gerly to the north. He found no strait in the coast, bare except for palm trees and mud villages of fishing folk. He turned back at the river Pánuco.

But Grijalva brought back to his cousin more reports of the hidden empire. It lay far inland, in a city on a lake ruled by a *Moctezuma*. Infuriated because Grijalva had made only a coastal survey, the governor of Cuba handed the search over to an adventurer with guts, one Hernando Cortes, a great lover of women. Nothing, apparently, was said about a strait. And Cortes, taking a tough fighting band of Christians, vanished from authority into the hinterland.

Meanwhile the aged pilot Alaminos had been deep in talk with De Garay, Governor of fertile Jamaica. He urged De Garay to explore the mysterious north. Now was the opportunity to do so, when King and Casa called for search for a strait. This man who had steered a caravel of the great Admiral may have hoped that at long last open water could be found to Cathay. He mentioned a "new passage of the Bahamas [where Columbus had landed]." Or he may simply have been on the track of the mystifying Gulf Stream, which flowed like a river around Florida, which he knew so well.

So it happened that in 1519 three vessels went to explore the circuit of the Gulf of Mexico.

They found the Father of Waters.

Apparently their skilled pilot and sea captain, Alonzo de Pineda, headed up the western coast of the Florida peninsula. No passage lay there, for "the land prevented their keeping to the course." They turned west, probing at the coast, which they found low and barren of interest but fertile. Here they came in time to a river both wide and deep. It impressed them because they sailed up it and took time to careen and repair their vessels, passing forty villages where friendly folk supplied them with fruit and food. (No conquistadors had been there, and Pineda took pains, although he carried weapons in plenty, to provoke no conflict.) They called the great river the Espíritu Santo. It might have been Mobile Bay, but seems to have been the Mississippi because in the chart marking their voyage made the next year the Espíritu Santo appears close to the Mississippi's position.

From there the searching vessels seem to have followed the coast west. Wherever they went, they ended up at the desert stretch of the Pánuco River (modern Tampico). They sent a chart back to Seville, and there the chart of 1520 shows the closed circuit of the Gulf of

Mexico. Rivers are marked on it, but no passage out. And a Spanish map of 1529 marks this coast as *Tierra de Garay*.

Alaminos was not defeated. He claimed that Spanish fleets could go from this new coast of the Pánuco and the port of Vera Cruz swiftly to home ports by following the "new passage" around Florida on the Gulf Stream northerly, to be borne on their way by current and winds due east to Spain. (This was the convenient route followed later by the Spanish plate fleets, homeward bound.)

Then at the end of 1519 came astounding news. The wandering Hernando Cortes had made his way through the wilderness to the miracle of the city on the lake, Tenochtitlán. There Spanish eyes beheld the treasure of Moctezuma, the Aztec.

"When we saw not one but many cities built in the water with towers of stone, with that straight and level causeway leading to them," a conquistador wrote, "we were amazed, and said it was like a legend of Amadis. Some of us even asked if it were not all a dream. I do not know how to tell of things that had never been seen before."

It seemed miraculous—this hidden empire of five million souls dwelling in ordered city life, sending to Hernando Cortes gifts of the sun in gold and the moon in silver, so massive and heavy that two men could not carry them . . .

Tidings of the unimagined Aztec Empire acted with explosive force on the Spanish venture into the New World. Men deserted the mines and plantations of the unrewarding conquered islands. They streamed from the governing city of Santo Domingo to take ship for the mainland.

It was the first gold rush of the New World. And it made certain that Spaniards, not Portuguese, would explore the southern shores of the Unknown Land.

The Wilderness Defeats De Ayllón

Nothing could have challenged the eager Spanish spirit more than the prospect of danger, riches, and a cultured slave population ready-made. Here was revealed their destination in the tormenting wilderness of the New World, more fabulous than Grand Cairo, nearer than the Spice Islands of the Portuguese east. Three expeditions set sail from the islands to the continent in the next years.

In the rush of preparation it did not occur to these other would-be conquistadors that Hernando Cortes had brought about his miracle by very practical means. Like Balboa, he had enlisted the aid of powerful natives allies (the Tlaxcalans, hostile to the Aztecs, who acted as guides). He had entered Tenochtitlán with apparent good-will toward the Aztecs, and he had been able to control the populace at first by making its lord Moctezuma a hostage. Above all, he had been capable of bringing his small army safely through a wilderness road.

In San Juan Island, the elderly Juan Ponce de León was an experienced soldier. He possessed his old patent to Tierra Florida. And Florida might reveal some such hidden city as Tenochtitlán. Quickly he threw out an excuse to the distant Casa and still more distant King:

"And now I return to that island, if it be God's will, to settle it . . . so the name of Christ may be praised there and your Majesty served with fruit from that land. And I also intend to explore the coast of said island further and learn whether it is an island, or whether it connects with the land where Diego Velásquez is."

(Diego Velásquez was the governor of Cuba who had sent out Cortes and now had a claim of his own to the discovered Mexico. Just where Mexico actually lay in relation to Florida was not at all clear in that year.)

With his old impetuosity but without his old strength Juan Ponce spent all his means to outfit ships, soldiery, colonists, and priests. He added tools, horses, and cattle, and set out in the stormy spring of 1521 to survey—by his own statement—settle, explore, and convert *his* Florida.

Four months later he was on the west coast where Córdoba had fared so badly. His priests harangued the natives, but Juan Ponce found no port suitable for disembarkation—or at least none that satisfied him. He led neither a competent exploration force nor a

well-equipped fleet of colonists. With cattle aboard he could not remain at sea for long. What actually happened does not appear in
the records.

But soon on the west coast of Florida, below Pineda's turning
point, Juan Ponce entered a bay (San Carlos, or Estero) and came
to savage battle with the Calusa people, who had powerful bows.
These Calusas may have driven Córdoba from this coast years before. Here Juan Ponce was wounded by an arrow in the thigh and
sailed back to San Juan to die. One of his vessels went off to quest
for gold, to Vera Cruz, port of Aztec land.

Francisco de Garay, Governor of Jamaica and, like Juan Ponce,
veteran of the early discoveries, also had a claim to the mainland
coast. *Tierra de Garay,* somewhere by the greatest of rivers, had
been won for him by the skilled pilot Pineda. Obviously his Garay
Land lay close indeed to the remarkable Mexico then being conquered by Cortes.

Now the competent Pineda had brought back to the Governor's
house at Jamaica a rough chart of the coast and also a crop of rumors
from the banks of the great river. These were rumors of the old sort.
Village folk on the river Espíritu Santo wore some gold nose rings
and throat bands. They had assured Pineda's crews that the gold
came from the back country, from a city beyond the river where
dwelt giants and dwarfs.

But now these rumors of the river linked up with the great
find of Cortes in the mountains. In a fever of suspense Garay spent
his fortune on an expedition. Grijalva joined him in filling thirteen
vessels of all sorts with hidalgos, horsemen, and halberdiers.

This time Garay sailed with his ships, and managed to lose several of them on the way. He had been careful to order his captains
to avoid conflict with the natives, and indeed had drawn up a model
plan of colonizing Pineda's fertile coast without making slaves of the
people there.

But he laid his course to the western side of the gulf, and landed
so close to Cortes's area that he came into conflict, not with the
natives, but with the hardened soldiery of that conquistador. The

consequence was that most of Garay's weapon men deserted him to join the invaders of Mexico.

Conflict was beginning between governors and adventurers; it would soon become in New Spain the strife of lieutenant against captain, of conquistador against conquistador. So great had been the stakes laid upon the scales of discovery by Cortes.

Lucas de Ayllón, a justice of Santo Domingo, was a conscientious official with wealth but no experience as an explorer. Since his island faced, as it were, the outer coast of the Unknown Land, he had planned for some time to explore it. From his Hispaniola the "new Bahama passage" of the pilot Alaminos led easily up past the islands to the nebulous coast line that might well open into the much desired western passage to Cathay. De Ayllón was happily wed, prosperous, and righteous. Yet he may have dreamed, as Bastidas had dreamed, of following the dangerous way of the conquistadors. He had sent out two vessels to explore the northern coast, ordering his captains not to take Indians for slaves. One ship had come back with seventy Indian slaves; the other had been lost. This matter De Ayllón, being a justice, had taken so to heart that he had gone to Spain to argue it, and there had heard the tidings of the Aztec Empire.

After years of preparation he did follow the example of the conquistadors, but sailed to his own coast with some 500 souls including eager Dominicans and Negro slaves and 100 horses. He had made his pledge to the Crown to search 800 leagues of the coast for "the passage to the Spice Islands."

How many leagues the migrants from Santo Domingo actually traversed remains unknown. Like Juan Ponce's mariners, they had trouble finding a sheltered bay with anchorage and a good town site among friendly Indians who produced food. (They were off the Carolinas, where the earlier ships had seized slaves.) They ended up before the autumn of 1526 on a river they named the Jordán.

The banks of the river were agreeable but marshy; beyond stretched dense forest without large villages or cultivated lands. The animals of this forest were hard to kill with crossbows or firelocks. It made a dark wilderness around them. (They may well have been on the Cape Fear River, since they estimated it to lie at 33° 20′ of latitude; just possibly they were on Chesapeake Bay.)

Having lost one vessel, they built a small craft out of green timber—the first ship to be launched by European hands in the Unknown Land.

That is the one certain thing they did. For the rest, the wilderness defeated them. They were not prepared for the fever of the swamps, or for the autumn cold of the north. The Indians sheltered themselves in long houses warmed by central fires; the Spaniards froze in cabins of boughs and on shipboard. De Ayllón died and strife broke out with the intractable Indians, with the rebellious Negroes, and with each other. The survivors left their river, and 150 regained Santo Domingo. The new-built bark, bearing De Ayllón's body, was lost at sea.

Now on the maps of the Unknown Land new Spanish claims appeared in the south. The continent behind the river Jordán became *Tierra de Ayllón,* and at its southern tip *Tierra Florida,* merging with *Tierra de Garay.* This ran along a hotly disputed boundary with the New Spain which the ruthless Cortes was shaping out of the Aztec Empire. The northern limit of New Spain was not known as yet.

After the landings of the little conquistadors the English claim to the nebulous northern coast set up by John Cabot thirty years before was pretty well forgotten.

III. The Search for the Middle Passage

The Fishermen Claim Codfish Land

CLOSE on the heels of the defeated little conquistadors came the trained explorers of the governments. As the Columbian discoveries of thirty years before had launched other fleets toward the new-found islands, the Balboa-Magellan discoveries started a race to find a passage through the new continents. It lasted through the decisive years from 1520 to 1529.

In those years world trade passed swiftly from the Mediterranean, to enter the Atlantic. At the same time the personal law of the late sovereigns of Spain changed to the demands of an empire. For in the autumn of 1520 its young monarch from Flanders was crowned at Aix, the ancient city of Charlemagne, as Charles V, Roman emperor. Charles Hapsburg won his election to that high office because Jakob Fugger the banker lent him florins enough to pay off the electors—taking as security for the loan a mortgage on silver mines in the New World. As ruler of the vestige of the Roman Empire in Europe, the youthful Charles faced troubles that were not all caused by the ferment of the Renaissance. There was the need of his own Flanders, the antagonism of the lords of Spain to a foreigner, the challenge of a stubborn monk, Martin Luther, who had written *On the Freedom of a Christian Man*. And there was the military challenge of the Othmanli Turks, whose young Sultan

Suleiman dared launch Turkish fleets into the Mediterranean. As the new Emperor, who was also King of Spain, contended with these opposing forces within the Old World, he would drain treasure from the New World to enable him to do so.

"The Spaniards have brought back two stands, one of gold and one of silver, and both pure without any alloy." So Peter Martyr informed the Pope, Leo X, who had been Giovanni de' Medici. "The gold stand weighs 3800 castellanos, and in the center of it rises the image of a man a cubit high, resembling a king on his throne . . . two golden necklaces, set with 32 red stones and with 123 green stones. I have seen helmets they brought covered with blue stones or scales of gold from which hang golden bells . . . a sceptre of gold set with jewels . . . and 24 breastplates of gold. They made gifts of such a quantity of gold that Cortes writes how, after melting the metal into ingots the royal share of one fifth came to 34,000 castellanos."

This first trickle of ingots was growing into cargoes of bullion soon to be brought home yearly by the Spanish plate (*plata*—silver) fleets. And in turn it would pay for the building of the great shipping required by Spain's new empire of the sea.

At the same time supremacy at sea was passing from the Portuguese to the dynamic Spaniards.

With their amazing ability to organize the Spaniards centered their effort in the Council of the Indies (surpassing the Junta of Lisbon); they taught navigation at the University of Salamanca and pilotage at the ports of Cádiz and Cartagena (dwarfing the pioneer School of Sagres). They tapped the brains of foreigners, making Peter Martyr first an instructor at Salamanca, then a member of the Council of the Indies—enlisting Portuguese map makers, and the matchless Magellan, translating Portuguese works on astronomy and the sphere, until Fernández de Enciso (one of the defeated conquistadors of Golden Castile) could publish in 1519 his first treatise, the *Suma de Geografía*.

At the same time the office of the Pilot Major enforced its monopoly of the new nautical instruments and the outfitting of transatlantic vessels. Fernando Columbus noted: "Whenever a master undertakes a voyage to the Indies, he must show his implements to the Pilot Major—his map, compass, astrolabe and sailing directions. Since the Pilot Major is the friend of the Cosmographer, if he sees that any map or instrument is not the work of his friend, he refuses to give his certificate to the master, and he keeps the instruments ... so that no ordinary person is willing to make such instruments for fear of the enmity of the Pilot Major and his friend. I who say this have witnessed it."

Locked behind the two keys of Pilot Major and Cosmographer at Seville, the master map, the Padrón Real, was presently to become the Padrón General of "all the islands and continent already discovered, or to be discovered." Shipyards were launching the new world vessels, carracks and galleons of four masts with lateen rig at bow and stern, two-deckers, giants of the ocean capable of bearing the steel-clad *tercios* of Spain, and migrants and slaves by the hundreds to and from the Indies. The decks were strengthened to bear the explosive force of large cannon, the hulls were rounded out at the waterline to withstand the shock of a broadside.

These warships were the instruments of a new and decisive force. One such galleon could take captive a fleet of defenseless merchant craft. Global sea power was in the making.

Before Dias rounded Africa, the enclosed Mediterranean had been the theater of war at sea of the Europeans. Now the immense sea routes of the outer world lay open, to be controlled by the nation with the most powerful battle fleet. In the Western Hemisphere the Spaniards were the first to accomplish that.

This issue of sea power would shape events in the Unknown Land more than any other single force.

In June 1520 two underprivileged monarchs of the Atlantic nations met together. Both being cut off from the expanding Iberian empires, they had much to talk about. One was the youthful Henry Tudor, eighth of the name, king of England; the other, who liked to be called the first gentleman of Europe, was Francis of Valois, first of the name, the Most Christian King of France. The field of their meeting being hung with gleaming draperies has been called the Field of the Cloth of Gold. Henry crossed the Channel, however, on a giant new vessel, *Henri Grace à Dieu,* commonly called the *Great Harry*. Its topgallant sails towered skyward, and it cleaved the water with a weight of 1500 tons. Francis could embark on the *Grand Louise,* a four-master splendid with painted shields and projecting cannon. These Anglo-French monarchs had at the moment no claim or particular interest in the Unknown Land.

Their fisherfolk had both. Men of Bristol brought in yearly valuable hauls from Codfish Land. One year the English Vice-Admiral William Fitzwilliam urged Cardinal Wolsey that warships on the west coast "be sent forwards for the commyng home of the new fownd Isle landes fleet."

Other fishing fleets made the voyage from La Rochelle and Dieppe, and they showed the way to the folk of Normandy. The markets of Europe had need of the cod from the new banks. Since the Portuguese fishers had preëmpted the harbors from Cape Race north, the French took the harbors south to Cape Breton, which had its name from them.

Unrecorded in the annals of empire, these fishing fleets waged their own conflict for the far northern coasts. A memorandum came to Henry VIII: *"In the kyngs hands*. Item—taken in the Cost of Normandy a shipp of Rouen wt XI men laden wt new fownd lande fyssh, containing IX thousand . . . prised at £ 120." (A Normandy fishing vessel from the New Found Land had been captured with 9000 cod worth 120 English pounds, silver—a very large amount for those days.)

These were straws showing where the wind blew unseen. And after the first news of Cortes's treasure reached Lisbon, a solitary Portuguese appeared like a wraith of the Corte-Reals in the New Found Land. As usual his real purpose remains a riddle—except that he did some rapid and skillful exploring and said nothing about what he found.

João Alvares Fagundes was a nobleman of Viana, a fishing port, who went across with the fishing fleet and some companions at his own expense. So the documents say; but they add that he was given a grant by "King Emmanuel, by the grace of God King of Portugal and of the Algarves, of this and that side the sea in Africa, lord of

Guinea and of the conquest, navigation and commerce of Ethiopia, Arabia, Persia, and India, etc." (Manuel's overseas empire had grown.)

From Cape Race, Fagundes, probably guided by the fishermen, traced the coast of Newfoundland south, probed into the Gulf of St. Lawrence, gave names that still endure to some islands and bays, and made a pretense of a settlement near Cape Breton, which was a sphere of influence of the French fleets. Thereupon in May 1521 he was rewarded with grants of the lands discovered "this side the line of demarcation with Castile."

Did the nobleman Fagundes really try to restore the Portuguese claim—now discredited—to this northeast corner of the new continent? Did he plan to make a base for his fishermen of Viana at one of the chosen harbors of the French? Or did he make a quick search for a possible western passage—the prize for which the new empires contended? Fagundes never explained.

Unexpectedly the French took a hand in the quest.

Their fishermen had been crossing also to Santa Cruz Land, or Brazil. There quietly enough some Portuguese Jews had taken refuge; one acquired a monopoly of the trade in red dyewood. They managed to live well enough with the native folk, although Brazil was being depicted upon maps with giant trees from which hung limbs of Europeans, severed by the hungry cannibals of lurid voyagers' tales. The Normans and Bretons traded for this wood, used in dyeing wool, and for monkeys, parrots, and poorish cinnamon. They also pillaged Portuguese craft.

Then Cortes began to ship his plundered treasures home, and the alert Bretons and Normans turned to the finer sport of waylaying "the silver ships." In 1521 Francis I went to war with Charles V, whose empire stretched around most of France. This gave the French "pirates" the opportunity to levy patriotic tribute on all the other transatlantic shipping of that day.

The spirit of this French resistance by sea was embodied in the fabulous Jean Ango, who kept open house near Dieppe for wandering poets and exiled Italian artists as well as pilots. He combined artistic appreciation with the new art of preying upon the sea. Among the habitués of Ango's house were a certain John the Florentine and a skilled pilot Giovanni da Verrazano, also from Florence.

The first of the two, John the Florentine (alias Jean Florin and Juan Flory in the chronicles), seemed to act at sea as Ango's lieutenant. Overnight he gained international fame when he seized off Cape St. Vincent the Spanish carrack laden with Moctezuma's gifts to Cortes. This treasure was intended for Charles, the Emperor. Peter Martyr knew the amount of it and explained methodically: "Were it all melted down—the shields, rings, jewelry, helmets and other ornaments—it would total 150,000 ducats."

All of this, or most of it, was delivered instead by the Florentine and Ango to Francis, now the enemy of Charles. It might have been sight of this spectacular treasure, or the urging of his sea captains, or more probably a whim of the volatile Francis that led him to exclaim, "I know of no clause in the will of Father Adam that gives all the outer world to my cousin Charles!" And Francis decided to send somebody to discover and so claim lands for France in the New World.

Naturally enough he called upon Jean Ango, who outfitted four vessels; naturally Ango called upon the most experienced pilot of his circle to make the ocean crossing. This proved to be Giovanni da Verrazano, who had sailed the eastern Mediterranean and possibly the other route to the East Indies. (Verrazano was *not* John the Florentine, alias Florin and Flory, as histories often assume.) Rumor persists that a clique of Italian merchants at Lyon backed the Ango-Verrazano voyage in the hope of discovering a passage to Cathay.

So much is clear, but it is not at all clear what Ango's four vessels did at the start off the European coast. They carried heavy armament; January was a bad month to attempt the North Atlantic crossing; one account from them relates: "We took our course along by the coast of Spain, which your Majesty will understand by the profit we received thereby." And Peter Martyr related with indignation before long how Spanish shipping was blockaded in port by the French pirates.

Whatever happened here at the take-off, Verrazano broke away from it in one small vessel, *La Dauphine,* manned by fifty Normans. He left the rocky point of Madeira January 17, 1524, to run down the latitude of 32° westward to the middle of the Unknown Land.

"These Were the Goodliest People——"

Little *Dauphine* (called *Dolphin* by the English) encountered storms that drove her north, to a landfall at about 34°, near the Cape Fear River. Verrazano quested south a bit, noticing the fragrance of the wooded coast; then, keeping warily off the wintry shore, he headed north. It is not surprising that he made the venture, like John Cabot, in a small vessel. A weatherly bark could avoid uncharted reefs, enter river mouths, and claw its way off a lee shore in a sudden gale where a great caravel or galleon might be helpless. (Columbus had lost *Santa María,* but had brought "lucky little *Niña*" safely through all kinds of weather.) For some time, until winter ended, Verrazano kept his vessel safely offshore, sending in boats well armed for wood and water, noticing the many fires which at night revealed the presence of unpredictable inhabitants. Warily he felt out the unknown currents and experimented with anchoring off sandy beaches. He had need to be cautious, because south of 32° he had been close to the forbidden Spanish Florida.

This caution, while he was off some low spit, at the Chesapeake or the Hatteras sandspit, led him to make a mistake that had remarkable consequences for a long time after. While coasting this narrow "isthmus" his masthead lookout sighted open water beyond it stretching to the west. "From the ship was seen the ocean of the east, which, without doubt, reaches to the extremities of India, China and Cathay."

Now Verrazano possessed no chart of this middle coast, which must have been unknown to his Normans. Perhaps one of his watering parties fell into pidgeon-sign talk with curious natives who described Chesapeake Bay as a sea—or even the great lakes to the west;

perhaps in this moment of early enthusiasm the Florentine navigator fancied that he had sighted, beyond the spit of land, Balboa's ocean here in the north. If so, he regretted it later and tried to deny it. But the report of "Verrazano's sea" spread to the map makers who tried to draw it upon the continent, and to searchers for the western passage to the far ocean, and fairly bedeviled European ideas for the next half century.

Verrazano himself does not seem to have been ordered to explore for a western passage. At the "isthmus" he made no effort to reach the waterway beyond, and presently in the Hudson River—where he must have felt the pull of the tide and found the water to be salt—he had no thought of following it inland. By his actions he seemed to be intent on exploring this missing coast line, above Spanish Florida and below the supposedly Portuguese Codfish Land.

At all events, after by-passing Delaware Bay, he believed himself to be in "another land." Spring had come, and he was relieved for his ship; the tree growth changed from the cypress and palms of the far south; the inhabitants no longer fled away at the coming of the Norman seamen.

Fortunately for the interested Italian he had not come among the Iroquois of the Great Lakes. The inhabitants here were the more gentle and attractive Mohicans, scattered in small palisaded villages through the eastern woodlands. Through woods so dense that Verrazano remarked that an army might be hidden within them—yet open enough for the explorers to pass freely where grew "fragrant flowers, wild roses, violets and lilies, yet all different from ours."

The people of these woods used their weapons chiefly for hunting; they cultivated moist land by the streams, growing the "three sisters": native corn, squash, and beans. At least the women did that, carrying water in clay pots and weaving some garments of animal hair; they braided their own hair, covered their loins modestly with soft furs, and kept prudently out of arm's reach of the admiring mariners from Dieppe. Evidently here the natives were meeting Europeans for the first time and liking them.

Contact with them was made only by accident, for the Normans had been careful not to set foot ashore where Indians gathered. One seaman, swimming close inshore to toss gifts to watching Indians, was pulled in helplessly by the surf. "With such violence he was cast on the shore that he lay bruised and stunned: which the Indians perceiving they ran to draw him out. The young man perceiving that they carried him began greatly to fear, and cried out piteously. So did the Indians cry out, cheerfully, setting him on the ground in the sun. Admiring him, they made him put off his garments, and they made a great fire to warm them."

After watching their mate resuscitated instead of being put to death Verrazano's people ventured ashore. Yet when presently they encountered in the woods a young woman "very beautiful and of tall stature" with small children, they attempted to carry her off. When she cried out wildly they released her, because they had a long way to go back to the ship, and went on "bearing away a child only."

Seeking, as always, a safe harbor, *La Dauphine* sailed easily into a "very pleasant place situated among certain little steep hills through which there ran to the sea an exceedingly great stream of water, very deep in the mouth of it. A great and laden ship may pass from the sea into this river with the tide which we found to rise 8 feet. Here we rode at anchor in a spot well shielded from the wind, and passed on with our boat only into the river . . . up to where it made a most pleasant lake about 3 miles in compass."

So Verrazano anchored in the bay of New York, perhaps by Staten Island, and rowed on into the Hudson River generations before the coming of Henry Hudson. This spectacular tidal waterway to the hinterland interested him less than the tribal folk of Manhattan and Hoboken, who covered their heads with the bright feathers of fowls. "Their small boats to the number of 30 came out to us from the shores very cheerfully with a display of much admiration—showing us where we might come to land most safely with our boat. Yet upon the sudden a contrary flaw of wind coming from the sea, we were forced to return to our ship, leaving this land with great discontent, for the great commodity and pleasantness thereof. We supposed it is not without some riches, for all the hills showed some mineral matter in them. We weighed anchor and sailed toward the east, for so the coast trended."

It was in truth a pleasant place, although windy, and not without natural advantages. Off Block Island the Normans threw toy bells and beads to the canoes that thronged around. The observant Florentine noticed how well the dugouts had been shaped by applied fire and flint and copper tools. These natives, he suspected, had a certain mechanical ability and a religion of their own; they had good manners and used ceremony at greeting and departure. As for precious metals they seemed to value only their usefulness.

"When they had caught our toys, they examined them with laughter and then came without fear aboard our ship, which they beheld as something marvellously made. There were two kings, one a young man. The elder had a chain about his neck garnished with stones of different colors. These were the goodliest people and the fairest circumstances we had met with in our voyage. They exceed us in bigness, and some incline more to whiteness, with long black hair they are very careful to trim and deck up. They are dark and quick of eye and of sweet and pleasant countenance.

"The women are of like beauty, and as well mannered. The elder sort dress their hair like the women of Egypt and Syria. They did not desire cloth of silk or of gold, but most of all the tiny bells and crystals of azure color.

"Neither cared they for things of steel and iron which we showed them in our armor, at which they did not wonder, only asking how it was made. The like they did with our glasses [probably burning glasses, or beads] at which they laughed and gave us them again. On their part they are generous for they give away what they have. When we entered into a haven, they came in great companies, their faces all bepainted, showing us this was a sign of joy, bringing us of their victuals and making signs where we might safest ride in the haven."

With such hosts at hand Verrazano lay for fifteen days in Narragansett Bay, and his men explored wide, fertile fields "where any seed planted would yield the best crops" and where the vine grapes

needed only a skilled hand to produce good wine. On *La Dauphine,*
Verrazano acted as host to a Mohican or Connecticut royal pair—
as he thought them to be. "The queen and her maids stayed in a very
light boat a quarter mile away, wondering at the noise and cries of
the mariners." Even as shore women and sailors today. And the
"king," like monarchs of this age, made long speeches to the visitors, and "beholding our apparel, and tasting our meats, courteously
took his leave and departed." More than that, shore parties were
much gratified by sport shown them by the monarch of the bay, who
strung his bow and, with his gentleman, raced up and down in the
pantomime of hunting.

Verrazano's practical Italian mind judged this country to be
ideal for corn, wine, and oil. The navigator in him rejoiced at exploring a bay nearly twenty leagues in compass, set with five small
islands, very fruitful and pleasant "among which islands any great
Navy may ride safe without fear of tempest or other danger." (The
American Navy shared his opinion three centuries later.)

Swiftly and yet prudently little *Dauphine* forged north and east
along the New England coast. Rounding Cape Cod, Verrazano was
struck by the change in the coast. "We found it to be another land,
high and full of thick woods of firs and cypresses such as are wont to
grow in cold countries. The people here differ much from the other
[Mohican-Connecticut] for the others seemed as courteous and
gentle as these were full of rudeness and ill manners. They clothe
themselves with bear and seal skins. So far as we could observe their
food came from hunting and fishing, with some fruits and a kind
of earth root."

Landing parties saw no sign of cultivated fields or open meadows. They traded only warily with these truculent red men. "We
standing in our boats where they came to the sea to stand on certain craggy rocks—they let down with a rope what it pleased them
to give us, and they took nothing but knives, fishhooks and tools to
cut with. Neither did they take any account of our courtesies. And
when we had nothing left to exchange with them, these people
showed every sign of disdain possible for any creature to invent."

These aboriginal Yankees had traded with Europeans before. Probably the Normans, strangers on the coast, stirred them to fear or ridicule. Sometimes they fled away after loosing a flight of arrows.

La Dauphine looked into the Bay of Fundy and coasted Nova Scotia to still another kind of country, without visible inhabitants. "We reached more pleasant meadow-land without forests, yet with high hills; we discovered 32 islands lying all near the [main] land. These were small and lofty to the view, having many windings between them, making many fair harborages as do the islands in the gulf of Venice and Dalmatia."

The voyagers were questing through the haunts of the fishermen of St. Malo and Dieppe. "Sailing northeast we approached the land that was discovered in times past by the Bretons, which is in fifty degrees." Some of the Normans, then, had knowledge of the landfalls of the Bretons; but at or near 50° they would be beyond Cape Race, heading toward the Labrador heights. And Cape Race was the unofficial boundary between French and Portuguese fishing grounds. Apparently the Normans understood that, for their narrative states: "Beyond this point the Portuguese have already navigated as far as the Arctic circle without reaching the limit of the terrestrial globe."

No word here about a strait to Cathay or their failure to find it. Verrazano and his crew had coasted the new land between Spanish-claimed territory and the northern, Portuguese, part of Codfish Land. They had surveyed landmarks, studied the inhabitants, and established a French claim of sorts to the fertile coast between Cape Fear and Cape Race. They also left us the most straightforward account, until then, of our eastern seaboard. Two of Verrazano's place names, *Acadia* and *Norumbega,* endured for a long time.

"Having now used up all our provisions, and having discovered about 700 leagues of new countries, and being furnished with fresh water, wood, and fish, we decided to return to France."

So Verrazano ends his story. He did return to Dieppe, in July of the same year, 1524. But, like John Cabot, he brought back no articles of tangible value. After that this last of the great Italian pilots disappeared into a haze of legends. Certain maps thereafter give evidence of another voyage of his; gossip among the ports relates that he went back to the New World and died there. His near-namesake John the Florentine certainly died on a Spanish scaffold.

Possibly he did go back on a larger ship, *Mary Guildford*. Her pilot was a nameless Italian of Piedmont who did not survive but guided the ship from London to the waters off the Labrador where little *Dauphine* had turned homeward.

Shadowy Cruise of Mary Guildford

She remains one of the shadow-shapes of the chronicles, losing her consort vessel in a storm, turning back among icebergs at 52°, following a polar current south to search for her lost companion. Until then her captain seems to have been seeking a western passage to Cathay.

Mary Guildford found herself on a coast all wilderness and moss without habitation or people. Her men sighted tracks of beasts, but no living beast. Then, at a good haven called St. John's, she found "eleven saile of Normans and one Brittaine [Breton] and two Portugual Barkes, and all a-fishing."

Evidently the wanderer followed the coast south, because she appeared after four months off the Isle of Mona, near Santo Domingo, capital city of the new Spanish empire of the sea. (The Italian pilot had been lost by then.) Never before had a vessel flying the lions of England been sighted in the Caribbean. Suspicious Spanish officials took the testimony of those who had any contact with the strange craft.

At Mona one Navarro testified that while loading his caravel with cassava, he had questioned an armed party of the Englishmen, who said their king had fitted out their vessel to go and discover the land of the Great Khan. Then what were they looking for in these islands? They had come, they said, from the "coast of the new land where Ayllon took his colony." They wished to examine the islands and give the King of England an account of them, and to take a cargo of dyewood home.

Then at Santo Domingo itself judges of the Audiencia testified to the secretary of the Casa de Contratación how the said ship had explored at command of the English King a certain region in the north between the Labrador's land and the Codfish land, to find a passage to sail to discover Tartary.

The burgess of Santo Domingo testified that he knew only how two sailors of said ship had been heard to say that they had set out to discover a certain strait near Norway, that they had been nearly frozen with the cold and had come to warmer waters to sell certain clothes and linen goods they had, and find a skilled pilot to take them back to England. . . .

Thereupon the high constable of the island had been sent to bring said ship into the harbor, but the justices understood that a lombard had been fired from the fortress, the stone of which passed near the said ship, on which account the said ship made sail and did sail off in the direction of Castile.

There were many pages of such testimony by puzzled Spanish witnesses, but no further trace of *Mary Guildford* after she had sailed at the cannon shot, to seek her home without a pilot.

She was the first of many English ships to seek those islands.

Gomez Turns Back at the Ice

Swifty and secretly Spain explored the track of Verrazano on her own account.

Estevan Gomez was one of the Portuguese veterans who followed Magellan to Seville, to draw the pay and privileges of an outer-seas pilot from the richer coffers of the new empire of Charles V. Possibly a neighbor of Magellan, and probably jealous of that greatest of navigators, Gomez had deserted Magellan in the strait the latter discovered, and had survived by bringing his ship back alone to Spain. Then, while serving Spain at the conference of Badajoz in 1524—where the rival Iberian sea powers failed to agree on the situation of the line in the Eastern Hemisphere, and the consequent title to the valuable Moluccas—he was called away urgently by the Emperor and given the mission of following after Verrazano.

Unlike Verrazano, however, the veteran Portuguese was smuggled to sea for the one purpose of finding a strait through the unknown portion of the North American coast. For once Charles, the Casa, and the merchants of Seville were agreed on what they wanted without any delay. As Cortes put it, writing from his stronghold of the Aztec capital, it was "an all-Spanish route, shorter than the Portuguese', to the Spice Islands." (Cortes was fitting out vessels of his own on the west coast of Mexico ostensibly to search for this same passage but really to explore up and down his own coast; yet he warned the Emperor frankly not to expect to find such a passage.)

Since both empires now claimed the Moluccas, possession of that rich prize would fall to the one with the most powerful fleet and the most practical salt-water route to the farthest east. Charles and the Casa now had the power, but the voyage around by Magellan's strait was almost prohibitive, owing to the width of the Pacific. By then the planners of the Casa, studying their Padrón Real, could be certain that no serviceable passage existed to the north of Magellan's strait, around the circuit of the Gulf of Mexico (explored by Pineda and mapped by Cortes). But what about the little-explored coast from Tierra Florida up to the fishing banks of the stubborn Portuguese? That very coast was being searched by the shrewd mercenary Italian by command of the archfoe of the empire, Francis of Valois.

It called for the utmost speed and skill, to search out what the Frenchmen might have discovered, or failed to find. Charles of the undershot jaw gave order, as King, to the ports of Biscay to fit out at once a caravel of fifty tons for "Stephen Gomez, our pilot, to go on a *certain discovery* at our order." (A ton of that day would be more than one and a half of today.) While the purpose of the voyage was not revealed to the public, it was laid down clearly in secret orders to Gomez. "To search among the many windings of our ocean whether any passage can be found leading to the kingdom of him we commonly call the Grand Khan . . . to discover eastern Cathay of which you have notice, as far as our Molucca islands which all fall within our sphere of influence."

Gomez did a good job, in fast time, and risked keeping at sea during winter (1524–25). It may be that before sailing from the Biscayan coast he heard rumors of the discovery by the French of the mythical "Sea of Verrazano." For the Italian Verrazano, unlike the closely censored Iberian pilots, talked freely enough about the lands and people he had come upon in the misty mid-region of the Atlantic. And it is said that Gomez, Portuguese-born, learned much from the fishermen of Viana.

But his report was made under seal to Casa and King; we know of his voyage only from the remarks of others. Apparently he took his small vessel along the route of the fishermen, making his landfall between 47° and 51°, circling either the north or south of New-foundland, probing into the Gulf of St. Lawrence, and then making a cast north along the bleak highlands of Labrador. Here he seemed to satisfy himself that open water stretched westerly between Labra-dor and Greenland, for Alonso de Santa Cruz, who talked with him, relates how "he agreed with the general opinion about the strait or passage off the Labrador's land, yet he convinced himself that this was not necessary to attempt because of the cold in those parts which would always be a bar."

Probably Gomez reached the Greenland waters in late autumn, sighting floating ice; his trained eye observed what it would take other pilots a century and a half to find out by hard experience, that the cold in this latitude would always be a bar to a ship's passage. But search for this northwest passage would go on, with waste of lives and treasure, long after him.

After that, Gomez seems to have got his small craft out of the ice zone with winter coming on. Heading south to warmer water, he probed up a broad reach he called Deer River, which might have been the Bay of Fundy, or the Penobscot. Either he missed the Hud-son or found no passage there—as happened at Chesapeake Bay. To the south there was nothing.

In the end he found no passage to the west between Labrador and Florida. He also made certain, probably with inward satisfac-tion, that the "Sea of Verrazano" did not exist.

"Gomez returned in ten months," Peter Martyr wrote to Rome,

"having found neither the strait nor Cathay as he had set out to do. He did discover agreeable and useful countries directly opposite to us. The justice Ayllon has explored the same countries with two ships. . . . The Spaniards have much to say of the nations inhabiting them, and of excellent ports and great rivers there—with great plains overgrown with ilex, oak and olives, where wild grape vines spread over the trees. But what need have we of what is found everywhere here in Europe? It is toward the south, not toward the frozen north, that our fortune is to be sought."

This diligent chronicler of a new world, now a bishop and a Councilor of the Indies, was growing older and more set in his ideas. With something like a smirk he relates the unfortunate incident of the return of Estevan Gomez, who, finding no wealth, dared bring back a cargo of slaves against the orders of the Council. "Your Holiness will hear a laughable fact concerning this voyage of exploded hope. When Estevan Gomez barely reached port, somebody leaped on a horse and without waiting to learn more, galloped to us, and cried, out of breath, 'Estevan Gomez has brought back a shipload of cloves and precious stones [which could only come from the real Indies].' This man hoped to be well rewarded by proclaiming how Gomez had brought, not slaves (*esclavos*) but cloves (*clavos*)—as he had understood the word! Thereupon everyone derided Gomez and his partisans."

The reaction at Seville was like that at Lisbon. Neither Ayllón nor Gomez had found a trace of the eagerly sought strait, or of riches to be traded for. On Spanish maps, thereafter, the northern coast appeared under a new designation—Land of Estevan Gomez. In Paris, also, Verrazano's account of fertile coasts to be cultivated easily stirred no interest. He had found only some copper and signs of other minerals. Of gold he reported no more than a trace of color. The sponsors of his voyage turned to other, more important matters. Jean Ango and the Florentine bankers sought trade from Santa Cruz Land-Brazil even at cost of a small sea war with the Portuguese. The adventurous Francis was taken captive in his war with the empire and imprisoned for nearly a year at Madrid.

For a few years the coast of North America was left undisturbed, because its forest barrier yielded no valuable dyewood and its scattered inhabitants could not easily be marketed as slaves.

Toward the end of the critical years, 1520–29, the quest of the sea powers turned south.

The Strange Case of Sebastian Cabot

Rumors came more strongly then of gold, silver, and even another hidden empire waiting for discovery beneath the equator. Following them with stark courage and ruthlessness, Pizarro was cutting his bloody way down the west coast of the southern continent, America, toward Peru. The rumors came also from the mouth of the tropical Amazon. *Somewhere in the mountains of the hinterland men resembling the white Europeans worked mines of silver.*

The merchants of Seville heard as much, and the strategists of the Casa considered it with caution. There was another waterway vast as the Amazon below the equator, the Fresh Water Sea of Juan de Solís, who had died before exploring it inland. True, Magellan had turned his back on it after two days. Yet it could be a passage to the western ocean. (By the reckoning of that time a river rising in a lofty mountain spine might flow in two directions, to the east as well as the west.) And the rumors of vast silver mines to the west quickened the Casa's desire to reach them before the Portuguese could claim them. Where the Line of Demarcation lay within the hinterland of Santa Cruz-America no one had ascertained.

So it befell that in 1526 a Spanish discovery fleet sailed for the estuary of the Plate, to run down the rumors of silver, to survey the line, and "to discover the Moluccas, Tarshish, Ophir, Cipangu and Cathay." The Pilot Major, who led this expedition, was ordered furthermore "to barter there and load his ships with gold, silver, precious stones, pearls, drugs, spices, silks, brocades and other precious things."

Now this is a rather fantastic order—for a fleet to ascend a river, find the passage to the western ocean, and trade thus lavishly in the far Indies. Probably it was so phrased because the Pilot Major had a habit of claiming he could accomplish such things. He was Sebastian Cabot, son of the silent discoverer of the New Found Land.

Through these years of plotting and counterplotting, of buying and selling of secrets and services, of contraband maps and contraband voyages, the figure of Sebastian Cabot appears at every turn like a daemonic cosmographer planning great undertakings but accomplishing little—yet ever adding to the fame of Sebastian Cabot. He is the one pretender among the great voyagers of the early days.

At provincial Bristol he makes maps for the Tudors, claiming first that he made the voyage of 1498 as a boy with his father, and then that he was the prime-mover of that voyage to the north (not true). Marrying a Spanish lady, he shuttles between Seville and London with great secrets to confide, alleging in Spain that he made a desperate voyage for the English to seek the northwest passage around Labrador land, to be turned back by ice and a mutiny of his crew (and historians for centuries would cudgel their brains to prove or disprove this arctic search of Sebastian Cabot). Yet Sebastian is certain that the passage can be found.

The Spanish monarch wins Cabot's services with a great salary and emoluments and gifts. Yet Magellan is chosen instead of him to make the desperate try for a passage to the south. When Henry VIII desires in 1521 to have him lead a fleet to search for the passage in the north, the Drapers' Guild of the city of London object stoutly to Cabot as captain, arguing bluntly "he was never in that land himself; he knows only what in his youth he heard his father and other men tell in times past." Whereupon Henry fails to get the money for his ships from the London merchants, and Cabot, now Pilot Major of Spain, is censored by Charles V for failing to pay (and keeping for himself) the pension of the widow of Amerigo Vespucci (the first Pilot Major). Meanwhile, behind locked doors in Seville, Cabot assures a friar from Venice (Cabot's native city) that he can sell to the Council of Ten the secret of the passage, "which I have discovered." He adds that he refused the offer of the English king for the secret because he is loyal to Venice.

When he was ordered to seek the passage by the Fresh Water

Sea of Solís, it may well have been that Sebastian Cabot stuck to his story of great secrets he had learned, and pledged himself to reach the far Indies and bring the specified cargoes. It seems inevitable that such a man in such a moment would seek to outdo Magellan. Curiously enough, Cabot reveals devotion for his wife by requiring a life pension to be paid her after his departure.

Like the guild of London, the merchants of Seville object to him as captain; opposing in this manner the Emperor's venture, they arrange to send a ship of their own on the quest for the passage and trade with Cathay. Cabot, getting to sea first with his fleet, manages to lose weeks in finding the coast of Brazil, and then to lose his flagship on a reef. Cabot, as commander, was first to leave the wrecked vessel. Hearing from survivors of the Solís ships—who had actual Peruvian silverwork to show him—of the rich empire inland to the west, he forgets about the passage in his eagerness to ascend the rivers. After naming the great estuary the Río de la Plata, from the new silver he has found, he ascends far up the Paraná to build a fort, named Sancti Spíritus. He pursues this river route into mountains where natives yield up more silver and tell Cabot of the "White King," who is the Inca, beyond them.

Then, near the inland frontier of the Incan Empire, his expedition is assailed by aggressive tribes, while others later capture his base at Sancti Spíritus, massacring the garrison. At this point the rival vessel of the Seville merchants appears in the Plate, with Diego García commanding, and after his efforts of four years Cabot returns home, having surveyed a thousand miles of rivers without finding a passage to the west. He is tried in Spain on charges brought by the survivors of his crews, fined and exiled to Africa—to be pardoned by Charles V, who may have had ideas of his own about what Cabot actually accomplished.

His spectacular career, thus far, influenced the future of the northern continent in two ways. His persistent story of the futile voyage to the arctic linked itself to legends of the barren coasts and ice-endangered seas—to the myth of the Isle of Demons, believed to lie off Greenland—and confused the imagination of Europeans. While the southern continent opened up swiftly to their view, the northern land remained much as it had been, veiled in legend of forbidding nature. Sebastian Cabot also took several Englishmen with him to the Plate, giving them their first observations of the great continent below the equator.

While Cabot was tracing out his rivers, three Spanish craft built on the west coast made a try at crossing the Pacific under command of Alvaro de Saavedra. One of the flimsy vessels made the crossing, but failed to beat its way back against the trade winds. Saavedra died at sea, and the survivors of his crew surrendered to the Portuguese.

After Cabot's failure and the loss of these ships that tried to master the Pacific, Charles V came to terms with the Portuguese in 1529, agreeing on the line between their empires and giving up his claim to the Moluccas in the east.

By then the incredible Spanish conquest of South America was under way. It went south as Peter Martyr urged, toward the wealth of the burning equator, toward the cities of the Inca and the untouched multitudes of human beings existing between the Peruvian coast and the silver of the Río de la Plata. And on the map of the Padrón General this southern continent was taking shape entire.

What the Maps Revealed

Old notions of geography are hard to kill. Probably Plato had been daydreaming about the vanished splendor of Crete when he described his long-lost land of Atlantis, but Atlantis became the persistent dream of millenniums after him. Such a myth once taken to heart by humanity becomes as bodiless and indestructible as human hope.

Even after two generations of transatlantic voyaging the legendary island of St. Brendan kept its place stubbornly on the new maps. True, it was removed from the now-familiar latitude of Newfoundland, to appear hopefully more to the south near Bermuda. Since nothing had been found of the isles of the Seven Cities, they vanished from the ocean, to be revealed on the little-explored coast, and presently to migrate inland as the Seven Cities of Cibola.

It was clear enough by now that the gold-roofed palaces of Cipangu lay far to the westward, far from Santa Cruz-America, which was more than an island, being a continent in its own right, dividing the two great oceans. But what of northern Asia, beheld by no voyager, with its elusive Cathay, and its still to be discovered country of the Great Khan of Tartary? The old notion persisted that this extremity of Asia leaned close to Europe in the north. It joined to the belief that the earth could not be as great in size as some of the voyagers made it out to be. Along the circuit of the equator perhaps it might be; but in the north—who knew the truth?

Even the practical pilot Verrazano had some doubt about the north within the Arctic Circle. The story went around that he described the northern continent as "another world, different from those we have known, by evidence of its size and nature. It does not join Asia, but perhaps it extends into Europe by way of Norway and Russia." (The old concept that Greenland formed a peninsula of Europe up in the arctic region.)

Other map makers, however, joined the unknown north of the New World firmly the other way, to Asia, Siamese-twin fashion (as Bartholomew Columbus and those who followed him had done). The Schöner globe of 1523–33 conceded that the great South Sea (Pacific) separated the land masses along the equator, above which they united. On this globe the Golden Chersonese blended into Mexico, while the Land of the Mongols occupied what is Wyoming today.

Another globe of gilded copper—known as the Paris Gilt Globe —copied this of Schöner. Bearing the modest title of "New and Exact Representation of the Entire Earth," it splices the extremity of Asia to Mexico, due south of Cortes's city of Tenochtitlán. It places Cathay at the headwaters of the Pánuco River, while the Desert of Lop lies a bit inland from *Terra Francesca* "newly discovered" (by Verrazano). Farther north, where imagination could run free, Codfish Land does duty as the tip of Siberia.

Now these cartographers were not merely sketching continents

at random. They might try to catch the eye of the public by pictur-
ing cannibals in quiet Brazil, or giants—of Vespucci's shore tales—
in Patagonia. But in the race to map the newly revealed portion of
the earth they tried to fit the reports of the new surveys with the
older, accepted geography and to keep the old myths in view. Their
work reflected accurately the ideas that reached them at the time.
The Paris globe clearly named the southern continent "America,
found in 1497," while its eastern bulge appeared correctly as "Region
of Brasil." Both globes dismissed the Columbian concept that the
New World consisted of islands, and the concept of Juan Ponce, of
seventeen years before, that the peninsula of Florida was the legendary isle of Bimini.

An Italian family of cartographers embodied their ideas in the
map of Vesconte de Maggiolo, in 1527, with rather remarkable
effect. The southern continent here assumes almost its natural shape,
but an imaginary strait (for which search had been made in vain)
divides the central isthmus with the notation "doubtful strait." Then
Tierra Florida ends abruptly with the intrusion of an entirely imaginary *Sea of India* about where Cape Hatteras should be. This is the
rumored Sea of Verrazano, which Verrazano denied but could not
banish. So his coast of *Francesca* appears north of it as virtually a
third continent. It all formed a neat picture in a cosmographer's
mind—Spanish America complete, up to the strait that ought to be
there, and the little-known Florida nicely severed from the very
hazy north, just then claimed by the French. It fitted every notion,
except the reality.

Reality was taking shape on the guarded Padrón Real, the
master map of Spain. And for the first time, in 1529, this was released to public view. Curiously enough, however, it was not given
out as a copy of the Padrón Real; it appeared in print as a world
map of one Diego Ribeiro, cartographer to the Emperor.

In that day of the last discoveries and the first accurate mapping
thereof the master cartographers demanded and received as great
salaries and bribes as the master pilots, who were allowed to wear
silk, and gold chains. Ribeiro, a Portuguese, had sold himself to

Seville with the Magellan group, had resisted the efforts of Lisbon to win him back, had helped prepare the sea charts for Magellan's voyage, had tapped the brains of Fernando Columbus just before the latter's death, and then had published apparently for the use of Charles V this unexpected "World Map of All the Discoveries." Why?

It is hardly likely that Ribeiro sold out the secret of the Padrón Real. He had recently been awarded a life pension of 60,000 maravedís. Perhaps the answer to the question—why was the empire's master map released unofficially?—lies in the map itself. It is called the New World, in accordance with the capitulation of Tordesillas, in 1494. But in it the famous line passes the continents harmlessly out in the Atlantic.

For the first time the eastern coast lines appear in their natural shape. There is no dubious strait, or fantastic sea of Verrazano—and almost no myths. Moreover here the Spaniards have mapped only what has been surveyed; unexplored spaces are left blank.

The northern continent appears as a coast line without an interior. Cortes's kingdom, entitled New Spain, thrusts up into a void. Beside this the northern shore of the gulf is inscribed, "Tiera de Garay—in all this coast there is no hope of finding gold." The southern Atlantic shore becomes "Tiera de Ayllon—yielding breadstuffs, wine and other things of Spain." Farther on the Indians are noted as living on maize, fish, and game and clothing themselves in the skins of beasts. Then to the north stands the "Tiera de Estevam Gomez, which he discovered by order of His Majesty. It contains great forests with the fruits of Spain, with the fish salmon and sole. No gold has been found." At Newfoundland: "The land of Codfish discovered by the Corte Reals, and where they were lost. Until now nothing valuable has been found except the codfish and they do not amount to much."

No territory at all is conceded to the French, and Portuguese claims are hardly admitted. The only foreign designation lies far to the north on Labrador: "This country was discovered by the English and there is nothing in it worth having." (In the years of the map's publication the English king was preoccupied with his marriage to Anne Boleyn, the excommunication by the Pope, and the birth of a girl child named Elizabeth.)

Quite clearly Ribeiro's map sets forth the claim of Spain to the New World entire, and at the same time conveys the idea that inquisitive foreign powers would find nothing worth seeking in it. And at that particular time the new fleets of Spain plied the coasts with no competitors in sight.

Only the armed fishing fleets of French and English ports persisted in coming to their New World bases.

It was inevitable that, with the coasts surveyed, the next effort would be to explore the blank space on the map, the unknown interior of the northern continent, and that this effort would be made by Spaniards.

So the map of Diego Ribeiro in 1529 marks a change. The age of discovery was ending, the day of exploration beginning.

IV. The Quest for Inland Empire

"We Had None of the Things Needed . . ."

SO far the voyagers had surveyed the coasts of the Unknown Land without attempting to penetrate the forest barrier of the shores. One, De Ayllón, had landed on a river to build a settlement, only to be defeated by the wilderness.

"We sent him back to New Spain," Peter Martyr wrote a little before death ended his own patient chronicle of the New World, "authorizing him to build a fleet to carry him to those lands where he will found a colony. Companions will not fail to join him, for the entire Spanish nation is so desirous of change that people follow eagerly where they are called. They are ready to sacrifice what they have for what they hope they can get."

The delirium of the myths still drew men from the bare hills of Estremadura and the quays of Cádiz. After the companions of Cortes uncovered an empire, a younger generation in Spain sought passage to danger and unlimited opportunity. The dualism of the Castilian personality impelled the newer generation of Spaniards outward. They felt the sense of mission as strongly as the craving for gold. With soiled satin cloaks draped over scabbarded swords they embarked on the fleets of empire—when had an empire been thrown across an ocean before in human memory?—elbowing companions who were the hooded servants of the Church seeking a harvest of pagan souls—where had a continent of pagan people been discovered before? They escaped from medieval law and age-old poverty, yet carried in their thoughts the medieval longing to behold miracles and accomplish what no human beings had achieved before. They envied the hardened and proved conquistadors; they themselves were ready to attempt the impossible, for which, however, they had not troubled to prepare.

While a certain Fray Bartolomé de las Casas brooded in the monastery of Santo Domingo, before sailing home to appeal to His Most Catholic Majesty for the treatment of Indians as human beings with souls, another noble-born Spaniard, Pánfilo de Narváez, received from that same Emperor Charles the title of Adelantado with power to enslave all Indians who, after being summoned, refused obedience to the Emperor and the Christian faith. He was authorized also to conquer and colonize the territory between Florida and the Río de las Palmas (Cortes's border). Already he signed himself Governor of Florida and Espíritu Santo (the Mississippi).

These titles assuaged his injured pride; he had failed in an attempt to supersede Cortes, being blinded in one eye during that combat; he longed to carve out with his sword another Mexico on the northern coast where Pineda had seen natives wearing ornaments of gold.

Narváez sailed with five ships from San Lúcar in June 1527, with sufficient armament to overcome any predictable resistance. His company of 600 had armored matchlock men, crossbowmen, laborers, with attendant priests and Franciscan friars. It did not include an experienced pilot, an interpreter, carpenters—except for one man—or supplies for more than the voyage. But the governor of a still to be found empire sailed with high hope and bright banners displayed.

His armament, however, diminished. At Santo Domingo many followers basely deserted to seek their fortunes in the *partidos*—the comfortable settlements worked by Negroes, yielding sugar, cotton, and hides. Because the pilots were not familiar, as they had boasted, with these waters, he lost two vessels in a hurricane off the dangerous southern coast of Cuba, and almost lost his captain ship on a reef. Then, when the surviving vessels were bearing up for the safety of the Havana, a storm blinded them, driving them north. When they sighted land ahead and entered a great bay, the pilots did not know where they were, but it turned out to be the west coast of Florida. (It was actually Tampa Bay, midway up the peninsula.)

There Don Pánfilo debarked, with 400 followers and 42 horses that had survived the storms. On this day, Good Friday of the year 1528, the explorers found a village vacated by its people, and they picked up a trinket of gold among some fish nets. To mark his entry, Don Pánfilo planted imperial ensigns and took possession of the country in the name of His Most Catholic Majesty. The horses were too weak to be of use. Since the pilots could not tell him exactly where they had landed, Don Pánfilo searched inland. He came upon inhabitants of the bay who made signs for the Spaniards to go away.

They had no interpreter, so they could only guess at the meaning of the strange Indians. Yet they came upon fragments of gold with woven cloth and bunched bright feathers, the like of which Don Pánfilo had seen in Cortes's New Spain. This encouraged them, especially when the Indians they caught seemed to tell them that the woven cloth and gleaming metal came from a region to the north, the country of *Apalachee*. There also, asserted the Indians, grew the maize on which the Spaniards must subsist, because the stores in the ships were about used up.

Several things impelled Don Pánfilo to order the march inland through his new dominion. They needed to find corn, ripe to be gathered. The objects they found seemed to prove they were near Spanish-occupied New Spain. One of the pilots believed there was a good haven in a bay not far up the coast, and quite close to the Pánuco, which Don Pánfilo knew of old.

Before deciding on this Don Pánfilo called a council of officers and hidalgos to ask their advice with his voice of a bull. Most of the members of the council were sick of the sea with its storms; the leader of the Franciscans declared that it was clearly God's will that they should avoid the sea henceforth. Only one officer, Alvar Núñez Cabeza de Vaca, treasurer-to-be of Las Palmas, objected. He insisted

they must not part from the ships until they had built a settlement
in a good harbor. Don Pánfilo then offered to put Cabeza de Vaca
in command of the vessels that would search by sea for the harbor.
This Cabeza de Vaca refused, being the descendant of a crusader
and son of a governor of Grand Canary. It would injure his honor
to choose the safety of the ships against the danger of the march by
land. Whereupon Don Pánfilo summoned a notary to make out a
certificate that he, the Governor, did but abide by the judgment of
the majority of the officers in taking his people by shore to seek for
a better land and a haven for the ships. He ordered each man going
to be given two pounds of biscuit and half a pound of bacon, and
they started north, leaving the ships behind.

But it was farther than they thought to the Pánuco; it was not
ten leagues, nor a hundred, but three hundred leagues. They did
not see the vessels or the crews again. Cabeza de Vaca, who had
advised against the march, was one of the four who lived to tell how
they found their way to Apalachee, after a chief carried on the back
of another, wearing a painted deerskin, gave the Spaniards maize.

There was no path in the dense forest where the skeletons of
trees lay as they had fallen. The swamps led to deep lagoons. The
air was alive with ducks, herons, and hawks; deer ranged the forest
and the Spaniards came upon a small animal that carried its young
in a pocket in its belly (an opossum). They found green maize
fields around the village of Apalachee, whence the men fled before
them but returned to assail them with arrows, and set fire to the
thatched houses of the village. The mounted Spaniards pursued
the villagers, who fled again to the lakes where they could not be
followed.

"These Indians were all archers," Cabeza de Vaca testifies,
"naked and spare of body, very large and active. They use bows as
thick as my forearm, and as long as eleven palms. With such bows
they miss nothing at two hundred paces. Some of our men were
wounded through the good armor they wore. Some of them swore
they had seen a red oak, thick as the calf of a leg, pierced through
with the arrows. The Indians attacked from behind trees and on

fallen trees, and they took away the Indians who guided us." (These
were probably Timucuan tribes.)

In midsummer heat the Governor's column, less than 300 by
then, sustained itself by maize, beans, and pumpkins found near the
scattered villages. Pánfilo Narváez ordered his followers to seek the
sea again to regain the ships; Cabeza de Vaca searched the coast,
coming upon inlets and sandspits but no trace of a harbor or the
ships. They discovered oyster beds that eased their hunger, as did
the fruit of the small palms. Indians were no longer visible, and long
starvation weakened the marching hidalgos, priests, and laborers,
without breaking their spirit.

"There were not horses enough to carry the sick who increased
in number each day. We saw on our arrival at the shore how little
means we had of advancing further. There was nowhere to go, and
the people were unable to move on, owing to their sickness. The
owners of horses began to plot together to ride off, leaving the Governor and the sick; but the hidalgos and those of gentle breeding
among them would not allow this plotting to go on, to disobey the
orders of your Majesty.

"After this the Governor called each of us apart to ask what we
should do to get out of so miserable a country. We agreed then on
a great and most difficult project, and that was to build vessels in
which we might go away. That appeared to be impossible. We had
none of the things needed for such building, nor any man who
understood ship building, and, above all, there was nothing to eat
while building them."

Not far inland there was an Indian village with food growing
from the ground, but by then the Governor's party could meet with
Indians only in combat. Animal life in the wilderness offered meat
to hunters, but the Spaniards were neither archers nor trappers. The
hope of gold in the next country no longer led them on; they desired
only to escape from "so miserable a country" to the Pánuco River
of Cortes's dominion. To do that, they attempted the impossible and
accomplished it in a way of their own.

"It was God's will that one of our company should come forth
to say he could make some pipes out of cane, which with deerskins

might be made into bellows [to fire a forge]. At that time any semblance of relief appeared good to us. We set him to work, and agreed to fashion nails, saws, axes and other needed tools from the stirrups, spurs and crossbows with the other iron we had. To sustain us while the work went on, we made four sallies to *Aute* [the Indian village on the St. Marks River; the Spaniards were then at St. Marks Bay]. All the able horses and men went, and brought back as many as four hundred fanegas of maize, but not without conflict with the Indians. Every third day a horse was killed, to be divided among the workers and the sick.

"We began work on the fourth of the month, with the only carpenter we had directing it, and on the twentieth day of September five boats were finished, twenty-two cubits [thirty-three feet] in length. They were caulked with the fibre of the palmito, and pitched with a resin of sorts made from pine trees by a Greek named Don Theodoro. From palmito husks and the tails and manes of the horses we made ropes for rigging. Our shirts and cloaks made sails, and saplings oars. Only by long searching could we find stones large enough for anchors. We flayed the horses, tanning the skin of their legs to make bottles to hold water.

"During this time some of us gathered shellfish from the coves of the sea, at which task the Indians attacked them killing ten men within sight of the camp. Some of them had worn good armor, yet we found the bodies transfixed by arrows. Not counting them, more than forty men died of disease and hunger here. The horses had been eaten, all but one. Then we embarked. The last boat was given to the Assessor and me, with forty-nine men. After our provisions and clothes had been loaded in, only a hand-span of the boat's railing remained above water. The boats were so crowded we could not move about.

"By necessity we were driven to hazard our lives in this manner, fleeing out to a sea upon which not one of us knew how to navigate."

The five flimsy vessels of the Governor of Florida and Las Palmas felt their way west along the Gulf coast, seeking the river Pánuco and other Spaniards. They threaded through the sounds, searching the river mouths, waiting ashore when the surf ran high. The water bags of green hide rotted, and the slowly starving Christians were compelled to search for fresh water on the land. Sometimes, then, they found dried fish and maize in the villages deserted by Indians at their approach. Their survival now depended on meeting with native people who had food.

When autumn storms set in, Narváez, who had the strongest men in his boat, persisted in going on, believing that they must be nearing the Pánuco. Instead they reached the Mississippi mouth. Here the current and a north wind separated the boats, carrying them out to sea. And here Cabeza de Vaca saw the last of the incompetent Narváez. "The Governor having in his boat the healthiest of the men, we could not by any means keep up with her or follow her. I called to him that since he saw how our weakness rendered us unable to follow him and do what he ordered, he must tell me how he wished me to act. He answered me that the time was past when one man should command another, and now each should do what he thought best to save his own life, and that was what he himself intended to do. Saying this, he departed with his boat."

It was odd that Cabeza de Vaca should survive, to tell how his commander deserted him. His voyage ended some weeks later on an island off the Texas coast. Here the Indians, probably a Karankawan tribe, had never met with Europeans before, and, astonished at sight of the white men draped in wet rags, gave them roots gathered in the sand of the shore and fish. Cabeza de Vaca and his companion officer, the Assessor, decided to take to their boat again, without consulting their Indian caretakers, to try to reach the mainland.

"When we dug our boat from the sand, we had to strip off our garments to launch her—we being in a state where to move the lightest things caused us great labor. We climbed into the boat two crossbow shots out in the shallows, when a wave came over, wetting us. We were naked in great cold, and our hands could not grip the oars. The next sea capsized the boat, carrying over the Assessor and two others who drowned beneath her. As the surf was very high, it threw the rest of us half drowned on the shore of the island. We lost everything we had in the boat—of little enough value, but worth much to us at that time. It was November and a cold wind blowing, so that we emaciated skeletons were nearer to death than to life.

"At sunset the Indians who had not thought we were going off, came to seek us again with food. When they saw us naked and so different than before, they became frightened and turned back. I went to them and called, making them understand by signs how our boat had sunk. Then before them they saw two of the bodies of the dead, and we others like to them. At that the Indians came and sat down among us, beginning to lament so loud with sorrow that their cries could be heard at a distance. It was strange to see these wild and untaught men howling like brutes over our misfortune. It made me and the others feel our misfortune all the more.

"The Indians built very large fires at intervals all the way to their habitations. When they saw that we had regained some heat and strength, they took us so swiftly to the next fire that they hardly let our feet touch the ground. In this manner we went to their habitations, where we found they had made a house for us with many fires in it.

"After our arrival they began to dance and rejoice. We did not so rejoice, for we expected to be sacrificed as their victims. Their festivity and our fear lasted all the night without sleep. In the morning they gave us fish and roots again, showing such good will that we were reassured, and lost somewhat the fear of sacrifice."

Having joined the hungering people of the western desert in this involuntary manner, Cabeza de Vaca and three others kept themselves alive for six years. He had, it seems, a genius for surviving.

After searching vainly along the Gulf coast for the missing Governor and his expedition the transport ships, which had been left to their own devices, returned to Santo Domingo to report the expedition lost to sight and probably dead.

The circumstance that Cabeza de Vaca did not die was to influence happenings in both hemispheres thereafter.

Jacques Cartier Sails Inland

Unexpectedly, again, the French came to explore. On a fair day, the twentieth of April of the year 1534, two small weatherly vessels of some sixty tons each left the haven of St. Malo with experienced crews. With Jacques Cartier captain, and supplies for eight months aboard, these vessels took the route of the fishermen and crossed to Newfoundland in a record twenty days.

Why they did so remains a question much debated. It is said they went to seek a "northwest passage" for the French, and it is said they went hurriedly to find gold like the Aztec treasure for Francis I. Yet Cartier, a solid sea captain of St. Malo, was hardly a conquistador capable of prospecting for gold among natives. No doubt both pilot and king would have been very happy to hit upon the missing salt-water passage to Asia. But evidence reveals that their purpose was to claim territory in the Unknown Land for France.

Since *Mary Guildford* strayed into the sacrosanct Spanish Caribbean, the kaleidoscope of Christian Europe had shifted with startling and increasing rapidity—with the Spanish veterans and German *landsknechte* of the Holy Roman Empire (of Charles) pillaging Rome and making the Pope captive in Sant'Angelo Castle, with German nobles protesting, and becoming "Protestants," arrayed with Lutherans against Romanists, league against league, and, politically, French against Spaniards, while the unpredictable Turks marched on Vienna, and Tudor England went through a convulsion of its own.

What happened on the seas, however, influenced Francis more than the continental conflicts, at which he showed himself a master of intrigue after the model of Niccolò Machiavelli's prince. Toward the east the dangerous Turks, guided by Suleiman, called "the Magnificent," were checked at the walls of Vienna and thereupon turned seriously to the sea. Their fleets, manipulated by invincible Khair ad-Din Barbarossa, penetrated the western Mediterranean, fairly bedeviling the armadas of the empire, of the Papacy, the galleys of St. Mark and the Knights of Malta, as well as Genoa the Proud. So the inner sea staged one of its last medieval pageants of oared galleys, slave-powered and manned by knights in battle. In this free-for-all fray for ports, loot, and somewhat tarnished glory Francis found his galleys and galleons outmatched by the armadas of Charles the Emperor, whose power encircled France. And Francis turned to an alliance with Suleiman, the enemy of his imperial foe —"an unholy alliance," the imperialists protested. Yet Francis, whose treasury was exhausted by then, hoped to gain from the wealthy Turks "a million in gold, which will be no inconvenience to the Grand Signior [Suleiman]" and a unilateral trade agreement which would give to hard-pressed France her first overseas Crown colony in the Turkish Empire itself.

With the Mediterranean such a welter of conflict the outer seas and the trade thereof began to assume almost magical attraction for the Iberian powers and French alike. The Atlantic in particular gained greater importance with the news of Pizarro's conquest of Peru.

Francisco Pizarro, a bastard of Estremadura, had tracked down the rumors of Incan civilization through blood and treachery, to emerge with Alagro and the pilot Ruiz from the miasma of rains and coastal jungles to the clean heights of the Andes. There, upon post roads leading to wealthy cities, Pizarro, now an adelantado of Spain, found Cuzco as Cortes had found the hidden Tenochtitlán. There he had fired his climactic volleys at the palace of Cassamarca, killing 2000 Peruvians. Before then he had taken captive the Inca Atahualpa. Captive, the Inca yielded up a ransom of 1,326,539 pesos of gold before being conveniently put to death. There, across the western sea, the Incan treasure proved to be even greater than the Aztec.

Undoubtedly the volatile Francis would have relished uncovering another such treasure in the west as well as the payment of gold on account by the Turks, yet he showed no particular disappointment at getting neither. (He did get the vitally important trade alliance with Constantinople.)

While it is always difficult to decide what the impetuous Francis —and the French Admiralty and merchants—wanted, it is clear enough what he did not want. Most urgently he did not want the monopoly of the outer oceans held by the empire, and by Spanish and Portuguese sea power. In the very year, 1529, that the Turks had turned back at Vienna these same Iberian powers agreed between them to halve the outer seas, from which trade flowed increasingly. They reaffirmed the old papal Line of Demarcation, as being a valid title to what they now possessed. In effect the Portuguese Crown claimed the Indies of the east, leaving to the Spanish Crown what it persisted then and thereafter in calling "the Indies of the west." That is, both the new-found continents except the bulge of Brazil. Now all of the northern continent lay, by this process of reasoning, within the Spanish side of the line. The French had no title whatever there except for the flags planted along the coast by the capable Verrazano, which had probably been made into loincloths long since by frugal Indian workingwomen.

Francis I, who had made the famous invocation of Adam's will, now challenged the line entire. The authority of the Pope, he remarked, was indeed supreme in matters spiritual, but it did not extend to dispensing in this fashion half the lands of the earth. Moreover, at that famous partition of the world, he stated, no king of France had been consulted, nor any other Christian monarch. The Most Christian King of France had a right to such new land.

While Francis was arguing after his fashion, French maritime merchants of the Jean Ango stamp had been acting in practical fashion, arming their vessels to trade across the Atlantic in Brazil. There the Portuguese had divided up the coast into captaincies for settlement, laying an embargo on trade by others, and enforcing their embargo by gunfire.

Their king, John III, explained that the ocean here was closed except to Portuguese vessels. "The seas," he proclaimed, "open to all people to navigate are those which were known to all and shared by all. But these other seas which were unknown in the past and appeared to be innavigable were discovered by great efforts on our part, and so other people are excluded from them."

Probably the Portuguese had no intention of asserting by this that sea power brings with it monopoly of the oceans. In the expanding world of that day the old concept of particular seas still prevailed—the Adriatic being the Venetian sea, the Baltic German, and the Caribbean certainly Spanish. And Portuguese strength, lacking manpower, was stretched thin to the far East Indies. Nor did the French consciously anticipate history in laying down the doctrine of freedom of the seas. Francis retorted quickly enough that "the sea, which is common to all, is free to all." And he gave *lettres de marque* to enterprising privateers to defend themselves against the Portuguese "who have been killing our poor citizens and merchants." In November 1533 at Marseilles, such a letter empowered a departing vessel to fight "for freedom to navigate on the common sea."

But with the Brazilian coast a theater of undeclared war between the French privateers and Portuguese guard fleets, and the Spanish Mainland ringed by fleets too powerful to challenge, there remained the northern coast, unguarded, unoccupied, and virtually unexplored.

There, ten years before, the competent Florentine captain, Verrazano, had marked safe harbors, valleys suitable for cultivation, and traces of valuable minerals in the hills. Moreover, there in the *Terre Neuve,* the enterprising fleets of Dieppe, Brest, St. Malo, and even Rochelle had wrested the best of the now-vital fishing banks from the Portuguese. Such fleets brought back also whale oil and bone, sealskins, furs, hawks, live wildcats, popinjays, and wild men. Perhaps "nothing of value," as the Spanish master map asserted, yet something helpful to a nation without gold. And there was always the chance of uncovering a sea passage to the Spice Islands which would be no longer than the Spanish route to their isthmus and down the coast of the South Sea to their new empire of Peru.

So it happened that in 1534 the French Court outfitted Jacques Cartier, a sound mariner of St. Malo, who spoke Portuguese and knew the route of the fishermen—who may have sailed with Verrazano along that very coast—to discover and claim the best territory for France. "And having discovered it, to place there colonies and forts."

The French intended to claim their share of the New World by possessing it.

In his skillful twenty-day crossing Jacques Cartier simply ran down the latitude of his home port, St. Malo—about 48°. In so doing, however, he arrived too early on the Newfoundland coast (May 10). The men of St. Malo encountered ice in which a polar bear hunted for seals. Prudently Cartier, whose skill fairly matched the incompetence of a Narváez, put in to a pocket harbor to wait out the ice and refit his vessels. He took note of the swarming sea birds, but saw no good in that dark coast of rock overgrown with moss, with "not a cartload of good earth." It must be, he noted, "the land God gave to Cain."

Whether by chance or design, the St. Malo captain had made his haven near the point where Verrazano had turned back ten years before. The Portuguese fleets no longer competed here with the French. Even if Cartier had not made the voyage with the brilliant Florentine, some members of his picked crews must have done so. There can be no doubt that they knew their way around this coast. While running along it they picked up landmarks with familiar names. As soon as the drifting ice cleared away, they called at the message center and haven of the French fishermen, "Brest Island."

Already this haven was haunted by memories that never survived in written records—by the ghosts of the Corte-Reals, and Fagundes, the nobleman of Viana, by the tales of Aubert of Dieppe, captain of *La Pensée,* who had started the whale hunting here, and who had begun the traffic in sealskins with the "wild men" of bark and hide canoes. (The Eskimo, although driven from the inland waters by the dominant Algonkins, clung to this coast.) The very names of the Brest haven bear witness to long occupancy. *Bon Esperance* Point and *Exquimaux* Island, and *Old Fort Island* indicate that this New World Brest had possessed more than one fort, and that the native inhabitants were well known to previous voyagers. Moreover, on leaving Brest, Cartier's ships met with a fishing craft from Rochelle that had lost its bearings, and they set it on a course for a good harbor.

And Cartier knew his way in from the seacoast. He turned north to narrow Belle Isle Strait, which had been christened the Bay of the Castles because it lay between towerlike basalt rocks. He understood that this was no bay but a great gulf (Gulf of St. Lawrence), which had not been fully explored by his predecessors, the mariners of Dieppe and Brest and St. Malo.

In this deceptive labyrinth of islands, false bays, and hidden straits Cartier proceeds with new zest and care—taking soundings, charting his course from point to point, and above all studying the nature and possibilities of the land he came upon. This is the task he has come to perform and he goes about it with immense pains. He makes sharp note of any mistake—"the land we had taken to be islands was firm [continental] land." He checks off worthless territory—"encircled by sand as far as the eye can see, overlaid by marshes and standing pools." And he exclaims at coming upon fertile shores—"these islands have the best soil we have found; one of their fields is worth more than all the New Land [*Terre Neuve*— Newfoundland] with goodly trees, meadows, fields of wild corn and peas in bloom as thick and fair as any you can see in Brittany."

Cartier and his messmates can name the varieties of swarming birds, and of course the fish they haul in—salmon, mackerel, sturgeon, cod—and the trees as well, the cedars, yews, pines, ashes, white elms, and willows.

Now they are making the circuit of the great gulf that opens before them to the west, and now the landmarks are strange, because they give new names to them, such as Brion Island, in honor of a patron of their exploration. With the warmth of June these chill northern reaches become gay with fragrant bright foliage.

Probing west into an unknown bay, Cartier exclaims at the heat, calling it the *Baie de la Chaleur,* hoping that it may prove to be the missing waterway to the west. "We went 25 leagues within it, and took notice of distant high mountains beyond the lowlands, but seeing that there was no passage at all, we began to turn back.

Sailing along the coast we saw certain wild men who were making fires and smokes . . . sending one of our boats to the bank, the wild men came out to us putting pieces of seals on boards and, retiring again, made signs to us to take them. We sent two men with hatchets, knives and beads to them, whereat they were very glad and came out in clusters bringing skins and other things they had, to exchange for our wares . . . some of the women who came not near stood up to their knees in water singing and dancing . . . in such manner we began to traffic familiarly they giving us whatever they had, until nothing was left them but their naked bodies."

Now in all this Cartier mentions only casually that he failed to find a passage to the west in Chaleur Bay. But before he is finished with this age-old method of trading, he manages to get a great deal of information from the "wild men" (probably Nascapi Algonquins). He learns how they live, where they fish, and how they think of religion. Apparently these citizens of the great gulf had met Europeans before—or heard about them—and were eager to trade for any kind of utensils. If the intolerant Narváez had met the Florida Indians on such a basis of friendship and fair barter, he might have survived his march inland. Already the French seamen were demonstrating their knack of getting on with the wild but human people of the New World. They do not call them Indians.

And before leaving Cartier takes a hard look at the countryside. *Le Malouin* is a son of farming folk. "It is hotter here than Spain, and the country is the fairest to be found, even if it be sandy. In every place it has trees or wild corn with an ear like rye, and small peas as thick as if they had been sown and ploughed over, and red and white gooseberries, strawberries, blackberries, white and red roses and many other flowers of sweet smell."

Like Verrazano, the St. Malo captain notices the wealth of wine grapes growing wild. This is something of a miracle to the Breton, as to the pilot from the Lombard vineyards. In fact Jacques Cartier, although he has seen no sign of a passage, is very happy at discovering the warmth and fertility of this inland side of the mighty Castles gulf. There is an idyllic moment when a score of native maidens break away from their men—the women here as at Manhattan were kept at a distance from the Europeans—and throng around to stroke Cartier's hands and shoulders, until he gives each admirer a small tin bell, whereat the girls go into their singing and dancing act. At the same time Cartier notices that the people here differ from the others in speech and poverty, possessing only fish nets "worth no more than five sous" and the bark canoes under which they sleep. For the first time he wonders if these simple folk cannot be converted to Christ.

Here, long after his landfall on the coast, *le Malouin* raises his claiming cross, of tree lengths thirty feet high, with the escutcheon of the fleur-de-lis and the inscription in capital letters *"Vive le Roy de France."* (This cross was placed on the sandy point of Penouille, it seems, and not on the Gaspé point, as often related.) For here the voyagers have passed the known landmarks and entered on new ground. After placing the great cross the French knelt in prayer, making signs to the interested populace to do the same.

This ceremonial, however, brought an unexpected reaction from the native audience. The chief of the Penouille-Gaspé folk came forward, but not cordially, wearing an old bearskin and with his sons attending him. He made the sign of a cross with his fingers and followed this with an oration about himself and the country around them. The French, who had been picking up native words as they progressed, understood the "captain" to protest that all this country belonged to him and the Christians had no right to put their mark upon it.

Whereupon the Bretons resorted to diplomacy, taking the protesting royal family to their ships, dining and wining them and giving them priceless gifts, colored shirts, red caps, steel knives, and hatchets. "We showed them by signs that the cross was set up only as a lead by which to enter the port, and that we would soon return to it bringing good store of ironwares and other things, but we would take two of his children with us, and bring them back to the said port again."

The wine or the presents prevailed. The chief left two of his sons, Taignoagny and Domagaya, with Cartier, bringing them a supply of fish for their journey on the floating houses, and assuring Cartier that his cross would not be touched. This friendly abduction of Domagaya was to have consequences unforeseen by the French.

Ironically, Cartier sailed past the mouth of the St. Lawrence—the river that would be always identified with his name—without perceiving it. Mist and storm veiled the great estuary and the ships crossed to the east cape of Anticosti. Yet the Bretons did perceive the pull of the tide at this point. If their single purpose had been to find a passage to the west, those mariners from the tide-swept Channel would surely have followed this tide in a way.

With the first east winds of the summer's end Cartier broke off his coastal survey and took counsel with his crews to decide what they should do. Either he himself knew or he was told by the others that the ocean would soon be in the grip of the autumn storms, which would keep the vessels in harbor here for the winter. They decided to head out for the Strait of the Castles (Belle Isle) and home. They found their way back as if on a charted course to the quays of St. Malo.

Now Jacques Cartier had little to show for his brief two months' sojourn around *Terre Neuve*. He brought no gold and explained with regret he had found no sign of a passage. Estevan Gomez had discovered more, to be greeted with ridicule at Seville. But the painstaking sea captain became the hero of St. Malo, the guest of the Court at Paris, and was praised by Francis the King as "my pilot of the western sea."

Evidently he had carried out his orders well. He had managed to break the barrier of the continental coast which had defied other northern navigators from Cabot to De Ayllón and Verrazano. He had explored, as it were, the entrance to the great unknown. In so doing he had lost neither a spar nor a man.

It might be said that, while the Spaniards had sought in vain the reality of wonders, the French had found the wonder of reality.

Among the things, little noticed, that he brought back there was a long list of words, quite a vocabulary, in fact, of the strange people of the west—"the language that is spoken in the Land newly discovered, called New France."

There was to be a new France beyond the sea. The persistence of the French in seeking it would create in time their proudest possession, Canada.

The Reason Why of the French

The two boys from the west, Taignoagny and Domagaya, naturally caused much excitement when they appeared dressed in European garments in Paris. The boys, especially Domagaya, testified to the truth of what Cartier's band had heard on the great gulf: farther inland there were kingdoms to be found in New France, kingdoms called Canada and Hochelaga and—far off—Saguenay.

Under eager questioning the Huron-Iroquois boys tried, as usual, to please their masters with their answers. Yes, Hochelaga was a town. Yes, the town had a wall around it, of wood. Gold, copper and silver? No, not in Hochelaga. Such red, yellow, and white metal came from Saguenay. They came down the great river Canada, a long way—a journey of many months.

Domagaya appeared to be telling the truth, and perhaps in his own mind he was telling truthfully all he knew. It turned out that by Saguenay he did not mean the river of that name near his home, but the region farther west, beyond the Ottawa, where the powerful Iroquois dwelt in long houses and possessed the copper of the great lakes.

But Cartier and the planners in Paris believed what they wanted to believe. Up this river in the kingdom of Saguenay precious metals might be found. And Cartier himself made another natural mistake. Having circled the Gulf of St. Lawrence in the two summer months, he swore that the climate was wonderful, and the nature of the place like to Paradise. That seemed logical to his listeners, who had the scientific notion of their day that climates in the same latitudes were the same everywhere. The Canadian winter, however, would be very different from winter in St. Malo.

In one other matter the French, or at least those who planned a second, larger expedition to be led back by Cartier the next year, were mistaken. For a reason often overlooked nowadays, they paid little heed to the fact that Cartier had failed to find a salt-water passage to Asia. It seemed to many of them that *le Malouin* had found his way to the entrance of Asia itself.

He would be charged presently to sail as captain and King's Pilot "to the lands of Canada and Hochelaga *at the end of Asia,* on the western coast."

That was Francis' idea, but not his alone. At this time eminent cosmographers believed that northern Asia extended into the unknown continent. The newest globe of the earth in Paris (known as the "Wooden Globe") had Cathay begin somewhat to the west of *Terra Francisca,* into which Cartier had found his way. The latest book of the discoveries, *Novus Orbis Regionum ac Insularum Veteribus Incognitarum* (Region of the New World and the Islands Unknown to the Ancients), had been published in both Basle and Paris in 1532. It combined accounts of Tartary by Messer Marco Polo and Haithon, King of Armenia, with the journals of Christopher Columbus and the *Four Voyages* (which refused to die a decent death) of Amerigo Vespucci, and the *Decades* of the late Peter Martyr, and others. The map illustrating this latest volume in Paris was made by Oronce Finé, ablest of French geographers, and it revealed Asia linked like a Siamese twin to the unknown continent in the north.

Now Francis I studied maps. A pension-hungry Portuguese pilot testified that the Valois monarch argued with him excitedly over maps that showed his territories in the west. Oronce Finé wrote, concerning his own new map of the world, "I designed this mappamundi for the Most Christian and Mighty Francis the King of France . . . that monarch who is adept in geography, was pleased with that map." On Finé's work, rather bare of names in the north, the great name ASIA extends from modern Siam to the vicinity of Manhattan. The most brilliant of the young mathematical geographers, Gerard Mercator (who would evolve the Mercator projection of the earth's sphere on a flat map), was copying Finé's concept closely.

Studying such maps, or even glancing at them, Francis, who

was naturally optimistic, could not escape fancying that a reliable explorer like Cartier could make his way *overland* to the markets of Asia, or at least to Cathay and the much-desired city of Quinsay . . . probably Cartier could work up the great river to Saguenay, and on to—who could tell?

The geographers were not merely doodling with fantastic ideas. The European voyagers by 1535 had opened up the vast oceans and the long coasts of the New World and Asia only in a southerly direction. From Balboa's South Sea they had probed northerly only into the Gulf of Cortes (Gulf of California). The Portuguese, and Magellan too, had not pushed north of the Philippines on the Asiatic side. The Pacific Ocean above some 20° north remained a blank. Yet Cortes's explorers had noticed the westerly trend of their unknown coast, while the Portuguese had charted the easterly trend of the China coast. If the two continents extended in this fashion toward each other, must they not meet somewhere in the farther north? All continents came together somewhere above the Arctic Circle. This conjecture was strengthened by the old notion that land must balance water in each hemisphere. If the great South Sea of Balboa contained only minute islands, there must surely be immense land masses in the unexplored north.

So far the geographers reasoned, and, except for Bering Strait, which would not be explored for two centuries, they reasoned correctly. And they had to guess what might be in northeast Asia. No one of record had ventured there since the missionaries who followed Marco Polo. An envoy or two had penetrated to the barbarous court of the Grand Prince of Moscow. It seemed that to the east of Moscow there was a river Volga and tribes which drove dog sleds and hunted reindeer, much like the wild Eskimo of the nearer land God gave to Cain.

In their maps the geographers had to fill in this void beyond Moscow with quotations from the Bible or Marco Polo, and landmarks left by Alexander the Great, who had penetrated it for some distance. They did the best they could. *No one from Europe had been there.*

Whatever maps he studied and whatever may have been his

thoughts about them, Francis beheld an enormous vista of the unknown stretching west from the region named after him, *Francisca,*
two thirds around the globe of the earth to the river Volga in Muscovy. Within that belt of darkness might lie undiscovered seas, gold
mines, or pagan peoples never seen by European eyes.

He told Cartier to "go west as far as possible."

Vista of a Continent

By early October of that year, 1535, Jacques Cartier was more
than a thousand miles inland from the entrance Strait of the Castles.
He was climbing a mountain that he named for his king *Mont Royal*
(from which Montreal would take its name).

Standing on the summit of the mountain, he looked out at
the vista of a continent. Beneath him there was an island in the
great river and beyond it the white water of rapids; the upthrust
of dark hills rose like waves to the north and south. The horizon
stretched away scores of miles to the west. Through the haze of far-
off valleys unknown rivers gleamed. There was no trace of another
sea. There was only the mass of a continent unmapped by Christians.

The solid sea captain of St. Malo must have had a moment of
inward joy. He had carried out his orders well.

Behind him in the last weeks lay faultless achievement—the
great river of Hochelaga (St. Lawrence) ascended by his two larger
ships, *Great Ermine* and *Little Ermine,* and the small *Merlin,* to the
town of Stadacona (Quebec), near which they lay in a safe haven in
a stream, except for *Merlin,* which had carried him and a picked
band with four noblemen upriver between majestic forest walls,
until he took to the long boats to find Hochelaga.

He had charted his route carefully, with soundings all the way,
guided by the two boys Domagaya and Taignoagny, who could
speak with the French now—keeping the friendship of the king,
Donnacona, at Stadacona, until the people there wailed at his de-

parture—treating the sick at mighty Hochelaga by prayer and laying on of hands, finding the wooden wall of Hochelaga as Domagaya had described it, and the houses of the people there fifty
paces long with twelve fires burning within. These were kindly
people and proud, masters of the towns toward the sea; when they
saw the French to be wearied, they picked up the voyagers and carried them on their backs. (These were some of the Iroquois, above
the great lakes.)

The land only waited for the plow to yield good harvests; even
without cultivation the fruit and grapes and nuts tasted good.

More than that, the Hochelagans had made gifts to Cartier of a
long knife of beaten copper and some lumps of melted gold. This
was the first evidence of gold in the new land and it fairly started
the French. Might not the riches of Asia or another treasure of
Moctezuma be found beyond the horizon?

The Hochelagans explained. The red copper came to them from
Saguenay. Where did that country lie? Beyond, to the west, there
was a river that led to Saguenay. The yellow metal came from their
own river, the great river below, up at its source. How far to its
source by boat?

The Hochelagans, it seemed, knew all about that. No boats of
bark passed up the white water, the rapids like the one near the
mountain. A path led around the white water here and at three
more rapids upstream. Once past the rapids it was a journey of three
moons to the source of the great river. And beyond that, what was
to be found? There was a sea of fresh water where dwelt a people
fierce in war and dangerous to meet. By way of proof, the king of
Hochelaga showed the French three pieces of flayed skin of a
man's head. These were scalps.

The gold meant little to the Hochelagans, who were pleased
to have steel hatchets, knives, and some wampum—for Cartier had
discovered this to be the native money of exchange—in return for
the ingots. They were more pleased when the French saluted them,
at parting, with a fanfare of trumpets.

That trumpet blast marked a climax of hope for Jacques Cartier.
At that moment it must have seemed as if he were well on his way

toward a New France both fertile and rich in metals. His first check came at once when the two longboats tried to ascend the *saut* he had seen. His rowers could not force their way against the rush of water. Did Cartier christen these rapids *La Chine* in irony or in hope? Certainly the seaman of St. Malo realized that this was no navigable route to the west. At Stadacona he had been on tidewater; here not even the little *Merlin* could pass.

Since autumn was closing in, with unexpected cold, he headed downstream quickly to his fort at Stadacona (actually on the St. Charles River) where most of the 110 men of his company waited. With spring, and the aid of the Hochelagans, he expected to resume the search for the source of the gold and the elusive kingdom of Saguenay. But he was not able to do that.

November brought to the river the breath of arctic cold for which the Frenchmen were unprepared. For more than four months they could only hibernate in their ships and fort on a frozen river. "We were held in ice two fathoms thick, and snow rising more than four feet, above the rails of our ships. All our drinks were frozen, and the ice thickened below hatches as well as above." It amazed the voyagers to see natives walking about on snow shoes, almost naked in this unbelievable cold.

The winter also brought its human tensions. Donnacona's people resented the journeying forth of the French to Hochelaga because this meant the loss of the trade of coveted steel weapons and tools of the Europeans. Although the hunters of Stadacona still gave meat and parched maize to the godlike white men, they had less food to spare in the hard winter and demanded higher prices, egged on by Domagaya and Taignoagny, who had been quick to learn values in trading, as well as their own importance.

Then scurvy struck the snowed-in encampment. Apparently Cartier had no experience with this dread disease of seamen, because he took it to be plague, caught from the natives, and he dissected the body of the first of his men to die to try to learn what the plague might be. When the scurvy was at its worst, only three or four of his company were able to keep their feet, and Cartier, who feared an attack by the Stadacona folk on his helpless company, explained to

Donnacona that he was keeping his men at hand labor within the vessels. As evidence of this, he had the few able men make a racket with tools and timbers during the hours of the day to deceive the Indians.

The difficult Domagaya, however, helped the French find a cure for the sickness, although unwittingly. "Our captain, while considering the sickness and how it increased among us, went forth one day to walk on the ice to the fort, and saw a band of those countrymen coming from Stadacona with Domagaya among them, who ten days before had been very sick with that disease, his knees swollen and his gums rotten and stinking. Our captain, seeing him whole again, was glad and thought to learn how he had healed himself. Domagaya answered that he had taken the juice of the leaves of a certain tree. Then our captain desired to be shown if such a tree were near, because, he said, he had a man stricken with the disease who had taken it from Donnacona's people. This he said because he did not wish to reveal how many of his men were sick. Straightway Domagaya sent two women to fetch some branches of it, therewith to show how to take the bark and leaves of the said tree, to boil them together."

By this extract of the bark of a spruce Cartier saved his sick. But he had lost twenty-five of his company. Short of men and supplies, he decided to return to France as soon as the ice left the river. There was the glad omen of the gold to be shown to his king, and he carried off Donnacona, chief of Stadacona, to tell Francis what was known about Saguenay.

On his way out in June he met with the fishing fleet of Brittany off the Newfoundland coast.

He had penetrated nearly a thousand miles into the continent, not without loss, and had brought back copper and gold and a witness to prove what could be gained by venturing further. But France was again at war with the empire, and Cartier's mission had to wait five years.

Because of the delay rumors from Paris began to reach the ears of the empire. The first two voyages of Cartier had been made under secrecy and neither he nor his Bretons did any talking. Now rumors from the French Court revealed that the silent explorer had found gold and his king was preparing to send, not three ships, but an armada to the western continent to claim and conquer—what?

In Valladolid, Charles the Emperor demanded an answer to that question—being vexed like a Laocoön with so many convolutions of the French, whose armies invaded Italy, whose merchants sailed to the ports of the Grand Turk, the most dangerous enemy of the empire in the Mediterranean, whose statesmen encouraged the rebellious Lutherans biting at the bowels of the empire. Spies gave Charles answers that were not reassuring.

Lagarto, the Portuguese pilot who had argued discreetly with the enigmatic Francis over the maps, reported that there *was* an expedition setting out to "the Indies" for gold, which he did not believe the French would find. Agents in the Channel ports sent word that the Admiralty there was fitting out as many as 125 vessels. Christopher Haro, merchant of the Pyrenees frontier, wrote that the old nemesis of the empire, Jean Ango—with other French merchants—was taking a hand in the Cartier project. At Toledo, Juan Tavera, the Cardinal, picked up a report that Cartier meant to settle in the New Land, although he was probably merely after gold.

Like many supreme commanders before him and since, Charles Hapsburg was exasperated by the vagueness of the reports. *Where* was Cartier bound for? To this *Canada,* 760 leagues from the French coast, or to the unknown destination 600 leagues beyond *Canada?* Which way beyond? South to the Spanish dominions, to Santo Domingo, and the route of the treasure fleets? Charles comprehended very well the desperate need of the French for gold and bullion; his own need was nearly as great.

Wearied and furious, Charles gave out a warning. If this sea captain Cartier sailed south into Spanish waters, the French would be treated as pirates, their vessels seized, and they themselves thrown over the rail to drown.

To all this Francis made ready reply through his ambassadors. Cartier's fleet was not bound for the dominions of his friend, the Most Christian Emperor, but for the discovery land of the French in the north. Surely the New Land must be free to all. "Surely," Francis himself retorted to the Spanish ambassador, "a land is not discovered by merely sailing by and looking at it!" (So much for the Spanish claim, based on the Estevan Gomez voyage; Cartier had been ordered to traverse the far territory, to build a settlement and forts.) "It is not discovered until habitations are built there and fortified."

To this reply the Hapsburg Court gave no belief. "If the Cartier fleet is indeed bound for that northern coast of little value," Charles demanded of his advisers, "what would prevent him from raiding Spanish possessions from there?"

As French preparations neared an end in the Channel ports and Jacques Cartier received his orders as captain and King's Pilot to sail to the extremity of Asia in the west, Charles invoked agencies of his own to take counteraction. He appealed for advice to no less a personage than the Adelantado, Hernando Cortes, who had been summoned back to Spain to receive honors and be kept at a safe distance from his rich conquest of Mexico. The Emperor also demanded action from the Casa de Contratación and the Council of the Indies. The Council summoned the ghost of a man to act for them.

He was waiting in Seville then, this ghost of a Cabeza de Vaca who should have died with Narváez, yet had been found by a Spanish patrol in the deserts north of the Rio Grande with three other skeletons of men including the African Estevanico. De Vaca, who had started out eight years before to become treasurer of Las Palmas, had returned to Spain to tell of what the four had beheld —the marvel of barren plains without limits, of herds of hump-backed cows that covered the prairies, and of cities lying beyond the northern horizon. When Cabeza de Vaca was asked by the Council to guide a fleet to track down Cartier on the coast of the northern land, he declined the doubtful enterprise.

Then for a while the Council of the Indies planned to send its fleet out under Cortes. In the end only two caravels sailed to track down Cartier. One, which cruised off the Cape Verde Islands, had nothing to report of him; the other, crossing to the Newfoundland terminal of the fishing fleets, reported that Cartier had passed that

point with five ships to enter the great river of Canada, there to
found a colony.

To explain the failure of the following year, some say that his
king had lost faith in Cartier; others conjecture that the aging master of St. Malo had lost confidence in himself during his long wait on
shore, or that he chafed under his subordination to Roberval. Nothing like that seems to have happened.

Francis sped him on his way with expression of "full trust in
his proud and painstaking pilot of the western sea," to whom he had
made a gift of *Great Ermine*. What is more to the point, the Valois
somehow managed to find the money (which he failed to do with
Roberval) to outfit five sizable vessels, with 400 men, including
miners, merchants, and farmers, with cattle and sheep, supplies for
three years, and even six longboats in sections, and the parts of a
windmill.

So Jacques Cartier sailed in the spring of 1541 for his river in
the west, there to establish the first Crown colony of France, and
thus claim a share of the new continent. This was what he had urged
should be done, and it put a great responsibility on him. The King
of France added to the responsibility at the last moment. For Donnacona—according to Lagarto—had convinced Francis that somewhere in the kingdom of Saguenay dwelt "people clothed like the
French, living in great houses like the Christians." "Persevere in
finding the Saguenay," Francis ordered Cartier.

At sea Cartier shows no failing of his old skill. He rides through
the usual storm off the coast of Newfoundland; running out of
water, he keeps the cattle alive on good Breton cider.

At the rendezvous on Newfoundland, however, he waits in vain
for his co-commander Roberval with the military personnel of the
expedition. Roberval, often called the "King of Vimeux" is a nobleman, a Protestant, an engineer, and tough soldier in contrast to the
seaman of St. Malo, but their duties are different—Cartier to direct
all navigation and discovery afloat, Roberval to fortify and command
the land works, becoming by letters patent "Lord of Norumbega
[the land named by Verrazano] Viceroy and Lieutenant-general of

Canada, Hochelaga, Saguenay, Newfoundland, Belle Isle, Carpunt, Labrador, the Great Bay [Gulf of St. Lawrence] and Baccalaos." All of which is to constitute the New France, above New Spain, north of 40° at the extremity of Asia.

When Roberval's ships fail to show after some weeks, Cartier can delay no longer. He takes the well-known route to Stadacona (Canada) and displays no fear in telling the people that their chieftain Donnacona died in France. He builds double forts, on the shore and the height at Cap Rouge a little above the site of Quebec. He sets the farmers to clearing and tilling fields around the forts. Then he "perseveres in finding the Saguenay." Pushing upstream with his longboats, he is helped by the Hochelagans to portage around two of the *sauts*. By the time he reaches the third rapids it is late in the season; two of his men warn him that the Hochelaga chiefs intend to attack their base forts with the Canadians. The kingdom of Saguenay with its fabled riches remains as invisible as ever—and Cartier turns back, speeding downriver to his forts, which must be held secure. There at Cap Rouge he sends two vessels back to report to France, but has no word from Roberval and the soldiers.

There his record ends, leaving the winter a blank, with Cartier a changed man at the end.

It is clear that the garrison at Cap Rouge did not suffer this time from scurvy. Yet twenty-five men died apparently in conflict with the natives. One other fact comes out—the gold and diamonds they stumbled upon, not in Saguenay, but near Cap Rouge itself. They filled ten barrels with yellow-veined ore, and several hogsheads with shining diamonds dug from the beach. Now since Cartier had wintered near there before without uncovering any precious minerals or stones, it might be that the miners brought on this voyage discovered them. The discovery must have been made before heavy snow set in, so the colonists had all the winter months to ponder the treasure they had unearthed. They were entitled to a third of the finds. Should they wait for the tardy Roberval, to share the treasure with the soldiers? Or should they speed to Paris with word of the discovery?

The Canadian winter tried them in more ways than one.

With the breakup of the ice Cartier made his decision, to hurry back to France. His mind made up, *le Malouin* would not change it. Perhaps he had boasted too much about the first gold taken from Hochelaga; perhaps he felt he must redeem his failure to discover Saguenay. Whatever the reason, he persisted in his fatal mistake.

Then, at the last haven of the New World, at St. John's on the Newfoundland coast, he ran into the Sieur de Roberval arriving with two vessels and the armed force.

Honestly enough Cartier showed the Lieutenant General specimens of his precious finds, and Roberval thought them good. But when Roberval ordered him to turn back to Cap Rouge, Cartier refused. He alleged, not altogether honestly, that a colony could not survive another winter there.

Whereupon the two commanders clashed violently. Roberval, an army officer, needed desperately to repair his own fortunes. The "King of Vimeux" had borrowed recklessly to outfit his two ships—until the portside brokers called him "King of Nowhere"—and he had raided the jails to fill out his company of 200 armed men. More, he had lingered for the winter in the Channel to raise money by profitable pirating of passing vessels until English and French alike had raised a hue and cry after him. He had women aboard, of various sorts. Possibly, a proclaimed Protestant, he hoped to establish a Protestant colony in the New World. Having in one way or another burned his bridges behind him, he would not give up his mission. Nor would Cartier change his mind.

They parted company there at St. John's, the soldier to go forward to the abandoned fort with a skilled pilot, Jean Alphonse, a corsair of Saintonge, while Jacques Cartier hurried with the westerly gales to his home port and king.

At Paris, Cartier brought his barrels of ore and precious stones to Francis, who had only a day to rejoice in them. When tested, they proved to be valueless iron pyrites, and mica or quartz crystals.

That ended the career of Jacques Cartier as King's Pilot. It gave birth to a proverb, "False as a diamond of Canada." The great achievement of the seaman of St. Malo in penetrating the unknown continent was obscured by the ridicule of his fool's gold.

The first French colony failed. On the St. Lawrence—as the river came to be called by accident, after the name Cartier gave to a bay outside it—Roberval brought his people through the deep freeze of the winter under the lash of cruel discipline, losing fifty by executions and scurvy. Determined but inexperienced, he dispatched Jean Alphonse in the spring to search for a passage to the north of the Gulf of St. Lawrence. The corsair-pilot of Saintonge was turned back by ice outside Belle Isle.

Roberval himself made every effort to reach the mythical kingdom of Saguenay near the head of the St. Lawrence. Losing men and boats in the rapids, unable to cope with the strange Iroquois, he retraced his way to the forts at Cap Rouge. Without a Cartier to guide him he could not penetrate the wilderness. Yet he may have reached the Ottawa. If so, he came within a short journey of the great lakes, homeland of the Five Nations of the Iroquois and the rivers that Champlain followed south long after him.

That summer of 1543 Francis sent ships under another captain to evacuate Roberval and his survivors. Discouraged by the failures and influenced now by his mistresses, Francis abandoned hope of winning his foothold in the New World. Not for sixty years, not until Samuel de Champlain forced a way through the wilderness, would the effort made by Cartier and Roberval be resumed.

There Exists a New France

In the Portuguese court there was amusement and some relief at the failure of the French to bring back gold. Where else, courtiers asked, could the piratical French have betaken them to be so harmlessly out of the way as to that obscure corner under the Arctic Circle? Charles V, however, saw nothing funny in it and wrote to his young son, Philip, in 1548 never to forget the danger that the French might bring to their Indies. Philip (who would be Philip II of Spain) was on his own account dedicated to the eradication of Protestants, nd belief in the Papal-bestowed title to all the lands of the Indies.

Spanish ships began to frequent Newfoundland waters, until Breton and Norman flotillas waged a sea battle with them and brought them as prizes to French ports.

For the fishermen persisted in making their summer voyages to the Grand Banks. In the cathedral of Dieppe the yearly service for these mariners became known as the "absolution of the New Lands."

With the persistence of ordinary folk in seeking food and profit the descendants of Jean Ango and the merchants who had sailed with Cartier pursued the traffic in furs, whale oil, and sealskins at their terminal of the New World, Brest, and beyond. Maintaining friendship with the coastal, Algonkian tribes, they supplied the native hunters with superior steel hatchets, traps, corded nets. In return the hunters brought them the choicer furs that commanded a good price in Europe. From the outer haven of Brest these unchronicled traders advanced their base to Tadoussac at the mouth of the actual Saguenay River.

Already the pattern of French endeavor was being set. It did not at first call upon missionaries to convert the pagan peoples; it formed alliance with the Algonkins—who made use of their new weapons to drive out to the Labrador coast their racial enemies the Eskimos— to aid the French *voyageurs* to penetrate inland with their trading posts.

The concept that there could be a New France beyond the sea did not die.

And it seemed to many of the small navigators that this New France might lie farther south, along the warmer rivers of "Norumbega and Acadia" (of Verrazano's voyage). This was actually the coast as far south as the Hudson, or even Chesapeake Bay. When he retired to his home in La Rochelle after forty years at sea, Jean Alphonse set up shop as a cosmographer and made a map of that far coast; on it he named the Penobscot River the *Rivière de Norvegergue,* and the shore southerly to the Merrimac he claims as *Terre de la Franciscane.* At the same time Roberval's pilot mentions one reason why the traders kept to the St. Lawrence route. The native people were friendly there, speaking some Basque and English as well as French. South of the *Terre Neuve,* however, they were bad, being fine archers, fierce, and intent on killing men with beards.

The concept of a new land of France blended with the persistent myth of a refuge to be found there. True, the islands of the Seven Cities had not been found, yet the aura of a golden age hung around the coast. Peter Martyr's "innocent, naked people" were on record, and by some transmutation of imagination these became the "noble savages" of Renaissance thought. Among them, beyond the sea, troubled spirits could find solace from the calamities of Europe, from wars and Turks. Ronsard wrote of the "port of the Happy Isles" awaiting distressed Europeans.

The poets had some tall tales from witnesses to feed their imagination. The Huron Donnacona had told of people in the hinterland who needed no food to sustain them, having no stomachs to fill; Lagarto, the Portuguese adventurer, testified that he had seen native people with wings who could fly down from trees to earth. Jean Alphonse spoke of the charmed *Isles de la Demoiselle*.

In fact around one particular Isle of the Maiden gathered an aftermath of legends of the Cartier-Roberval voyages. As the story took shape, Marguerite had been a maiden parted from her lover by the harsh Roberval, who marooned her with her nurse on an isle near Great Mekattina, near Brest. (He actually abandoned some criminals on an island.) Here the fair Marguerite was defended from demons (perhaps a legacy of the medieval Isle of Demons) by the solicitous Virgin. Her stay ended happily for Marguerite because a passing fishing craft sighted the smoke of her fire and took her off. Thereafter Marguerite became a fixture of French lore, being written into the *Heptameron* of that other Marguerite, of Navarre.

Such fantasy was the fashion of the age. Before Cartier's death he was visited by one of its stoutest champions, François Rabelais. The creator of Gargantua's and Pantagruel's travels in a new fantastic world wanted to make notes of Jacques Cartier's voyages. Despite the mockery of Rabelais's pen and the ridicule of the "Canadian diamonds" the seafaring folk of St. Malo respected their Captain Jacques Cartier.

At the turn of the century a historian mentions him as "Jacques Cartier who by his voyages gave to his king the New France which is now called Canada."

After his death the name *Nova Francia* did appear on the maps above the *Terra Florida* of the Spaniards. Before then, in 1541 the most careful of mapmakers, Gerard Mercator of the Netherlands, gave a new name to the northern continent—America. It seemed to him, as the two continents took shape, that the name of the south should be given as well to the north.

The name stuck to North America.

The Seven Cities beyond the Horizon

In the four years from 1539 to 1543 there was the probability that North America would become a Spanish province, a far frontier of the Holy Roman Empire under the rule of Charles Hapsburg. During those years three expeditions set out from the Spanish south toward the heart of the continent. One kept to the sea and the Colored (Colorado) River; the other two penetrated overland, one from the southeast corner, the other from the southwestern desert barrier. Both of these ventures by land had their starting impulse in the story Alvar Núñez Cabeza de Vaca told, or did not tell.

At first De Vaca had told the truth about his incredible ordeal in the unknown deserts of the north. As the solitary educated survivor of the Narváez death march, he had been greeted at Mexico City—more than 3000 miles distant from the site of the fort at Cap Rouge—with a fiesta and the hospitality of Don Antonio de Mendoza, the Viceroy. A man returning to the artificial magnificence of chanting in church and bullfights does not regain at once his old personality of a nobleman at large in such a city. Anxiously Cabeza de Vaca demanded that the Yaqui Indians who had guided him thither should not be taken as slaves by the slave-raiding party of Spaniards which had brought him back to civilization. For a few days, too, he could not bear to put on heavy cloth garments, or sleep in a bed. The palace of proud Mendoza appeared fantastic, with its trumpet calls, Indian servants, and wines and spiced meats on the table. The man who had walked for days without food from a shore where shellfish had given out to a valley where berries had ripened could not manage to make clear the reality of his wanderings to the listeners at the Viceroy's table. . . . He could not tell them of Spaniards carrying off the dried and preserved flesh of their dead comrades. . . .

Cultivated fields? Yes, he had met with them three or four times in the six years. On one river there had been houses of thatch and mud in the fields. Great cities? No, nothing of the kind—except that the Indians from the western hills told of large houses rising to the heights, where people wore woven cotton. Yes, he had found a precious stone, hard and blue—not sapphires. . . .

So he told the truth to the listeners of New Spain, and then departed home to the Court at Valladolid. Mendoza kept the other three survivors, hearing more promising tales from the African, Estevanico, who had learned to talk after a fashion with the Indians of the north. *After* the brooding De Vaca had gone, the Viceroy began to think more and more about the immensity of territory to the north of his dominion. Two of the survivors gave him no help because they refused to retrace their steps into the wilderness; they married and stayed determinedly within city limits. But the odd fellow Estevanico would go back among the Indians who had believed him to be a medicine man of great power. The more Mendoza thought about the region where the Seven Cities *might* lie, the more he wished to explore the route of De Vaca's wanderings. Somewhere beyond might lie the missing Sea of Verrazano—or this might prove to be the long-sought strait leading direct to Asia.

In due time Mendoza applied for routine permission from the Court in Spain to send north an exploring party of forty-odd horsemen. No harm in that, and little cost. When permission was refused, the Viceroy became angry and alert. There in Spain, it seemed, Cabeza de Vaca was applying for a grant as conquistador to the new lands; it might well be that the derelict nobleman had kept knowledge of vital riches of the hinterland to himself—which Estevanico babbled about freely. It might be. After further thought the energetic Viceroy dispatched Estevanico with an enthusiastic friar from Peru, a certain Friar Marcos born in Nice, to report on what actually could be found beyond his frontier. There was also Don Francisco Coronado, making a name for himself at the age of twenty-eight by suppressing unruly Indians as well as the rivals of the Viceroy. When Mendoza the Viceroy heard that a certain Hernando de Soto was to come to Florida as Adelantado, he hurried Coronado off along the route of Friar Marcos. . . .

In Spain, Hernando de Soto had warnings enough to keep out of the lands of Florida. After nine years Don Pánfilo Narváez, who had ventured thither, was certainly dead with most if not all his noble company. Yet De Soto, a man "of inflexible mind and little speech," applied for and received the grant vacated by Narváez as Adelantado of the Lands of Florida. The ghosts of Juan Ponce and De Ayllón did not trouble him.

De Soto came from that breeding ground of conquistadors, poverty-ridden Estremadura. He had risen to rank under patronage of the cruel and successful Avila of Golden Castile, and had gained nobility of a kind by marrying Avila's daughter. A skilled and ruthless soldier, he had led a rescue mission to Pizarro in Peru, returning with a fortune in gold and silver. At Court the Emperor himself took a fancy to the veteran captain, actually stopping to chat with him and borrow money from him. Apparently De Soto possessed everything even a Castilian could desire, except the glory of a conquest of his own. Perhaps his wife, the daughter of a conquistador, reminded him of that. By then all the best of South America had been preëmpted by others. But there remained unclaimed the whole of North America and each year rumors described this continent as vaster in size and greater in danger—thereby adding to its attractions in Spanish eyes.

After news of the fabulous wealth of Peru reached Spain, several other adventurers sought for the privilege to conquer Florida. Incan Peru and Aztec Mexico had been hidden from search until rumors reached the Christian captains. Might not the tidings of Pineda, of gold up the river of Espíritu Santo, be the clue to a richer Peru beyond the seaboard of Florida? Moreover the Emperor in those years desired that the continent be explored for the strange sea known to his enemies the French as the Sea of Verrazano. Neither Pineda nor, apparently, Narváez had explored up this mightiest of rivers. It might well flow from the missing sea.

De Soto meant to hold the favor of Charles Hapsburg, monarch of the New World empire upon which the sun never set, and Charles was just then beginning to be angered and concerned by the progress of Cartier up the great river of Hochelaga. However, according to one of his gentlemen, Hernando de Soto was intent on finding "another treasure of Atahualpa" (the Inca in whose capture and ransom De Soto had played an active part).

He must have had one bearing on such a prize in the north—the Seven Caves. Indian slaves taken in the Yaqui region told of the Seven Caves in the hinterland, forty days' journey across the deserts, where the people traded gold for feathers brought by the Indians. The experienced De Soto must also have known that such captive Indians had a way of answering what their Spanish masters wished to hear. . . .

Then Cabeza de Vaca arrived as if by a miracle from that very region. True, Cabeza de Vaca denied seeing any evidence of wealth when De Soto talked with him. He made much of the hardships of the blundering Narváez company—yet he sought for the title of conquistador of those lands. This apparent contradiction may have stirred suspicion in De Soto. De Vaca refused to go back to the mysterious country under his orders.

Moreover after a while this enigmatic Alvar Núñez changed his tune. (As the sole explorer of the northland, Cabeza de Vaca found himself the center of flattering attention at the Council and Court and, to increase his importance, he began to hint that he had actually been near the lost Seven Cities. "I and the others have sworn," he admitted, "not to speak of certain things revealed to us there." The other three survivors were not in Spain to testify one way or the other.) If Cabeza de Vaca had tidings of the hidden Seven Cities, it might prove to be the region of gold described by the Indian slaves as the Seven Caves. The number was the same, and the locality almost the same. . . .

These rumors induced many wealthy hidalgos to sell their property to buy outfits and ships to take them to the New World.

De Soto should have been warned by Cabeza de Vaca's refusal to go back there. Instead he threw part of his great wealth into an expedition stronger than any sent out hitherto—621 experienced soldiers, with some 200 horses, excellent weapons and armor, a pack of hunting dogs useful against Indians.

By his estimation such a force of Spaniards could fight its way into any part of Florida, if well led and fed. He meant to lead it himself, and he had worked out a way to feed it. In the Indies he embarked cattle and a herd of thirteen swine which De Soto meant to serve a remarkable purpose. He was not gambling as De Ayllón and Narváez had gambled; at need his regiment could force its way back to the shore where the ships would be awaiting it.

Having learned from Cabeza de Vaca of Narváez's route, the new Adelantado of Florida decided to make his entry at the same point, perhaps meaning to use for his base the town of Apalachee, where Narváez had turned back. He had sailed from the same port, San Lúcar, in 1539. His skill brought the expedition without a check to Apalachee.

De Soto had managed to bring this far everything necessary to explore the hinterland of North America except a navigator who could tell him where he was.

On the River, a Cleopatra

He should have been warned by finding Juan Ortiz. This survivor of the Narváez company looked like any naked pagan of the wilderness except for the purple weals of fire torture on his withered body, and his stammering cry of "Seville—Seville" to the Castilian lancers who rode him down. But De Soto saw in Juan Ortiz a Godsent aid, a perfect interpreter. Yet Ortiz, who had roamed the glades of Florida with native tribes for ten years, could tell the new Adelantado of no wealth to be found except perhaps in a town of many people 100 miles away. De Soto marched that way, toward Apalachee, because he had learned in Peru that the way to a hidden empire lay where populations increased and housed themselves in towns.

He broke through the wilderness barrier easily enough. His caballeros and hardened pike, crossbow, and arquebus men kept to his iron discipline and cared not at all where they might be moving so long as they had the hope of gold ahead of them. "The one idea of these cavaliers," testified in later years young Garcilaso de la Vega, "was to conquer the next kingdom, to search for gold and silver; to other matters they paid no attention." Garcilaso could judge the Castilians; he was born of Spanish-Incan parents.

The name of Juan Ortiz seemed to them to be an omen of gold. Negro slaves tended them, and captive Indians, chained in files, carried the baggage. They hungered at times between villages. But the natives yielded up parched corn and prunes, to add to the growing squash, persimmons, cabbage palms, and giant wild turkeys. Meat lacked because the pagan folk had no domestic animals other than the dogs the Spaniards relished. De Soto did not expect his arquebusiers to hunt the elusive wild game; he preserved his thirteen pigs for breeding, not eating, until they multiplied—gorging on the rich forest mast—to three hundred in a year. Not once did this expedition kill one of its cherished horses for food. When they found horse skulls with the feeding troughs and debris of forge fires where the Narváez derelicts had built the ships, they christened the ill-omened place the Bay of Horses. Nor did they shirk the fighting that marked their way up Florida and through the Cherokee villages; that, by the Spanish code of honor, made conquest more memorable. On their part the Cherokees remembered tortures inflicted by Narváez's captains, and they barred the way of these new Christian invaders with bitter resistance. This roused the Spaniards to cold anger.

If is often said that the Europeans, who possessed gunpowder, horses, and armor, rode like supermen among helpless Indians. But once the Cherokees overcame their natural dread of the strange, galloping horses, they attacked the mounted Spaniards in swamps or river fords where the beasts could not charge and the riders could be overthrown into the water where their helmets and breastplates hampered them. On foot the veterans of the *tercios* soon found that the native warriors could outrun and outswim them, and usually outlast them. As for gunpowder De Soto appears to have given away to a Florida cacique the only cannon he lugged along. His clumsy arquebuses proved ineffective. The powerful Indian longbow outranged the European crossbow—"the Indians loosed six or seven arrows while the Christians loaded and aimed their weapons once."

The advantage of the Spaniards lay in their breastplates and fine steel hand weapons, immensely superior to the small wooden clubs, stone hatchets, and copper knives of the natives. But more than that was their discipline and the *élan* which made them the most dreaded fighting force in Europe of that day. The Indians, however, displayed tactics of their own and a spirit almost as unyielding. They wearied the invaders by simulating attacks during the nights when the Spaniards tried to sleep, and they built novel defense works in forests.

One of these defended the approach to Apalachee, where, Garcilaso, the educated half Inca, explains, "the Indians withdrew only a little at a time, being unwilling to yield up any more ground than could be won by the sweep of a sword. Where our horses might have run at them, the Indians fastened lengths of wood between the trees; where the forest was too dense to pass through, they cleared pathways which allowed them to fall upon the Christians who could not attack them in return . . . where the Indians could spread out among the trees they caused us great affliction by attacking from both sides the road. They did this with system, for those on one side waited until the others had withdrawn before releasing their arrows in order not to wound their own men."

De Soto's veterans won this metropolis of the Indian peoples by cutting their way through to the "palace" of its ruler. By holding the chieftain hostage the Spaniards enforced obedience. In capturing Apalachee—and avenging the disaster to Narváez's company—the Europeans obtained food enough to last them out the first winter. Yet they had to endure partisan warfare by native bands holding the forest outside the cultivated areas.

This was no warfare of ambushes and flights of arrows as might be supposed; it was the determined contest of one people against another, one code of fighting against another. De Soto, an unyielding commander, was experiencing the mute and continuing resistance which kept the European intruders from making a livable settlement within North America for more than a century.

Resistance sprang up at the sound of the axes of a firewood party at work, or against a mounted patrol of foragers. Cherokees and Creeks alike soon realized that they could injure a mounted in-truder most by killing his horse. Once seven caballeros ventured out of Apalachee, as quarantined soldiers always do, to quest for food and perhaps a toothsome dog. "As they wandered about, looking for such things, they came to five Indians who awaited them with bows. These Indians drew a line upon the ground and threatened to kill any one who crossed it. [A certain invitation to the belligerent cava-liers of Castile to come on.] Not relishing such mockery, our Span-iards closed with their challengers who took their bows and killed two horses, wounding two more and severely injuring one rider. One Indian was killed but the others escaped on their feet, for these people are indeed very swift and are not hampered by clothes."

This challenge was not accidental. Nor did the native warriors usually avoid hand-to-hand conflict with Spaniards if the soldiers were on foot. Another party of seven, including five halberdiers of De Soto's guard, became bored with the winter camp and ventured out against orders to look for amusement or profit in another village. The seven had gone only two hundred paces into a cornfield before they were attacked. Hearing the sound of it, a rescue party ran out from Apalachee, to find the halberdiers and one other Spaniard transfixed with arrows, while the only survivor, a powerful man from Badajoz, lay helpless with arrows through his thighs under the corse-let, his shield broken, and his head beaten so that the bone of the scalp was bared. For nearly three weeks, while his wounds healed, his comrades jested about the beating he had had, and asked the man of Badajoz if he would challenge his foes to single combat, to avenge the injury he had received by being set upon by so many. Then, very slowly, the surviving man-at-arms explained what had really happened, and put an end to the jesting.

"To make you understand," he told his mates, "who the Indians of this province are—without detracting anything from those of us who are dead—I want to tell you with no joking of the courtesy and valor of those Indians that day. More than fifty of them came out in a company to look at us. But when they saw we were only seven without horses only seven of them stepped forward, the others withdrawing a little distance and abstaining from the fight. Those seven and no more attacked us, jumping in front of us and deriding us while shooting arrows. Then they closed with me by taking their bows in both hands and beating me—I do not tell this to glorify myself—to the state in which you found me. Now I do not plan to challenge them, because they might ask what such a challenge were worth. This is how it really happened, and I pray that God may keep you from a similar misfortune."

The veterans of Spain agreed among themselves that the strange fighters of Apalachee felt themselves equal to the Christians who were not mounted on horses.

De Soto's technique of travel through his new dominion failed at times because of the stubbornness of his new subjects, the Indians. Captive caciques slipped from the hands of his guards; captive bearers, even when chained, turned on their masters and had to be thrown to the packs of savage dogs. The Indians feared the dogs and horses, but, unlike the more civilized folk of Peru, they had little dread of the armored white men. Accordingly De Soto, a resourceful leader, made use of diplomacy. Realizing that the people of Florida had no reason to love Christians, he forbore any attempt to convert them to Christianity until they should be conquered; instead he offered them peace, pledging himself to pass through their province, taking only necessary food and bearers to transport it to the next province. Wherever Indians had heard of the Christians, such a pledge to move on quickly won their earnest co-operation.

The conquistador used such diplomacy when he encountered the first woman ruler, somewhere on the upper Savannah River. Thereupon this lady of Cofachiqui came in person to meet the Adelantado from Spain, who had heard that she ruled a large population and possessed gold. She arrived at the riverbank in a boat with eight maidens, all wearing clean linen garments, their boat being towed by canoes paddled by warriors. "The scene, although somewhat less spectacular, resembled that in which Cleopatra came forth to welcome Marc Anthony on the river Cydnus"—or so it seemed to Garcilaso de la Vega.

It was, indeed, a scene of ceremony on both sides. As usual De Soto had his portable chair to enable him to sit in dignity; the attractive brown lady (*señora*) of Cofachiqui also had a chair produced by her subjects. Willingly she agreed to give up half the food stored in her town. Owing to a plague the year before, her people had little reserve of food for themselves. As to housing, she would clear her own house for the Adelantado and half the town for his captains, besides building huts of branches for the ordinary men of the army in the fields outside. As to transport, she would furnish the army the next day with rafts and canoes to go up the river.

"The Governor [De Soto] felt deep gratitude because at a time when her land suffered from want, the lady had offered more than he requested. He assured her in the name of his lord, the Emperor of the Christians and King of Spain, that her kindness in service would never be forgotten."

To such an obliging young woman ruler Hernando de Soto could be charming. But Cofachiqui, although comfortable, proved to be only another Indian town; its gold turned out to be the usual bits of copper. Moreover the young lady of Cofachiqui was discovered to be merely the daughter or even the niece of the Queen of Cofachiqui, who had hidden herself in the forest rather than meet with such strange men, leading such strange animals. (The enlarged herd of swine must have arrived by then, although how the Spaniards contrived to make pigs travel on through lush spring growth remains a mystery.) Yet the discreet princess made amends for the discourtesy of the queen. While discussing the matter with the Adelantado, she removed a great string of pearls that she wore, as large as hazelnuts, and told Juan Ortiz that she would offer it to the Adelantado if her modesty did not prevent. De Soto, however, reassured her most courteously. "Make clear to her that I shall esteem the honor of having these pearls from her hands more than the value of the pearls, and her act in giving them will be in no way immodest because this is a matter of friendship and peace between strangers."

Whereupon the young lady of Cofachiqui pleased the Castilians even more by revealing to them that great quantities of pearls—"more than the entire army could carry away"—had been stored with the dead in the tomb house of her family. Yet here again the high hopes of the explorers were frustrated. When they broke into the burial house they found thousands of the shining white jewels, as the princess promised, but only seed pearls, or the larger ones from fresh-water mussels. Even they were damaged by heat because the Indians had cooked the mussels before extracting the pearls.

For a moment excitement seized the Spaniards when they found what they thought to be an enormous emerald, which proved to be clear green glass, made in Europe. It lay among other odd treasures, tarnished rosaries, and rusted iron axes. They were vestiges of De Ayllón's expedition.

The Women of Mavilla

Although they took the lady of Cofachiqui on with them, and she behaved as obligingly as before—sending messengers ahead to warn strange townships to receive the army of the Emperor in peace—she seemed to deprive them of any greater fortune, which by now the cavaliers of Spain felt that they deserved by reason of their great and courageous exertions. Although the new dominion opened before them with elusive beauty, the towns became fewer and the cavaliers and their horses hungered. They followed the rumor of gold mines up to the headwaters of the rivers, to find only some copper deposits, and to have their way barred by stark mountains (the Blue Ridge of the Carolinas?). At this obstacle the Adelantado led them south, toward the sea.

Actually De Soto seems to have tried to reach cultivated areas again; moreover he knew that his ships would return to the coast that summer with food supplies. In the vast wilderness of his dominion-to-be he had found no evidence of gold; some of his soldiery complained at the senseless marching, and a few sick, with Negro slaves, deserted to the security of the Indian villages. By now the marchers had added young women slaves to their company; exasperation increased among them because De Soto refused to slaughter more of the herd of pigs for meat.

Aware of these tensions, De Soto tightened discipline, and increased the pace of his column. So it happened that the column was strung out over miles when it reached a palisaded town named Mavilla (probably near the headwaters of Mobile Bay).

They were greeted here by the usual parade of dancers with songs and gifts of fur, and guided into quarters within the wall—the forty horses of De Soto and the advance being tethered in a grove outside. Luis de Moscoso and another officer warned De Soto that the Indians here were massed in numbers, all being armed men with few women, and no children or old people. In spite of that De Soto entered Mavilla to examine his quarters and agree on the food and *tamemes* (bearers) to be supplied the Spaniards. At the same time the long baggage train of the captive Indians began to enter the gate. Since the last weeks had been peaceful many of the Spaniards had laid aside their heavier weapons, to be carried by the Indian bearers.

No one agrees as to how the battle began in Mavilla. Whether the warriors launched a planned attack, or whether a captive Indian cacique, Tastaluca, refused to answer a Spanish officer, or a halberdier tore the marten-skin cloak from a warrior, it flared up from the enmity latent on both sides. For the first time in North America tribes had gathered into a sizable army to resist the invaders. And Garcilaso pays tribute to the "spirit and valor" of the Indians.

It took the Christians altogether by surprise. In the piazza the trained soldiers bunched together and fought their way out of the streets into the open. They ran to cut the tethers of the horses before the cherished animals could be killed by Indian arrows. Their baggage and many of their weapons remained inside the wall of Mavilla, where the captive Indians were released from the chains and armed to fight their masters.

For a half hour the De Soto column faced disaster. The main body of soldiers came up in haste. The badly punished Spaniards found themselves outside the palisade of the town, outnumbered by the exultant warriors who held it, with their supplies inside. De Soto commanded that no horses be taken into the streets, where they might be slaughtered by the bowmen on the roofs. There was only one thing to be done, to force a way in and to take Mavilla, like any besieged town, house by house.

It took nine hours of remorseless struggle through the burning houses. "At this time the Indians realised that their forces were weakening, while those of the Castilians were growing stronger. Summoning their women, they commanded them to take up the weapons of those dead in the streets. In this way they could at least bring death upon themselves and escape becoming the slaves of the Spaniards. When this order was given many of the women had been fighting with courage beside their husbands. In consequence they now bore in their hands many of the swords, halberds, and lances that the Spaniards had lost, and they turned these things against their owners, wounding numerous men with their own arms."

Few Indians, male or female, survived the conflagration and the weapons of the trained soldiery. But that night in the smoking ruins not many Spaniards kept their feet unwounded. Their medical supplies and dressings had gone up in smoke with most of the baggage, the trove of pearls from Cofachiqui, and their food. A witness says they cut open the bodies of Indians to extract fat and oil to dress their burns and hurts.

While forty-seven of De Soto's men were killed in the action, thirty-five died later of wounds. Almost as disastrous was the loss of forty-five of the remaining horses. Spanish chronicles tell of thousands of Indians destroyed in the holocaust at Mavilla. Probably, however, the Indians of Mavilla suffered no more than the Spaniards.

The nine hours' struggle had reduced the hardened Spanish soldiery to exhaustion. Garcilaso relates how one man without a wound died at the end of three days in which he did not speak, eat, or sleep. Before then many veterans of Peru had become disaffected by the failure to find any kind of wealth in Florida. "To this disappointment was added the incredible fierceness of the battle of Mavilla."

It forced De Soto to change his plans, and changed the strongest of the Spanish expeditions into a journey after a mirage.

The Three Hundred Who Were Lost

Before Mavilla, De Soto had heard from Juan Ortiz that captive Indians had sighted his supply ships at their rendezvous about thirty leagues to the south (probably in Mobile Bay). His plan had been, it seems, to join them, to build a base on the bay, and fetch colonists from Cuba to begin cultivation of the land, and thence to explore the whole of his new dominion. With the second winter coming on he must have needed the supplies in the vessels, which he might have reached in a week.

Instead of doing so he ordered his men to set to work to temper again the steel weapons damaged in the conflagration. He ordered Juan Ortiz not to reveal the nearness of the vessels. And he marched away from them to the northwest, an act of seeming madness.

Afterward one chronicler explained that De Soto sought to reach food in Indian villages there. A Portuguese gentleman from Elvas said that he "determined to send no news of himself until he should have discovered a rich country." De Soto himself went about the camp at night alone and cloaked, listening to the talk of his wearied followers. Garcilaso also heard of the grievances of the men: "Since they had discovered no gold or silver, they were not at all content to populate a place here in spite of its fertility. They said they could not dominate such warlike people who were so resolved to be free. They felt they could never bring the Indians here under their yoke. They could see no reason to waste themselves away, little by little in this land. Instead they should leave this evil kingdom and take ship for New Spain or Peru which were rich countries and already won."

De Soto had gambled his fortune on finding another New

Spain; many noblemen had done likewise to join him. Now even the pearls of Cofachiqui had been lost in the fire. He had sailed from San Lúcar as Adelantado and Governor of Florida, and he would not leave it while any hope remained. It must have been clear to him that if he marched down to the ships he would lose most of his fighting force; without that he could not resume his search of the hinterland.

Apparently he counted on two possibilities. Somewhere to the west a great populated center might still be found. The great river might lead to the western sea.

So he turned blindly away toward food in the west, and the great river. Garcilaso says, "From that day, a discontented person whose own people had betrayed his hopes of perpetuating the land, he never succeeded in anything for his well-being, and it is believed that he never attempted anything of the kind."

One man's will drove the enduring company into the wilderness. De Soto did attempt to find what he could, but failed to track his myths to earth. Food they had on the river bottoms that winter, but their winter camp was burned by the always-resisting Indians; they stormed a palisade built by these enemies, only to find no town behind it—the wooden wall had been built across their line of march to halt them. They reached the bank of the great river, the Mississippi, in its spring flood, when they had to labor for a month to make pirogues to cross it; they could not ascend it. And the enemy waited, in ceremonial attire, on the far side. Chiefs of the bayou region beyond told the Spaniards that the land to the north was bare of cultivation and grazed over by wild animal herds. That could not be the way to a hidden empire.

De Soto heard of mountains in the west that yielded precious metals (the Ozarks?). But months of marching failed to bring them to a trace of silver. They lived out the next winter in snow, and the cavaliers and halberdiers learned to trap rabbits, to add to the rationed hog meat. They also made themselves new garments out of animal hides. When Juan Ortiz died, De Soto at last consented to turn back.

By then, however, he had no clear idea where they might be.

For three years they had wandered inland from the coast, and the gentleman of Elvas at least could relate only vaguely how many leagues they had journeyed in what direction. De Soto thought, apparently, that by following one river into another, southerly (he may have followed the Canadian into the Arkansas), they would reach the coast and the ships that might still bring them the longed-for supplies from Cuba. All rivers flowed into the sea eventually.

But he came out on the Mississippi again, without a trace of the coast to be discovered. It was spring again, and mounted parties sent south to explore were turned back by swamps and flooded bayous. Indians of the area could not understand the Spaniards' pantomimed description of the coast. It could not be near them. The Indians thronged around them, and De Soto ordered his captains to march on a neighboring village, to kill all the males, to make the Spaniards so feared they would not be attacked again. This was done only too well as a spectacle, for other tribes gathered to watch the exploits of the inhuman armored men, who struck down women with their children (a thing seldom done in Indian warfare) and released warriors mangled with wounds to be an example to others.

"The Governor, already ill of fever . . . fell into deep despondency at sight of the difficulties that lay between him and the sea."

Witnesses say that when he died De Soto left property amounting to two male and three female slaves, three horses, and seven hundred hogs. "From that time on, most of the people owned hogs; they lived on pork which they had not done before."

Luis de Moscoso, who took over the command, tried to convince the Indians who came seeking "the lord, the Governor" that De Soto had not died. When he noticed them collecting around the loose earth of the grave, he had De Soto's body dug out at night and carried secretly to a boat. The skin cloaks of the dead man were filled with sand and secured about him before he was taken from the shore and dropped into the flood of the great river.

Moscoso Finds the Sea

It took the company of the dead Adelantado more than a year to reach salt water. Luis de Moscoso and the cavaliers knew one fact beyond dispute; somewhere to the southwest lay New Spain and Christian towns. They marched in that direction. They reached the blistering banks of the Red River and climbed through sandy pine-lands, to dry prairies where game fled away from them swiftly. Although they had mastered some of the Indian hunting techniques, they could not manage to feed themselves on the wasteland where Cabeza de Vaca had starved. Few horses or hogs remained; the people of these plains had no food stored up. The Spanish soldiery could not advance farther by land. Probably on the upper Brazos River they turned back to follow their trail east to their last winter camp on the great river.

Here they set to work as Narváez's band had done, to build barges that would float them down the Mississippi. Having learned much about the timber of their Florida land, they managed to put together seven "brigantines." These heavy floats were calked with hair, fiber and hogs' fat—nails were cast from the melted metal of slave chains and stirrups. Mats were woven and raised along the rails to guard against the now-dreaded arrows of the people of the river.

Moscoso's shipbuilders avoided the greatest mistake of Narváez's unfortunates; a certain Maestro Francisco of Genoa, an engineer, contrived to put together a pair of water kegs for each vessel before he died. The spring floods helped the cavaliers launch their un-wieldy craft.

They had a moment of chagrin when a fleet of Indian canoes bade them farewell by speeding past in full panoply of feathers, cloaks, flashing paddles, and flying arrows. The soldiers took their punishment and steered down the flood for more than 600 miles.

From the shoals of the Mississippi mouth they turned west,

edging along the sand bars and inlets to avoid being carried out to sea. They sustained themselves with prayer, and kept alive on fish and the stagnant water of streams. When they entered a brown river with villages and cultivated fields, they scrambled ashore and kissed the ground.

It was the Pánuco; some of the villagers wore Spanish garments and one man knew the Spanish word for scissors. They called for the cacique of the nearest village and he came out, "bringing eight Indians with Spanish hens, corn-bread, fruit and fish and also ink and paper."

So in September 1543 after more than four years of wandering the army of Hernando de Soto regained contact with civilization. By a remarkable feat of endurance 311 survived, to march in their leather and furs into the street of the settlement of Pánuco.

More than that, these veterans of the vast prairies and river routes of the unknown hinterland looked with scornful eyes on the undignified makeshift of a settlement. Garcilaso, who was of noble Inca blood as well as Castilian, gives their opinion of Pánuco as he heard it from survivors.

"These people had no gold or silver mines; they eked out a living from the yield of the earth and breeding a few horses to sell if anyone would buy them. They lived in dwellings of thatch and clothed themselves in more [native] cotton than Spanish cloth. Altogether, the Spanish soldiers realised that this town was no more than a miserable beginning of cultivation in a land inferior to the one they had left, where they could dress in the finest chamois leather, or capes of marten and other magnificent Florida furs. There indeed they had no need to plant mulberry trees to raise silk, for the mulberry trees grew wild, along with walnut groves and abundance of grapes.

"And now as the soldiers made this comparison, the glory of the many fine things they had discovered in so many provinces increased. They remembered the pasture lands and woods and rivers, and the great wealth of pearls they had scorned, and the splendors they had beheld when each man had fancied he could be the lord of a province."

The Explorers Leave the Hinterland

De Soto's expedition had surveyed with its eyes some 350,000 square miles of North America; it had gone north perhaps to 38° of latitude, within a few marches of the Missouri River. In four years the survivors had gained a clear concept of the great size of the northern continent as well as the nature of the land. One chronicler conjectured that the "Great River" (Mississippi) extended inland for 800 leagues, which is not far beyond the truth. They had mastered the wilderness and developed a technique of travel that worked. They had passed through the mound-dwelling region, among people of Iroquoian and Siouan stock with fairly high culture.

The boasting of the soldiers, however, did not conceal for long the hardships of the undertaking. A Spanish expedition inland needed to travel on the food supply of Indian villages. In North America, unlike New Spain or Peru, the population was small and scattered, and moreover inclined to fight for what it possessed. As Garcilaso phrased it, the soldiery could not dominate "such a warlike people who were so resolved to be free."

After 1543 for a long time no attempt was made by Spaniards to conquer territory east of the Mississippi. In the autumn of that same year Roberval was sailing home from the St. Lawrence with the remnants of his expedition. The quest of the European powers for inland empire, legendary or real, was ending for a generation or more. After 1542–43 an intensification of warfare in Europe and on the Mediterranean occupied the Old World powers.

√ The year before, Francisco Vásquez de Coronado had limped back disheartened from his search for the Seven Cities of Cibola.*
After his failure Spanish authorities abandoned temporarily the exploration of the land west of the Mississippi.

*The detailed story of Coronado's expedition is given in the volume of the Mainstream of America dealing with the Southwest—*Glory, God and Gold,* by Paul Wellman, 1954.

Because they had expected so much from his mission Coronado's fruitless search seemed to them to be disastrous.

He had been the first to break through the age-old barrier of the Rio Grande and its desert fringe. For centuries this had separated the peoples of the north from the Aztec-Toltec empire. Only "apache" roving tribes—Cabeza de Vaca's hosts—inhabited this limbo. Spaniards of the conquest, probing north from Tenochtitlán, had been discouraged by finding no precious metals to reward them or native cultivation to sustain them. They could not force a way across the waterless plateau without grazing for pack animals, beset with raids of the Apache people.

It was a return of the delirium of the myths that launched young Coronado with the high hopes and blessing of Mendoza the Viceroy, with a traveling colony of soldiers, idle nobles, Indian servants, and Indian allies northward from the trails of the Sierra Madre— hardly the disciplined striking force that followed De Soto, but better supplied with pack animals and herds of self-moving meat. Friar Marcos, who had explored the way ahead of it, had made a rather truthful report of what he had seen. From afar he had sighted a pueblo city on a rock. But, like Cabeza de Vaca, the earnest friar talked about wonders he had not seen. As so often happened, the listeners of New Spain had imagined more than they heard, until even priests in the pulpits of the cathedral exhorted them to venture north to find the lost Seven Cities with treasures of gold and jewels and a pagan population to be brought into the fold of the Church. Then, too, there was the illusion of an approach to Asia somewhere in the north, leading travelers dry-shod to the wonders of Cathay. If the wandering Seven Cities were not up there, as Friar Marcos seemed to see them from afar, then other cities of Asia might be found a little way beyond the deserts.

Once they left familiar landmarks behind the motley explorers of New Spain became pretty well lost. One amateur geographer insisted that they must strike north by the compass, for "the country between Norway and China is very far up." It was farther than he thought.

In finding the pueblo towns, the Hawikuh of the Zuñis and the quiet populations along the upper Rio Grande, Coronado's people were exasperated because they had not found the reality of their myth. True, the Zuñi confederacy of Shi-uo-na—"Cibola"—possessed seven such "skyscraper" cities, the same number as the legendary sites of fugitive Christianity, and some wealth. True, some 25,000 humans dwelt there, or thereabouts. But delicious fruit, tortillas, good grain, fine pottery, and deftly woven cloth did not yield tangible, portable wealth. Nor did turquoises in plenty and a little silver compensate for the missing precious stones and pure gold. Friar Marcos was called a liar, and two hundred Indians were burned at the stake for stubborn resistance.

Exploring parties sent northwest and east reported discovery of natural wonders but no confirmation of legend. The Grand Canyon, that vast purple wound in the earth, seemed to bar the way to China. The Teyas, or "Texas" Indians yielded up only turkeys. The expedition, accordingly, turned east across the marvel of the Staked Plain, and then took a compass course northerly in pursuit of a fresh rumor. Quivira, a country where flowed a river two leagues in width in which sailed canoes with twenty rowers on a side, and great lords sitting on the poops under awnings. "The lord of Quivira itself took his nap under a tree hung with little gold bells which chimed in the wind. In Quivira ordinary lords ate from dishes of gold, and drank from jugs of gold."

So said an Indian who had been to Quivira, whom the Spaniards christened "the Turk" because they fancied he looked like one. Disappointed in the pueblos of Cibola, the Spaniards hoped for treasure at the rainbow's end at Quivira. They found only the prairies.

The Great People on the River

It is often said that the Indian called the Turk lied to them. By so doing, the story runs, he hoped to lead Coronado's party astray in the wastes where the inhuman Christians would die of starvation, or something. The Turk himself alleged as much before he was strangled by order of Coronado. But an Indian's death speech is usually a private matter, given from motives of his own. Perhaps the Turk had told the explorers the truth as he knew it. Perhaps they themselves imagined more than he told them.

Certainly they did not find themselves in a starvation country. After leaving the pueblo center they circled eastward, down from the great plateau, across the headwaters of rivers—one might have been the Brazos on the lower reaches of which Moscoso's company was to turn back—and then, guided by the Indians, journeyed east of north, by their compass.

They entered the sea of grass, the prairies of the buffalo. These strange beasts seemed to the men from Spain to be cattle with the humps of camels, the shoulder hair of woolly sheep, and bare hindquarters of lions—with beards that trailed the ground. The Spaniards marveled at the green expanse where the trees grew beneath them in arroyos watered by streams, and "a man stood alone with the bowl of the sky all about him." They were completely lost in this endless plain without landmarks. Many of those who strayed from the column had to wait for sunset or sunrise to learn where west and east might be; some never found their way back to the line of march.

Afterwards in New Spain the chart makers could not be certain where Coronado had marched to Quivira. His people marveled at the wild flowers and green growth, so different from the dry plains of Castile. They paid it the highest compliment: "It was a finer land than Spain."

Yet it stretched before them interminably. The inhabitants dwindled to families of hunters that pulled down their hide tents and packed their belongings on powerful dogs, to move away at the approach of the Spaniards with the strange horses. These hunters grew no corn, and the wild plums and grapes made wine of sorts but no bread for the invaders.

They slowed their march in this land of illusions where the "cattle" raced past them for hours without herders. Some who had counted their paces said they had come more than 900 leagues from New Spain. Others insisted that a woman wandering in from the east claimed that she had left different Spaniards on a river, nine days' travel distant. This must have been De Soto's hard-pressed company. But Coronado's people were too uneasy by then to investigate the woman's story.

They reached the great river of the Turk's country. This, probably the upper Arkansas, was as wide as he had said. And farther down it De Soto's men had seen enough of the long canoes "with twenty paddles" on a side, and the chieftains seated in the sterns under mattings. But where were the cities and the golden bells that chimed in the breeze, and the bowls of gold?

Farther on, the chained Indian, the Turk, maintained. If the men of Coronado had kept on they would have reached the towns of the Pawnees, where the round huts were roofed with coils of grass and the copper implements resembled gold. Probably the Turk was a Wichita, kin to the Pawnees, who had achieved a rude culture of their own in settled communities. In the estimation of the other plains dwellers the Pawnee folk were "the great people." To them the Turk may well have been leading his captors.

The Spaniards admitted that the black earth here yielded ample crops. The land lacked not for water and indeed could produce "all sorts of commodities." Yet the Wichita huts did not resemble the Quivira they had imagined. A chieftain summoned from the plain beyond the river came before them nearly naked, with only feathers adorning his head, and hunters attending his person. After that Coronado executed the Turk.

At this journey's end Coronado, a man of less decision than De Soto, summoned his officers to council and reached a decision to turn back to the Zuñi pueblos for the winter, before snow hindered travel over the grassland. (It was then mid-August.) In the southern towns the Indians had food stored up. With the spring the Spaniards could return to search for Quivira.

But they did not come back to the prairies.

The Indians of that other settled society, the Zuñi confederacy, revolted against the exactions of the conquerors, who treated them as subjects of a distant emperor. Francisco Coronado suffered from an injury, but more from despondency at his failure to bring in any evidence of the Seven Cities or a Quivira suitable to make a rich province of Spain. Once within their own frontier, many of his people deserted him. There the Indians of his own province were in revolt. When he faced the Viceroy again, Coronado found Mendoza "very sad, because this was all the outcome of something about which he had felt so sure."

Oddly enough, as happened with the veterans led back to Pánuco by Moscoso, many of the soldiers who returned to the shelter of Mexico with Coronado felt that they had missed a discovery that might have been made. Something vital had awaited them beyond their last encampment, and in some way they had failed to keep their rendezvous with fate. Baltasar de Obregón, writing a history many years later, has this to say of them:

"The return of their general greatly offended the soldiers of Coronado's expedition. They desired to know the secrets of that great land and its termination in the sea. They had seen indications that they were approaching the sea of the north, where the strait of the cod [Codfish Land and the missing northern strait blended in their minds] was located. If this strait and coast are discovered, it will be very important for your Majesty and Spain, because of the trade therefrom and because the voyage to Spain will be shortened. . . . I have made certain from old discoverers of the lands of New Mexico and Quivira that there are no provinces with such good houses, lands, climate and metals as these. There are no such extensive lands, none with so abundant provisions of cattle and maize or with such great expectations. . . . These lands are cold, provided with fine water, mountains, and valleys suitable for all kinds of grain and cattle. Persons have been seen there wearing bells of low-grade gold brought from distant lands in trade."

This sounds like propaganda for the Spanish conquest of the northern continent, but if Obregón meant it as such, he was not alone in longing for possession of the vast and unclaimed lands. Some of the veteran soldiers took to their pens to urge others to go north "to make discovery of the better land which we did not find." Aged Pedro de Castañeda, a chronicler of their march, insisted that if

Coronado had taken the other way, up the Rio Grande and across the Cordillera, he would have come to the lands "on the edge of Greater India." Again the missing end of Asia.

But the Turk who had promised golden bells was dead. Coronado, completely disheartened, retired to his estate. Mendoza, feeling the disgrace of failure, resigned as Viceroy of New Spain to go to conquered Peru. The barrier of the deserts and the Rio Grande remained as before between the settlements of Mexico and the peoples of the north.

Now De Soto's march through Georgia had touched the heart of the continent, in reaching the stable society of the Caddo-Creek peoples, on the sites of the older mound dwellers, yet his Spaniards passed through without leaving traces (except the few deserters). They seemed to be forgotten in a generation or two. The Cartier-Roberval thrust into the northeast coast, which failed to reach the Iroquois society, did leave a tangible link behind it in the continuing fish-and-fur traffic at the Tadoussac terminal. Embattled Europe had increasing need of the "New World fish." By the end of the century the value of the fish from the Grand Banks would exceed half that of the yearly trove of precious metals taken from the mines of the south in Spanish America. And the value of the take of fur in the north would increase yearly. It was a case of natural products outweighing in the end the quick gains of looted gold, silver, and jewels.

On the other hand the Spaniards, then or later, accidentally gave some livestock to the native peoples. Hogs straying from the De Soto herders thrived in the lush riverlands; the Indians also soon began to steal them from the herds on the march, and by so doing acquired a meaty domestic animal. Horses traded or stolen from New Spain became the ancestors of the herds that supplied Indians with their first mounts. When the Spaniards had appeared on the scene with their battle chargers, often protected by chest armor, the Indians had been unable to understand that the horse was no more than an animal—they had no domestic beasts of their own except the wolflike dog. Often it was a shock to the natives to see a rider fall from his saddle—thus dividing the man-horse entity into two parts which still lived. When, after generations, the tribes of the plains caught and tamed this spectacular wild beast, a change took place in their way of living. In leaving their settlements to follow the migrations of game—the horses enabled them to kill fleeing buffalo—they became more active and more aggressive. Their weapon, the powerful bow, could be used effectively from the back of a horse.

Almost unnoticed, basic foods from the New World would give strength to European populations. While turkeys would be transported to the country that gave them a name, and tobacco would follow as far, the simple potato root would invade the fields from Ireland to Germany. From Spain corn and the strange tomato vine and new varieties of beans would enrich Italian farms. Such rarities, attracting little attention at the time, soon became more vital to Europeans than the eagerly sought spices of Asia.

Silver in the earth, not in the halls of an Inca, brought back the Spaniards by slow degrees to the north, along the Sierra Madre. The mines of Zacatecas drew them up over the plateau. Search for new veins of ore in the western ranges would bring them back in time to the Zuñi pueblos beyond the Rio Grande, but in a different manner. The age of the conquistador was passing. This northern region became, not a New Spain, a frontier of an empire, but a New Mexico subsisting on its own products. While the miners explored, the missionaries built small settlements without the aid of a viceroy. Around their mud-brick churches rose rudimentary schools in the mission compounds where Indian families could find shelter as human beings as well as laborers. This was the great gift of the Castilian personality to the New World. And at that time only the unpredictable Spaniards were capable of sharing their culture with the common folk of a strange continent.

Even while the armed forces of De Soto and Coronado were retreating from the depths of the northern continent, Bartolomé de las Casas, now Bishop of Chiapas, was arguing before His Caesarian Majesty, Charles V, the case for the persecuted Indians. It was really an appeal to the modern Caesar who held the title of King of Spain.

And Las Casas did not mince words with expediency: "As for Your Majesty, these Indians hold you to be the most cruel and impious of princes, when they see the cruelty and impiety your subjects commit." (The conquistadors who marched to conquest through blood, the governors who ruled for the benefit of their pockets, the encomenderos who extracted metals and food from expendable slave labor.)

What would Isabella have said of this? Las Casas asked cuttingly. Pagan folk had a right to their lands. Attempts to take lands by force of arms were against the will of God. "The Devil could not have worked more mischief than the Spaniards have done, spoiling the countries in their rapacity, treating the natives like beasts."

For such actions of his captains and plantation holders—illegal by Christian law—Charles himself was responsible as king, and enforcer of the law. So Las Casas argued and won his case at Court. He even caused the rule in New Spain to become more humane. The mission schools gained somewhat, and the slave plantation and slave mines suffered accordingly.

But neither the fiery appeal of Las Casas nor the reluctant agreement of Charles could change the nature of the Spanish dominion, which stretched now to the limits of the empire, in the pathways of the conquistadors. Just then Villalobos was attempting to seize the *Islas Filipinas* in the far east (contrary to the treaty of 1529). Those islands close to the Moluccas were named for Philip, the zealot son of Charles who would be King of Spain and ruler of a vaster empire. While in Europe the empire fought its internal religious wars, and strove to hold the North African coast and Mediterranean trade routes against the advancing Turks, Spanish shipping and manpower were drawn far afield. The provinces from New Spain to the Plate River could not continue to exist—and pay revenues— without the aid of Indian labor.

Nor could the Indies fleets man their ships now without sending forth criers and trumpeters to the docks of Andalusia to drum up vagabonds and even Jews and Moors to serve the Christian king in the new world.

Obregón, measuring the area of the new conquests, estimated

that 3000 leagues (more than 9000 miles) lay between the Strait of Magellan and "Quivira." Spanish manpower no longer sufficed to hold the antagonistic centers of Cibola or the wide prairies of "Quivira." When map makers charted the newly explored north, they marked Cibola more or less where the pueblos were, between the Rio Grande and the Grand Canyon; but "Quivira" wandered on their maps from the seaboard of modern Texas to Lake Winnipeg.

Another writer, Vasco Tanco, expressed the wastage of manpower in a single sentence: "There are six Spanish adventurers; one goes to the Indies, another to Italy, another to Flanders [in the wars], another is imprisoned, another is bound by a lawsuit, and the sixth becomes a monk; and in Spain there are no other people than these six."

V. The First Frontier

Where the West Coast Led

THE mystery of the north was nowhere as baffling as on the Pacific Ocean. This unlooked-for and inconvenient watery waste seemed to grow larger with every discovery. It contained neither landmarks nor traditions, and it behaved differently from the other known oceans and seas. Whales, which kept to Codfish Land in the Atlantic, appeared off the western shore of New Spain. There the ocean billowed gently, a true *mare pacifico,* yet Spanish caravels seeking to cross from Asia were driven back by demoniac winds. Where did it end in the south, and where in the nebulous north? No one could tell.

Southerly, Castilian ships had explored the coast beyond Peru to the strait Magellan found. Northerly only the hardheaded Cortes had ventured to search at first. From shipyards at Acapulco, manned by Indian labor, small vessels had gone up into a red sea, the Sea of Cortes. Then to the westward land appeared, whether an island or main. Francisco Ulloa had reported: "We had always in some manner land to both sides of us, making so great a country that I think if it continues further, it will need many years to conquer."

He reached the end of this great gulf (Gulf of California) yet beheld from his masthead mountains to the north so lofty that the curve of the earth—so he thought—hid their base. Then, rounding the point of the unknown peninsula, Ulloa disappeared into the sea. Many of his crew turned up later, but the fate of Ulloa himself remains a mystery.

The feuds of dour Cortes with his rivals and with the Viceroy from Valladolid crippled such search by sea. Cortes voyaged home to plead his case before the Emperor, with less luck than Las Casas had. Honored by the title of Marquis, he was kept henceforth in bitter idleness in Spain. He lost his most valued jewels, his share of the Inca's treasure, that he carried with him in a storm at sea when he accompanied the Emperor in the futile siege of Algiers.

Antonio de Mendoza, who directed exploration after that from Mexico City, was not a Cortes. He dispatched Hernando de Alarcón north along the coast, to follow Coronado in the quest for the Seven Cities. Alarcón had a knack of invention and a Rabelaisian love of laughter. Duly hugging the shore, he weathered the storms that came out of nowhere, and duly reached the end of the gulf at a river that split the desert with its broad brown flood. Unable to make headway up it, this versatile sea captain took to his longboats, threw hawsers ashore, and had his boats towed up it by admiring native men.

This river (the Colorado's mouth) Alarcón christened the "Good Guide." While his flotilla forged slowly upcurrent, he amused himself by appearing on shore as a dictator sent by the sun from the sky to make peace and give judgment among the Yuma people, who had seen no such bearded white men before. It was no easy role to play, but Alarcón proved equal to it. When the native men warned him off in his small boat, putting stakes in between him and the shore— "which when I took thought of them, I began to make signs of peace. Taking my sword and shield, I cast them down in the boat and set my feet on them. By this token I made clear to the Indians that I desired no war with them, and that they should do likewise. Also I took my banner and cast it down, causing the men with me to sit down as well. Taking up the trade gifts I carried I called that I would fain give them away . . . suddenly one man came out from shore with a staff whereon certain shells were set, and I took it and embraced him."

This technique won Alarcón friends among the Yumas, who questioned him, through an interpreter, to prove his relationship to the sun, which the quick-witted adventurer had noticed they reverenced.

Yumas: (with pantomime) "The Sun is high above us, he moves swiftly across the sky. How is it you were able to come from him here to the earth near us?"

Alarcón: "You have watched the Sun. At the beginning of the day and at the end of the day he touches against the earth. At that time I came from the Sun to here."

Yumas: "If in truth the Sun sent you to us, why did you not appear before now?"

Alarcón: "I was a child then. I could not come until I was old as I am now."

The country with its sandstorms and scarred ravines did not interest the worthy captain. When the Indians appeared warlike on his shore excursions, he drew up his little company, sounded off trumpets, and started to march toward them. He set mastiff dogs to pull down offending Indians. This sport he varied by watching dancing in the village streets and finding out about their marriage customs. In so doing this Quixote among explorers managed to get tidings of Coronado's progress far inland. It came to him by the desert grapevine, accurately enough—how the black man Estevanico had been put to death for posing as a magician. The Indian news commentators could tell him nothing of the Seven Cities, but they said that other men with beards and with swords and weapons that flamed and roared were approaching a place called Cibola.

Indians: "Are you truly a son of the Sun?"

Alarcón: "Yes."

Indians: "Those Christian men at Cibola said that likewise."

Alarcón: "That may well be."

Indians: "Will you join with them?"

Alarcón: "You need have no fear of them. If they are truly sons of the Sun, they are my brothers and will be loving and gentle as I am."

At this he related, "They seemed to be somewhat satisfied."

Finding the Good Guide River so difficult to ascend, and judging that Coronado's party was drawing away from him inland, the impulsive Alarcón apparently gave up the water route as a bad job. After fifteen days of towing he took his leave courteously of his Indian hosts, and shot back down the current in two days and a half to salt water. He took away a map made for him by the Indians, and left a cross set up, beside a homemade chapel, by virtue of which he claimed for his king all lands watered by the river. Alarcón must have been the first European explorer to set foot, in this fashion, on the soil of California.

Later, to explain why he had been unable to reach Coronado, he claimed that he returned up the river for more than eighty leagues, without coming across a trace of him. That part of his story may be embroidery. With such gifts for travel in the unknown country it is a pity that Alarcón had been injured upon the river and died soon after.

At the end of the summer of 1542 two ill-built vessels fought their way north along the coast of the modern state of California. The coast seemed to be an unending rampart of bare brown hills, without a safe harbor. And this the men on the exploring ships desired very much to find.

Westerly gales drove the ships in upon the rocky points and the surf fringe of this shore, unseen before then by European eyes. Luckily for the captain some small islands lay conveniently off-shore, with coves on the sheltered sides. Once the captain of the vessels, Juan Rodríquez Cabrillo, found such a miniature haven in the cove of Avalon at Santa Catalina Island. When the weather cleared, he crossed to the mainland where he found a bay in nice-looking country, with green arroyos and many inhabitants. Noticing the smoke from many fires in the valley here, Juan Cabrillo christened it the *Bahía de los Fumos*. The Valley of the Smokes happened to be the site of Los Angeles City today. Then Cabrillo, a resolute commander, made sail to the north to search for a better harbor.

Cabrillo was a Portuguese in Spanish pay, an experienced

navigator who had come out long since with Narváez to the Spanish
Main; for years he had served obediently in suppressing Indian
revolts and navigating new-built ships along the west coast of New
Spain. By way of reward for his services he owned an estate that did
not quite support his family with the children growing up. Thus
he had, it seems, no desire to risk his neck in pursuing a myth. Too
well he realized that his two vessels of some 200 tons burden had
more weight than weatherly qualities. The new shipyards at Acapulco had fitted them with frail cordage and cotton sails, their decks
lay open to the weather from clumsy poop platforms to bows, and
their planking absorbed water. The chance of their riding out an
autumn northwesterly blow on this shelterless coast could be estimated as fair, no more. His crews, owing to lack of able seamen,
included the sweepings of Acapulco and some Indians who did not
stir a hand on shipboard, one priest, and, besides himself, three
competent pilots. His instruments helped little in determining his
latitude.

Cabrillo could only guess that he had come more than a thousand miles from Acapulco, past the point where Ulloa had vanished
into the sea. Blown about as he was now, he could only be certain
that he had progressed north by west. Of what might lie ahead of
him he had no least idea. Yet, being a man to carry out orders, the
Portuguese kept on, working his way into the unknown north.

At a bare point (Conception) the wind struck his unhandy
vessels again, and he fell off to leeward, running south to another
island (San Miguel). At this point he should have turned back to
run before the wind for safety in New Spain, but he chose to follow
out his orders instead.

His orders were too vague to satisfy a practical seaman. He was
to follow Coronado by sea and aid that young nobleman if possible,
and to find the great River of Our Lady leading into the continent,
or else the missing strait that would open the continent to Spanish
ships westbound to Asia. Actually the Viceroy, exasperated by the
gasconade of Alarcón on the other river and by the uncertain tidings from Coronado, had made a last gamble on these ships and the
dependable Cabrillo. Coronado had told of crossing a main river;

it might flow out to this coast. And if the sea of the Atlantic explorer, Verrazano, existed, it might connect with the ocean in the north. *Something* must be found to reward the great labor and expense of His Excellency, the Viceroy.

As to Coronado's progress the anxious Cabrillo discovered, as Alarcón had found out, that he had no trouble in keeping track of it. The Indians kept him informed.

The strange coast fairly swarmed with native people, thronging down from the hills to watch the fascinating behavior of the floating houses of the children of the sun. They paddled out in swift, stately canoes; they gossiped with the Indians of the vessels when parties landed for water and firewood. The appearance of the white, bearded men at sea, as well as at the cliff of Hawikuh far inland, had become the one great interest of the tribal folk, poor folk with long hair and few possessions (the Chumash tribes). Apparently runners sped between villages with the latest invasion news.

Cabrillo's crews gathered the gist of the news—how other Christians marched inland. How far? Five days' journey. Seven days' journey. Men with beards and dogs and with weapons like theirs had been seen far to the north. Sons of the sun marched, like them, heavily, to *Shihouna* (Cibola). They killed people, many people.

One Chumash bearer of news gave his version running along the shore as the Spaniards passed. He imitated a galloping horse, and a rider throwing a lance. There, inland, behind the hills!

(Coronado was actually retreating by then to the border, while Moscoso was leading his party back to embark on the Mississippi.)

These Indians had no corn for the seamen; the maize grew only inland. Did they know of a river flowing into the ocean? Yes, there was a river to the north. Very large? Certainly large.

But the native concept of rivers turned out to be dry watercourses, or streams flowing down the gullies. Cabrillo, rounding Conception at last, came upon nothing resembling the legendary River of Our Lady. Storms buffeted his vessels; the hills became dark with pines. Rounding a point, he came into a likely-looking bay, at the mouth of a small river (Monterey Bay). For two days he searched it for a safe anchorage and found none. Again they ran south for shelter, back to San Miguel Island.

He had made, however, one exciting discovery on this baffling coast. It tended north and *west*. So it led, inevitably, toward Asia.

How much distance he had made to the west since leaving Acapulco Cabrillo could not know. (He had run more than 22° of longitude since leaving port.) Nor had he any means of estimating how near or far the outer islands of Asia might lie. Being a Portuguese and in touch with a viceroy of Spain, Cabrillo may have been aware that the east coast of Asia above 35°—above Cipangu, or Nippon's islands—remained a blank to European knowledge. By his own estimation he had passed 40° of north latitude on this coast. So long as the coast tended west, he was drawing nearer to the mystery of northern Asia with each week. If he could drive his vessels on, he might yet land in triumph on the undiscovered end of Cathay.

He did not live to go on. The Indians of San Miguel proved troublesome. In hurrying to the aid of some men who were attacked Juan Cabrillo broke the bones of a leg in a fall, and probably gangrene set in, for which there was no remedy. On his authority as Captain General he gave the chief pilot, Bartolomé Ferrer (or Ferrelo), charge of the ships, to take them on "in the service of God and His Majesty."

When they gave testimony after the voyage, some of his crew related that he led them "near to the isles of the Moluccas." This testimony is usually dismissed as part of the general misinformation of ordinary seamen of the time, comparable to the remark of the soldier of Coronado that "the country between Norway and China is very far up." Spaniards just then thought longingly of possessing the spices of the Moluccas, and Cabrillo may have encouraged his dubious seamen by telling them they were voyaging toward such a prize. But the evidence reveals how he and the men alike were struck by the westerly trend of the unknown continent. It lessened above Point Conception.

One witness said that if Cabrillo had not died "he would have discovered the country of spice and the Moluccas, as he had a deter-

mination to outdo the capatains before him . . . his wife and children were left in poverty."

That might have been the impelling force behind his determination to go on.

Bartolomé Ferrer, the chief pilot, took the two vessels on up
the coast through the winter storms. His course from "The Captain's Island" led north by northwest. He must have passed by the
entrance of San Francisco Bay, as others did for a long time, without
being aware of its safe haven behind the hills.

How far he went is a question much debated. If the ships
reached 44° they were off the Oregon coast. If the great river they
heard of was the Columbia, they came near to the waterway they
had sought.

They went through freezing cold, along a coast where the surf
kept them from landing. Mist darkened the days, and the shore
itself became dark with tree growth above which rose white snow
summits, the Sierras Nevadas. Finally the leaking vessels became
separated in a storm.

Ferrer's ship may have turned back at Cape Mendocino. Beyond
that point, at 40° north latitude, the land draws back toward the
east. It also changes in aspect, with forbidding rock points and the
impenetrable growth of redwood forests. Cape Mendocino was
marked conspicuously thereafter on Spanish charts, and appeared
on other maps.

Be that as it may be, Ferrer made the long voyage home and
found his consort off the Isle of Cedars. With their sails shredded
and rations reduced to a pound of biscuit a day, the two vessels
dropped anchor at Navidad on the home coast in April 1543. They
had accomplished a remarkable feat of navigation.

They arrived a few months before the survivors of De Soto's
march strode into Pánuco on the opposite coast.

After that Spanish exploration of the northern continent ceased
for two generations. In spite of Cabrillo, Coronado, and De Soto
the mystery of the northern limits of the continent remained unsolved. Although Ferrer brought back a chart with names given to

points on the west coast, these were erased later by a rival who chose to write in names of his own.

Although Ulloa and then Cabrillo had made certain that the land discovered in Cortes's day, the length of Alta California, was a peninsula and not an island, it began to be mapped as an island and remained so on most European maps for at least a century. The impression gained ground that beyond the "Isle of California" the coast line was not known.

Curiously enough in all this obscurity the name of California stuck to maps. Seamen had read in a popular romance of the day how an island of *California* in this sea was the home of exotic Amazons. While no such interesting island had been found by the explorers of the Pacific, the romantic name appealed to people and it endured.

The diary of the dead Cabrillo had made use of it for the first time.

Cabrillo and Ferrer had made certain that no westward passage existed on the continent, at least as far north as Cape Mendocino. The "strait to Cathay" remained a myth, but a most enduring myth. Hopeful cosmographers in the European courts merely moved it farther north on their newest maps.

This ghostly waterway also acquired a name—the strait of *"Anian."* That came about because Anin or Anian had been described by Messer Marco Polo as a rich province of Cathay. Actually he was speaking of Annam. As the fabulous Seven Cities migrated on the maps from the ocean west of Portugal to the pueblo dwellings by the Rio Grande, "Anian" made an even longer journey to the coast of China and then north into the unknown area. There it was joined by the fabulous Cathay of the Great Khan, which the Portuguese had not discovered on the real coast of China. Once situated in the nebulous north, Anian became by some transmutation of imagination the strait that led *to* Cathay, which the French had hoped to hear of beyond the Saguenay.

More than that, it joined in ghostly fashion the quest of the dead Corte-Reals, for "The Strait of the Three Brothers." That also must lie in the undiscovered zone of the north.

About this time a really remarkable rumor went the rounds of the European courts and cabals, far from the reality of the continent of the voyagers. It was said in well-informed circles that a wandering Netherlands captain had taken his vessel past the Newfoundland, into the strait of Anian; he had sailed past the splendor of Quivira and reached the objective of all voyagers since Columbus the Genoese, the rich port of Quinsay in Cathay.

It was no more than a rumor, added to a myth. But search for the strait of Anian was to play a part in future exploration as vital as the growing conflict of the sea powers.

The French Come to the River of May

Rivalry among the Atlantic nations had sent vessels questing across the ocean; some privateering craft had used their weapons against government transports. Now for the first time the wars of Europe were to affect the coast of North America.

It began at three o'clock in the afternoon of June 22, in the year 1564, at a shallow river mouth of the gardenlike Land of Florida. Here and then a devout gentleman of France, René de Laudonnière, anchored a large war vessel and two small craft under his command. Noticing a swarm of dolphins playing around the ships, Laudonnière named the place the River of Dolphins. (It would bear the name of St. Augustine later, when the first Christian settlement of North America was built upon it.)

Because he found this river too shallow for his vessels, the French gentleman ordered anchors weighed and sails spread; cruising to the north, after two days, he found the haven he sought. This he had visited before and called the River of May, having landed there on a May day. It seemed to him ideal for the fort he had to build, and he disembarked his goodly company of colonists and soldiers, delighted with the fragrance of the tree growth, the brilliant waterfowl and the spring bloom of this promised land. Out from it ran a stately chieftain followed by tall sons, greeting the

French gentlemen as old friends, calling them brothers in his own speech and *"Amici—amici"* (*sic*) in their own. The people of Florida danced with joy at beholding the French again; the chieftain insisted on taking Laudonnière upriver a way to see the stone column standing there on a sandy rise, bearing the arms of France.

Laudonnière had helped to set the column in place; now he found it wound around with wreaths of bay, with small baskets of corn beneath it, put there by the Indians, as if the stone pillar that marked the French claim to Florida had been a god. To show their good will, the Indians kissed the pillar, motioning the Frenchmen to do likewise. Accordingly Laudonnière and his officer embraced the stone "so that we might draw them into closer friendship with us . . ."

This idyllic landing of hopeful French military colonists so far from the Gulf of the St. Lawrence, explored by their countrymen, appears to be accidental. Yet it was the direct result of happenings in Europe during the last years.

A few miles out from the pleasant River of May (the St. John's) flowed the warm Gulf Stream. On that stream, as the pilot Alaminos had ascertained long before, ships could be carried north to the belt of westerly trade winds. This way Columbus had sailed; now the treasure fleets of Spain used the route. Yearly the ships took on the gold and silver of the mainland mines, at Cartagena, Nombre de Dios, and Vera Cruz. Assembling then at the Havana, they formed a convoy—guarded now by war vessels against raids of privateers—to round the cape of Florida and pass up the Bahama Channel on their way to Cádiz. And now each year the plate convoy carried tons of the precious metals.

The Atlantic Ocean had become the thoroughfare of New World trade, a near-monopoly of the Spanish Empire. In sixty years of navigation across it the shipping had grown more seaworthy; it followed great circle courses, along charted routes. The strange variation of the magnetic compass during the long east-west passage had been marked down. Old legendary terrors had pretty well disappeared; the windless area of the Sargasso Sea was known and avoided. Raking bows and handy spritsails, with nine sails spread on towering masts, had given speed to the vessels. They could head close to the wind and ride out the storms, escaping the endemic shipwrecks of the Nicuesa-Ayllón days.

The Spanish galleon with its tiers of cannon had replaced the Portuguese *nau* as mistress of the outer seas. Yet in the narrow seas of Europe the long French *galéasse* challenged the massive but clumsy galleon of Spain.

These new fleets put to sea in medieval splendor of bright sails bearing the insignia of royalty, of swallow-tailed banners of identity, with fanfare of trumpets and chanting of hymns at the vespers hour, when all vessels came forward to salute the Admiral's ship. Their mission was to carry cargoes along the routes of the world, with cannon and powder to defend the cargoes. Before long, in the wars that were beginning, they would be altered to the swift fighting frigates to escort the vital convoys, and line-of-battle ships to destroy all opposing fleets.

Along the seaboard of encircled France mariners demanded bases of their own across the ocean—islands or trading terminals such as those monopolized by the weakening Portuguese and the dominant Spaniards. Their most popular writer, Rabelais, echoed the desires of his countrymen when he related the adventures of the giant Pantagruel in seeking a Utopia within far Cathay. The "most renowned" Pantagruel used the sea slang of Dieppe and sought to make an enormous navigation by which a fleet might by-pass the Sea of Ice to voyage "to farther India in less than four months, which the Portuguese can barely do in three years." Despite some slight exaggeration Pantagruel's idea is clear enough; he wanted to find a northwest passage for France.

But in France during the years from 1542 to 1562 religious conflict had itensified. Luther's single message had borne fruit in varied Protestant faiths, in the reform that brought upon it the Counter Reformation, and within France ranged Huguenots against Roman Catholics. The strife between "Lutheran" and "Papist" would transcend national boundaries and tear Europe internally for most of a century. In France it so happened that many seamen of Normandy and La Rochelle turned to the new faith, thereby becoming heretics in the eyes of the Catholics of Spain, who had no reason to love them otherwise.

Inevitably there had been projects to make settlements for Protestants on the coast of the New World. Roberval may have planned that at Cap Rouge; certainly Gaspard de Coligny, now the most farsighted leader of the Huguenots, attempted it without success on the coast of Brazil, along the route of the French trading vessels. Such a venture would draw off the most restless Huguenots from French soil, and relieve the dangerous tension there. It would release the underground religion to a new land where religion could be free; it would also secure the political objective of a French colony in the New World—a base across the Atlantic.

The voyages of Cartier and Roberval had made clear that the northern coast, the haunt of the fishermen, was too cold. Cartier had contrived to live out the winters on the St. Lawrence, but had refused to be responsible for a colony there. After the failure of the ill-prepared Huguenot settlement in Brazil there remained the possibility of the Florida coast. While Spanish—and therefore Catholic—power had a firm grip on the Caribbean and New Spain, the coast to the north seemed to be without occupants. The Huguenot leaders knew little of the region between Florida and Newfoundland, but they understood that Florida was something of a paradise, near which passed the Spanish treasure fleets—two aspects that appealed to overseas-minded Frenchmen. True, Verrazano had turned back from Spanish waters, and they had no detailed accounts of *Tierra Florida*. To fire their imagination, however, they had the voyages now published by the Italian Ramusio. This gave the early account of another Frenchman, Friar Marcos of Nice, who has seen from afar—so the printed volume said—the splendors of the Seven Cities of Cibola. And European readers fancied that Cibola might lie only a little way inland from the coast of Florida.

Gaspard de Coligny was high in favor at Court, and was then Admiral of France, although he had no experience at sea. Determined to explore the possibility of a migration to Florida, he outfitted two small vessels in 1562 for a reliable navigator of Dieppe, Jean Ribault, with René de Laudonnière as lieutenant, to make a

test landing, and this they did at the river they called the River of
May. There they left a small fort and a volunteer garrison while
they returned hastily to report that Florida was indeed desirable as
a promised land for Huguenots. More than that, the Indian inhabitants had replied to Ribault's questions about the gold and silver of
Cibola by assuring him that Cibola could be found inland, some
twenty days' march. (Where the Appalachian Mountains happened,
in reality, to be.)

But then the religious tension exploded into warfare within
France; Coligny, Ribault, and Laudonnière were unable to send
vessels back to Florida; their garrison in the promised land, after
waiting in vain for supplies, built a bark to return across the Atlantic
and was picked up, starving, off England. When the truce of
Amboise ended the civil conflict for a space, the Huguenots felt
more than ever the need of a refuge in America. At Court, Coligny
argued that his venture would secure for France a strategic port on
the shipping routes.

So Laudonnière sailed back that June of 1564 with his three
ships and eager company of Huguenot nobles, and veteran soldiers
and mariners of Normandy looking for new opportunities. They
had ample supplies and even four women, but no farmers. They
landed with a conviction that this time the colony must not fail.
And they embraced the stone pillar with the Indians "so that we
might draw them into closer friendship with us."

At first the Huguenots kept the friendship of the Timucuan
native people. They made a good settlement on their river, in warm,
moist corn country where "uncounted stags grazed, wherein were
the fairest meadows of the world, and grass to feed cattle." They
raised and entrenched a strong fort, and the Indians roofed the
buildings—"in less than two days, for the Indians never ceased from
working, fetching palm branches and interlacing them." They
swore alliance with the native leader, "to be friend to his friends
and enemy to his enemies." They broke ground, planted some seed,
and then sounded the trumpets to call for prayer of thanksgiving—
"We sang a Psalm of thanksgiving unto God, beseeching him to aid

us in all our enterprises that all might turn to his glory and the advancement of our king."

With such a bridgehead happily secured the largest vessel was sent back to France for supplies and reinforcements. The embryo colonists named their post Fort Caroline in honor of the young King Charles, and settled down to wait out the winter and the coming of Jean Ribault with the fleet from France.

In ten months the situation changed for the worse. Food failed during the winter; the rudely cultivated fields yielded little harvest; the Timucuas brought in maize and roots generously enough at first from their own harvests, then they tired of feeding their white allies, who had altered from exciting children of the sun to arrogant armed beggars.

The traces of gold and silver did the most damage. While exploring the tributary rivers the ex-soldiers happened on a little gold dust washed from the sand of the streams by the Indians. These Indians explained that such precious metal in the streams came from the mountains out of which the streams flowed; search parties prospecting for gold-bearing rivers and gold-keeping native kings got themselves involved in the tribal feuds by trying to play one people against another. Then, running out of tradable trinkets and food alike, they traded their services as firing squads for a little white and yellow metal. The native *paracoussies* (tribal chieftains) discovered that a few armored Europeans could win skirmishes for them with a few volleys. But in so doing Laudonnière broke his pledge of friendship with the first *paracoussie* who had hung the garlands on the French occupation pillar. That earned him the contempt of his Indian ally, and led to the killing of two valuable carpenters who pulled some ears of corn from an Indian field.

These Huguenots came from the hardheaded *bourgeoisie* of small French towns; having been soldiers for the most part, and traders and artisans as well, they simply tried to make their old skills serve them in this strange wilderness with its hardships and tempting opportunities. When one of the sudden Florida storms passed over them, loosing thunder and lightning, the nearest Indian village caught fire. The Timucuas believed this destruction came from the supernatural cannon of the Europeans, and they sent messengers to beg Laudonnière to cease bombarding their village. Again the Huguenot leader made a mistake. He accepted credit for the phenomenon of the storm, and explained that the failure of the Indians to obey him "was the principal cause wherefore I had discharged my ordinance against them."

His Indian allies, instead of obeying him, moved away some sixty miles, beyond the range of any cannon. His soldiers, now mutinous, demanded to be led to the interior, to ripening fields of maize and "the passages to the mountain of Appalache out of the foot whereof there runs a stream of gold or copper as the Savages think."

The march inland through now-hostile country brought on conflict. In this the experienced French soldiery fared better than the Spaniards, except for De Soto's veterans. And, like Garcilaso, Monsieur d'Ottigny, Lieutenant in Command, paid tribute to the tactics of the native Americans. "He had to deal with such kind of men as knew how to fight and to obey their head. Their manner in this fight was that when two hundred had shot [their arrows] they retired and gave place to the others behind. All this while they kept foot and eye so ready that as soon as they saw our arquebuses laid to our cheeks, they were on the ground [as the volley came] and instantly up to answer with their bows. And they were as quick to fly if they saw us about to come to take them, for there is nothing they fear so much, because of our swords and daggers." Oddly enough, as with De Soto, it was a native queen who aided the marauding Frenchmen most generously. To her they showed all their courtesy. "Captain Vasseur in my name," Laudonnière relates, "gave certain small trifles to the Lords, to the Queen, to the maids and women of the villages. Whereupon our [river] boats were straightway loaded with meal, after they had made our men as good cheer as they could devise."

Laudonnière was a nobleman with a conscience, sympathetic alike to his men and his unpredictable Indian enemy-friends; his instinct was for justice, not his own advantage. He lacked the quick imagination and ruthless determination of the Spaniards.

They had expected the relief fleet to reach Fort Caroline by April 1565. "The month of May approaching and no manner of succour coming from France, we fell into extreme want of victuals, being constrained to eat roots and a certain sorrell of the fields. Although the Savages were returned by this time to their villages, yet they succoured us only with some fish, without which we would have perished by famine. Besides they had given us before now the greatest part of their maize and beans. The famine held from the beginning of May until middle June. During which time the poor soldiers and craftsmen being too feeble to work, did nothing but go, one after the other as sentinels to the crest of a hill near the Fort, to see if they could discover any French ship.

"Finally, being frustrated in their hope, they assembled all together and came to beseech me to take action to return to France. They considered that if we let pass the season for embarking on the sea, we were not like ever to see our country again."

The Huguenots ignored their greatest danger. Some mutineers led by a pair of seamen had taken a pinnace to go after greater treasure than pinches of gold dust or grains of corn. Near at hand lay the ports of the Spanish Main, and through the Bahama Channel passed veritable treasure ships. With the ache of hunger in them the foragers in the pinnace were ready to take any risk. Fantastically, they did surprise and capture a Spanish vessel with a lading of silver. Intoxicated by success, they put in to an island to take on water before heading back to Fort Caroline. There they were captured. And the Audiencias of Santo Domingo and Havana learned from them of the Huguenot colony and its plans.

Other mutineers made off with a larger bark, first forcing Laudonnière at pistol point to sign a passport for them and hand over a flag. Some of these came back in a small boat after failing to attack a cathedral during Sunday Mass.

Laudonnière had not been able to prevent the pirating; he could only guess at the consequences. Daily he expected the relieving fleet to arrive with the capable Ribault and ample food. When he faced the mass meeting at the fort, he assured the soldiers that he would take them back across the ocean. Yet since they had not vessels enough for the whole company, they would need to build a large galliot. He asked the shipwrights among the men how long it would take, given timber and cordage, to launch such a vessel. The shipwrights pledged the company that the new galliot would be ready for sea on the eighth of August.

All the longing of the Huguenot soldiery centered now upon that eighth day of August and the launching of the clumsy sail and oar galliot. Yet those same days were to decide the future of the coast of the Land of Florida.

Being commander, René de Laudonnière was in a measure aware of that. By the third of August he became "tormented in mind" because work on the galliot lagged—owing to the killing of the two carpenters—and they had seen no sign of a vessel from France. In his anxiety he walked out that day to a small hill to be alone with his thoughts. It went to his heart to leave so fair a country, to which he had been sent by his king. In spite of some conflict he believed the lords of the Indians, his neighbors, could be firm allies; they had given him what aid they could afford . . . the land was rich in commodities, if not in gold . . . if he had to sail away he would burn the fort and settlement rather than leave it for others to occupy . . . if only aid could reach him from France, to enable him to hold on . . .

"As I walked I descried four sails out in the sea, at which I was exceedingly delighted. I sent immediately to advise those in the Fort of this, and there you would have thought them to be out of their wits, so much they laughed and leaped for joy.

"After the ships had cast anchor, they sent a boat toward land. Whereupon I caused one of mine to be armed, to go speedily to meet them, and to know who they were. Fearing lest they were Spaniards I set my soldiers in order and in readiness. Until Captain Vasseur and my Lieutenant who had gone forth to meet them, returned and brought me word they were Englishmen."

John Hawkins Views the Coast

The English ships did not put in to the River of May (St. John's) by accident. In London Town the young queen, Elizabeth, and her sea lords and councilors had heard the tale of the first French refugees from distant Florida, and Jean Ribault's tale as well. Their curiosity aroused, they wished to know more of this wild French venture to the unknown coast across from England. Sixty and six years had passed since the silent Italian pilot calling himself John Cabot had sailed that northern coast with little to say and nothing to show for it—save the flags he had planted there and the few poorish furs he had taken therefrom. . . .

But these were Spanish seas, the route of the treasure fleets of the Catholic Majesty, whose right and power no English trader might challenge. In London heads were shaken when the anxious Ribault begged aid for his Huguenots against the Catholic Majesty. Yet his tale was written down and printed for Englishmen to read, under the title of *The Whole and True Discoverye of Terra Florida.* And a tall armed ship of the Queen, *Jesus of Lubec,* was loaned to young John Hawkins of Devonshire, sailing out of Plymouth with three other vessels to pick up Negro slaves off Africa and sell such cargo as best he could in the new ports of the West Indies of Spain.

It seems that on this voyage John Hawkins, son of the notable African trader, William Hawkins, was to look in at the coast of Tierra Florida, and especially at the Frenchmen now planting themselves there; he was to view the products and people of this strange America, as some called it, and to spy out a profit, if any there was, upon the coast for an English trading venture thither. In so doing, on no account would Master John Hawkins risk or lose Her Majesty's great ship, *Jesus of Lubec.* . . .

Hawkins, who was learning his way around the Atlantic, ran risks which he failed to report in taking on his cargo of Negroes (some Portuguese trading vessels thereby losing the same cargoes) and he disposed of them quietly (such traffic being contrary to the law), but, being a resourceful shipmaster, he took away large profits in pearls, silver, hides, dyewoods, and some jewels. Then, carrying out his unwritten orders, he headed for the Florida cape, and had an uncomfortable meeting with the Gulf Stream, which carried his vessels aback, even with all sails set and drawing. Collecting his ships together again and riding the main current to the north, Hawkins set himself to examine Florida, supply himself with drinking water, and find the port of the missing Frenchmen. To aid him in this, he had a pilot from Dieppe, who knew the mouth of the River of May.

He had also been briefing himself by reading Peter Martyr. "Those people of the cape of Florida," he relates in his report, "are of more savage and fierce nature and more valiant than any of the rest. This the Spanyards well prooved, who being five hundred men intending there to land, returned with few or none of them, but were inforced to forsake the same [land]. Of their cruelty mention is made in the booke of the Decades."

That is, in the *Decades* of Peter Martyr—probably the disaster to the armada of Juan Ponce de León.

With a quick eye for detail Hawkins backed up his quotation by a description of the weapons and fighting characteristics of the Timucuas. He noticed how they painted themselves "to shew themselves more fierce" and washed off the paint after an action. Their bows were of yew, somewhat like the English longbow, beyond the strength of Negroes to pull. The arrows of reeds, very long—"they shoot very steady. The heads are vipers' teeth, bones of fishes, flint stones, silver or points of knives which they have gotten of the French men, or in want of these, a kind of hard wood, notched, which pierceth as far as any of the rest."

Hawkins notes that the natives had a system in their warfare. "Being in the woods, they use a marvellous policy for their owne safeguard . . . although they are called by the Spanyards *Gente triste,* that is to say, Bad people, yet have the French men found them so witty in their answers that by the captaines owne report, a counsellor with us could not give a more profound reason."

Probably the captain of *Jesus of Lubec* was the first educated observer from England to sight this strange coast. He made the common mistake of believing the Florida Peninsula to be an island, but otherwise missed very little. He noticed the small fish with wings that flew over the wave tops, when pursued by swift bonitos— only to be caught by darting waterfowl. He heard how Floridian girls—he seldom calls them Indians—brought about miscarriages to preserve their figures, and he marked the names and habits of the swarming animals.

In final evaluation, he decided, "the country was marvellously sweet, with both marsh and meadow ground, and goodly woods. Sorrell grows abundantly as grass. Also great plenty of deer come down upon the sands ... the houses are not many, for in one house an hundred of them do lodge—they being made like a great barne, in strength not inferior to ours. For they have rafters of whole trees, and are covered with palmito leaves. In the midst of this house is a hearth where they make great fires all night, and they sleep upon certein pieces of wood hewn in for the bowing of their backs, put one by another all along the walls. They remain in their houses only in the nights.

"The commodities of this land are more than as yet known to any man. The land itself is more than any Christian king is able to inhabit; it flourisheth with woods of cedar and cypress, and apothecary herbs such as *storax liquida,* turpentine, gum, myrrhe, and frankinsence with many others whereof I know not the names ... the ground of Florida all the year long is green as any time in the summer with us. I have seen in the other islands of the Indies such increase of cattle that twelve head of beasts did in five and twenty years raise a profit of a thousand pounds yearly in hides, and the ground of the other Indies is not to be compared to this of Florida."

The sea captain, who had no knowledge of tobacco, mentions its use as a dried herb put into a clay cup at the end of a cane and ignited. "The Floridians when they travell do suck the smoke through the cane, which smoke satisfieth their hunger without meat or drink."

When John Hawkins landed at Fort Caroline, he brought ashore with him the longed-for luxuries of civilization, bestowed with cheery humor. To the famishing Huguenots he brought barrels of meal, kegs of wine, baskets of beans, wax for candles, and salt for meat. Laudonnière greeted him with ceremony and squandered the last of the settlement stores in hospitality, slaughtering the few chickens and sheep kept for breeding. All officers wore their best apparel and laid aside their weapons.

Either the generosity of the Englishman, at sight of the suffering in the fort, or orders that he failed to mention led him to offer to transport the colony back to France in his vessels. This Laudonnière refused, for "I stood in doubt lest he might attempt something in Florida in the name of his mistress [Elizabeth the Queen]."

And on his part Hawkins had impressions about the desirability of the land and the mismanagement of the French that he kept for his report. "Some of them would not take the pains to fish in the river before their doors but would have all things put in their mouths . . . the ground doth yield victuals sufficient, if they would have taken paines to get the same; but they being soldiers [Hawkins was a seaman from a farming country] desired to live by the sweat of other men's brows; when they had peace the Floridians made weirs to catch sufficient fish, but when they came to war, the Floridians took away the same, and then would not the French men take the pains to make any more."

Nor did he think well of the piratical raids of the mutineers on the Spanish ports. Yet when Laudonnière, after consultation with his soldiers, asked to buy one of the English vessels, Hawkins agreed readily, and took payment in artillery and powder instead of silver, which the garrison feared might arouse the cupidity of the English traders. And on leaving Hawkins, moved by pity, offered to give fifty pairs of shoes to the destitute Huguenots. Laudonnière's pride could not accept charity, so he gave his note for the shoes. Hawkins accepted the note without comment.

With such ceremony on both sides they parted. The English fleet cruised north along the coast. Storm conditions seemed to trouble Hawkins, anxious for the great ship loaned by his queen, and his food ran short, perhaps owing to his gift of supplies to the French colony. But his report gives no evidence of exploration north of the River of May. He was seeing this coast for the first time, yet he mentions nothing until they managed to catch some cod at 130 fathoms "upon the bank of Newfound land." Meeting there with two French fishing craft, the English bought more cod for gold and silver at a just price. Then they rode the westerlies home to Cornwall.

At Fort Caroline, with a new sound vessel in his hands, with his company demanding departure, Laudonnière could no longer refuse to embark for France. They baked the fresh meal into bread, filled water casks, and manned their vessels to wait for a favorable wind.

As they waited, seven sails appeared at sea; Jean Ribault came into the river with the fleet from France. It was then August 28. With fresh food, ample supplies, and a great contingent of armed men and laborers, and eight good vessels anchored in the roads, the ordeals of the Huguenots seemed to be over. Joyfully the veterans and new immigrants began to unload the vessels and enlarge their quarters.

That same week the fleet of Menendez de Avilés, Adelantado of Florida, came in sight of the river.

"There Rose So Great a Tempest . . ."

No one man ordered the destruction of the Huguenots on the River of May.

The *asiento* or contract carried by Menendez de Avilés bore the signature of the King, Philip II of Spain. Philip, however, strongly desired peace with France. In the bare hills above Madrid this visionary monarch of the New World empire had ordered the building of the Escorial, the palace that was to resemble a monastery. There in a room bare as a cell Philip dreamed of governing his dominion, not as his father Charles had done, on horseback or in the thronged courts of Europe, but in isolation devoted to the service of God. He thought of his empire, so far removed from his person, as marked out by the cathedrals now rising wherever the sun rose, as far as the cities of Mexico and Lima, and the islands where the French pirates raided.

In Philip's mind title to the New World entire belonged to Spain by virtue of the papal decree of more than sixty years ago. It had always been Spanish, and he had the responsibility to maintain it so. Among the massed documents that surrounded him was an order of Ferdinand and Isabella to one of their captains, Alonso de Ojeda—*"Para que atages el descubrir de los ingleses por aquella via."* Stop the discovery of the English by their route. The route of one John Cabot toward the New World of Spain that some senseless geographers had named America, when it was and must be the West Indies of Spain. And Philip had among his current papers the petition of his Casa de Contratación to drive the Frenchmen out of their port "because it is in the Channel of Bahama, the passage of the Indies of great importance to the service of Your Majesty."

Even so, Philip took time for meditation before acting. The matter of Florida touched his conscience in an odd way. Some years before Dominican friars petitioned to make a settlement there among the Indians, as the outspoken Bishop of Chiapas, Las Casas, urged. They had gone in to the west coast with colonists and Negroes, women and children, led by an aging captain, Tristán de Luna y Arellano, who had served with the disappointing Coronado. De Luna's effort to make a settlement had failed by reason of the hostility of the Indians, who had opposed the ill-fated De Soto in the same way. Philip had ordered Florida evacuated. Now the heretic Huguenots had appeared there, to claim the east coast.

That raised the question of title, debated not long since by his imperial father and the French monarch Francis: the question of the title given to Spain by Alexander, Vicar of Christ, as against the claim of voyagers who intruded and fortified themselves as Ribault and Laudonnière were doing. More than that, his ambassador at Paris reported how the French insisted that this coast had been discovered by them long since and named *Tierra de los Bretones.* This was dangerous, because Spain could never allow the French to claim that their outlandish country of the Bretons extended down to the Bahama Channel. If the French Court would withdraw Laudonnière's garrison instead of dispatching Ribault's fleet to strengthen him, the issue could be avoided without bloodshed.

But Philip's military counselor, the Duke of Alva, thought and said otherwise. Spain was the sword arm of the Counter Reformation, and the King its commander; there was now no way to avoid war with the massed Lutherans, especially where the heretics were led by a man as determined as Gaspard de Coligny. Inevitably the Huguenots, most determined of the Lutherans, must be killed off. And in France, under the regency of Catherine de' Medici, the Duc de Guise was taking measures to accomplish that. If the Huguenot cancer in Florida were allowed to fester within that northern continent, it would contaminate the realm held so tenuously overseas by a few Catholic missions.

At Alva's urging Philip consented to outfit a fleet strong enough to capture the Fort Caroline of the Huguenots on their river.

Then Ribault sailed with his convoy for Florida.

When the news reached Madrid—and Spanish espionage carried it thither swiftly—Philip ordered the departure of his combat fleet commanded by Pedro Menendez de Avilés, a zealous Catholic who would carry out the letter of a command.

The command was to voyage from the Florida cape to the New Found Land, to survey all bays and report on them as harbors, to search the entire coast for settlers or corsairs of any foreign nation and drive them from the coast.

At the same time Menendez was to make a settlement himself, taking with him to accomplish this 500 Negro slaves, male and female, along with artisans, farmers, livestock, and tools. His ten vessels would also transport the fighting force of 500 dependable soldiers and seamen.

Beyond this command—no easy one to carry out—Philip, always sparing of money, made a contract with Menendez, who paid most of the expense. *If he succeeded,* the single-minded captain would be rewarded as Adelantado (here, in the sense of Governor) of Florida with return of his own fortune, and possession of territory, honors, and trade privileges in the New World. By this one-sided contract Menendez would be impoverished and disgraced if he failed; if he succeeded in carrying out his commands he would become the wealthy viceroy of a new dominion.

Probably Menendez paid less attention than Philip to the profit-and-loss side of the *asiento;* he was a soldier with one idea, to strike the first blow gloriously in the undeclared war against the heretic Lutherans.

There was a brief moment of ceremony when the flagship of Menendez drew in to the French vessels anchored in the river mouth. Banners were displayed and the Spanish trumpets sounded, and the cry went across: "Gentlemen, whence comes this fleet?"

"From France."

"Gentlemen, are you Catholics or Lutherans?"

"Lutherans and men of Captain Jean Ribault. And you?"

Menendez stood under his banner to answer punctiliously, "I am Pedro Menendez de Avilés, by rank captain general of the armada of the King of Spain. Be aware that in the morning I shall come aboard your ships."

That much for the code of almost forgotten chivalry. There followed the victory of this one man's determination in spite of obstacles. Menendez's vessels were scattered by bad weather; he was weaker in numbers, stronger in discipline than the unprepared French. They possessed a fortified island, well supplied—his people were penned upon decks, wearied at the end of a long voyage.

The crews of the anchored French vessels did not wait for morning, but slipped their cables and put to sea where they easily kept their distance from the heavier Spanish craft—even following as Menendez at last put in to a haven. This was at the River of Dolphins, some twenty-five miles down the coast from Fort Caroline.

At tidings of the Spanish landing Jean Ribault took command from Laudonnière, who suffered from sickness. To the seaman from Dieppe it seemed all-important to engage and destroy the enemy's vessels during the unloading. Laudonnière and other officers pro-

tested against leaving the fort, but Ribault had his way. Indians from
the other river told them how the Spaniards had seized some of
their houses, and were building trenches around the village (where
St. Augustine would stand). Ribault argued that the invaders must
be allowed no time to prepare themselves; he could sail to the River
of Dolphins, capture or sink the ill-manned vessels there, and return
in two days—before the Spaniards could possibly move against
Laudonnière at the fort by land. The shore was pathless, ridden with
swamps.

When Ribault sailed impatiently, he took all the larger ships
and almost all the armed men. And his attack might have succeeded
if it had not been for the storm that rose to hurricane force off the
Florida coast. Watching from his beachhead, Menendez noticed how
the French ships were driven out to sea and scattered by the wind
before they disappeared into the curtain of rain.

"The very day he departed," Laudonnière relates, "there rose so
great a tempest that the Indians themselves told me they had seen no
worse on the coast . . . we delivered candles and lanterns to those
going around the ramparts to keep the watch because of the foul
and foggy weather. The night between the nineteenth and twentieth of September, La Vigne kept the watch with his company,
although it rained without ceasing. When the day was come, and he
saw that it rained still worse, he pitied the sentinels and, thinking
that the Spaniards would not come in such a time, he let them depart in, and he went himself to his lodging. In the meanwhile one
man had somewhat to do outside the fort and my trumpeter went
with him. Up on the rampart they beheld a troop of Spaniards coming down from a little hill. At once they began to cry the alarm, and
the trumpeter to sound it."

Menendez was advancing out of the forest with most of his
500 pikemen following. Gambling on the chance that the French
ships would be helpless at sea for a few days, he had brought his
force through the flooded swamps in the storm, a few miles a day
for three days, until they climbed over the muddied ramparts of Fort
Caroline. In that welter of rain no cannon could be fired; nor could
the eighty-five civilians, women and old men, with the sick Laudon-

nière, make any stand against the wearied marching Spaniards who cut down every man in their path.

When some survivors reached the small craft in the river, the exulting men of Spain tore out the eyes of the dead and threw them toward the boats. They sank one vessel with gunfire from the fort; the other got away with Laudonnière on board, and eventually reached safety in England.

To the resolution of Menendez the storm added its disastrous force. The Adelantado hurried back with part of his command through the waist-deep floods of the shore, to his encampment on the site of St. Augustine. There he learned from Indians that masses of Frenchmen were wandering along the lower coast, and he marched in that direction.

The French had come ashore from Ribault's wrecked or foundering vessels. Collecting into two bands, they were trying to make their way back on foot to their fort and food. Coming to each group, with his disciplined soldiery, Menendez showed them spoil from Fort Caroline, in proof of its capture. The starving and exhausted Huguenots had the alternatives of a futile last resistance or surrender. What happened to the first group Menendez explained in his report to his king.

"They came and surrendered their arms to me, and I had their hands tied behind them, and put them all excepting ten to the knife."

Ribault's party was the last to be found, making its way north on rafts along the inlets. The sea captain offered the Adelantado a ransom in gold for the lives of his men. "It grieves me not to accept it," the grim Menendez replied, "for I have need of it."

In this case the French musicians were spared with those who declared themselves Catholics. Ribault was not among them.

In comment upon him Menendez wrote to his king, "I think it very great fortune that this man be dead, for the King of France might accomplish more with him and five thousand ducats than with other men and fifty thousand ducats; and he could do more in one year than other men in ten, for he was the most experienced corsair and navigator of the Florida Coast."

There had been no battle, and hardly a blow struck in this victory of Menendez. His debts were paid, and the honor he gained by driving Huguenots from the North American coast was forgotten in the religious wars that soon gripped Europe. Reading his report at the table that served him for desk, Philip of Spain wrote in the margin of it, "As to those he killed, he has done well. And as to those he saved, they are to be sent to the galleys."

When news of the extermination of the Huguenots in Florida reached Paris, Catherine de' Medici and her weak son sent a protest to Madrid that was more formal than purposeful. To this in his own good time Philip gave an incisive reply. The "incident of Florida," he wrote, had been the just chastisement of men who were not vassals of the French King but robbers who had seized upon territory of the King of Spain.

That ended the incident. The French Crown could not afford to antagonize the world empire of Spain over the loss of a Huguenot colony. Catherine, who had supported Coligny in the project, now let the Spanish Ambassador understand that no French fleet would go again to Florida.

One did so, however, without the knowledge of the government at Paris.

Coming of the Privateers

The triumphant Menendez could not immediately carry out his orders to survey the coast north of Florida. He had too much to do in making the St. Augustine site habitable, and in restoring Fort Caroline, which the Spaniards renamed San Mateo. Then, too, the Indian peoples did not take kindly to the rule of armed Spaniards. In 1567 Menendez returned to Madrid to receive his honors and obtain more supplies and further orders. His absence was felt the next year.

Dominique de Gourgues, gentleman of Gascony, captain, and friend of the slain Ribault, was a war veteran who had served as prisoner on the Spanish galleys and had pulled an oar as captive of the Turks. Escaping and making his way back to the coast of France, Gourgues learned what had befallen Ribault; he sold his property, borrowed from friends, obtained a permit to sail the Atlantic to capture Negro slaves, and departed, ostensibly on this mission. He was "furnished with three ships of middling burden, having in them a hundred and fifty soldiers and fourscore chosen mariners. Having endured contrary winds for a season, he went on shore at the Isle of Cuba . . . two hundred leagues distant from Florida where the captain disclosed unto them his intention which hitherto he had concealed from them."

Up to this point, at least in the eyes of Spanish observers, Gourgues had been carrying out a trading voyage, like that other Lutheran, John Hawkins. But now, without waiting for a full moon, he entered the Bahama Channel. With all his men he was resolved to take vengeance on Menendez's soldiery. Passing by the River of May, the French vessels were saluted politely by the guns of a new fort. Courteously returning the greeting of the unsuspecting Spaniards, Gourgues sailed forty miles or so up the coast and landed to begin his operation of revenge.

This is often described as a corsair's raid that panicked the imperial garrison of Fort San Mateo during a Sunday dinner, and Easter Sunday at that. Actually it was a carefully planned attack by the French veterans upon Spanish troops in superior strength, in three well-built forts. The only thing lacking to the Spaniards was Menendez. The battle might have gone the other way if it had not been for the Timucua Indians.

Led by Saturiba, once the nearest neighbor of Laudonnière, the Timucuas thronged to welcome the French voyagers; in council, after exchange of gifts, their chieftains offered to join Gourgues with 400 bowmen. The sagacious Gascon already had survivors of the Fort Caroline slaughter to guide him and renew alliance with the valuable Indians. From them, and from a refugee soldier who had escaped to the Indians, Gourgues learned the plan of the forts and routine of the garrison.

The French made their approach march wading through the

swamps to the quiet river. There, aided by the Timucuas, they observed the forts for a day, planned the difficult operation of attacking the positions in turn. The gist of the Gascon's plan was to put
the Timucuas in ambush—where the devastating Indian bows could
be used to advantage—on the side opposite the point of his attack on
a position.

Although the Spaniards were caught loafing after dinner, the
watch at the first fort managed to fire a culverin twice at the charg-
ing Huguenots. Before the man could load the small piece a third
time, an Indian "who had not learned to keep his place in rank" ran
to the palisade and killed the guard with a spear. As Menendez's
soldiers had done, the French raced through the entrenchments,
killing the garrison. They then entered a small bark which had been
brought up to gain the second fort by water. Again the Timucuas
broke ranks to get at the enemy by wading and swimming. The
garrison, running from the French, came into the fire of the Indians,
and none of them escaped.

Behind the ramparts of the third fort—the original citadel of
the Huguenots—the Spanish commander chose to sally out boldly
with sixty arquebusiers. The sallying party was cut off and slain
where it stood, back to back. The remainder of the garrison tried to
escape, only to be caught. The last survivors were hung on the same
trees where Menendez had executed the last of the Huguenots. Beneath them the merciless Gascon burned upon a plank the legend:
*"I do this not as to Spaniards and seamen, but as to robbers and mur-
derers."*

This may have been an echo of Philip's phrase, that Laudonnière's Huguenots had been slain, not as vassals of France, but as
robbers.

Afterwards the Timucuas aided the French in burning and
razing the three forts on the River of May. In spite of the exultation
of the Indians over the victory and spoils Gourgues took care to
make the return march to his anchored ships in military formation
with weapons shouldered. Evidently he had been impressed by the
power of the Indian attack.

So much the Indian allies mourned his departure that Gourgues

took it on himself—whether as an expedient, or in sincerity is hard
to say—to promise that the French would return within twelve
moons with an army of their king and an abundance of weapons
for the Timucuas.

The ships of Gourgues sailed from Florida May 3, 1568.

"Coming to Paris to present himself to the King to signify to
him the success of the voyage, and the means he had to subdue this
whole Country to his obedience (wherein he [Gourgues] offered to
employ his life and all his goods) he found his reception and the
answer given so contrary to his expectation that in the end he was
constrained to hide himself a long space at the Court of Rouen . . .
which grieved not a little Dominique de Gourgues."

When Spanish men-of-war quested along the coast after them,
other members of the expedition went into hiding at Huguenot
centers. Whatever the avenging Gascon may have hoped to carry out
in Florida, the mass migration of Huguenots to the new land was at
an end.

For a long time no other fleets visited the eastern coast of North
America. St. Augustine, no longer one of a chain of Spanish settlements, became a garrison post, an observation point on the Bahama
Channel. It marked a new frontier between Spanish Florida and the
unoccupied north.

The "Third, Troublesome" Voyage of John Hawkins

Unaware of Gourgues's devastation of the Spanish forts, John
Hawkins was nearing the Indies on a southern course in May 1568.
As usual he had the Queen's ship, *Jesus of Lubec,* with the smaller,
weatherly *Minion* and four small craft. Of these the handy *Judith*
was commanded by Francis Drake, a young and resolute seaman
of Devonshire on his second cruise in western waters. As usual
Hawkins had a cargo of slaves out of Africa. His mission was to sell
this cargo—as the Portuguese had done before him—in West Indian
ports illicitly for sugar, hides, dyewood, and gold and silver coin for

the profit of the house of Hawkins. Since he handled contraband cargo, he was careful to keep within the law otherwise.

But Hawkins had had a hard time on this, his "third, troublesome" voyage. Storms and poisoned arrows of Africans had troubled the English with sickness; they had lost many men by taking part in an African tribal war to gain a full cargo of slaves. Moreover, when he approached the officials who had been his customers in the cities of New Spain, he found them rigorous in refusing to buy his goods —until he broke into a large seaport and held it as security to drive a bargain with the Spanish officers for his slaves.

Hawkins sensed a change of climate in his trading in the New World ports. He had, however, no means of knowing the cause: that the Spanish governors were infuriated by tidings of the disaster in Florida—that bishops were writing to the Crown in Madrid, complaining bitterly against such *cimarrones* of the sea, piratical Lutherans, agents of the devilish trade in black humans who usually ran away from their new masters. Just then in Spain the furious Menendez was urging the dispatch of galleons to purge the seas of the English-Norman-Breton corsairs. (The term corsair at that time meant a contraband trader, and mariners from Dieppe and La Rochelle often joined in ventures with their less experienced fellow Protestants from Plymouth.)

Even so, Hawkins might have got clear of the Caribbean with scanty profits in his chests if it had not been for the *"furicano."* This hurricane wind drove his battered vessels back to the west, and he was forced to put in to a harbor to refit. The harbor happened to be San Juan de Ulúa on the island just off Vera Cruz, where the Spanish treasure transports were loading, and the guardian galleons assembling under command of the Viceroy of New Spain. The harbor itself lay under the guns of protective castles—being no more than the narrow space behind a new breakwater. When the English vessels limped in to San Juan de Ulúa on September 16, 1568, they moored rail-to-rail with twelve Spanish ships.

Under the circumstance Hawkins, alert to danger, made clear at once to the port authorities that he would take not so much as a "groat's weigh" of the tons of gold and silver he fancied to be alongside; instead he would pay in coin for the food and materials he needed. (Actually the ships at San Juan de Ulúa had no such treasure aboard.) But the next day thirteen ships of the treasure convoy came in sight of the haven. Alive to the tensity of the situation, the English sea captain made a hard, blunt bargain to keep the peace. He was in a position, he claimed, to sink the treasure transports with cargoes valued at 1,800,000 pounds sterling; yet he pledged a truce, and demanded it of the Spanish commanders, for time enough to take on his supplies and repair his rigging; at the end of the truce he would sail from the port in peace. The truce was sworn and announced on all vessels by sound of trumpets, and the Viceroy's fighting ships moved in to their moorings. "It was meant in all fidelity on our part," Hawkins wrote in his report, seemingly with truth.

As the galleons came in on a Thursday, there ensued confusion while the English vessels pulled over to new moorings, and Hawkins noticed movement of troops among the Spanish vessels, with shifting of artillery in the shore positions. Many English seamen were occupied on the shore. Before recalling them Hawkins sent the master of *Minion* to protest to the Viceroy against the unfriendly preparations. The English master did not return. A trumpet blast from the Spanish flagship of the Viceroy gave the signal to open fire on the English vessels.

There ensued the Pearl Harbor of the Elizabethan seamen.

Those on shore were overwhelmed and slain, except some few who reached the *Jesus*. The Spanish galleons swung to the rails of the smaller English trading craft. "The great ship which had three hundred men placed in her secretly immediately fell aboard the *Minion,* but by God's appointing in the half hour time of suspicion we had, the *Minion* was made ready to avoid [draw clear] and so, loosing her headfasts [bow moorings] and hauling away by the sternfasts, she was gotten out. The *Minion* being got out, they came aboard the *Jesus* which also with very much ado was defended with the loss of many of our men. Two other ships assaulted the *Jesus* at the same instant, yet after some little time we had cut our headfasts and gotten out by the sternfasts. Now when the *Jesus* and the *Minion* were gotten about two ship's lengths from the Spanish fleet the fight became so hot on all sides that within one hour the Admirall [flagship] of the Spaniards seemed to be sunk, their Vice-admirall burned and one other of their principal ships seemed to be sunk, so that these ships were little able to annoy us.

"Then all the Ordinance upon the Iland [shore of the port] did us so great annoyance that it cut all the masts and yards of the *Jesus,* so that there was no hope to carry her away; also it sunk our small ships [except for the *Judith*] whereupon we determined to place the *Jesus* on that [shore] side of the *Minion,* that she might be able to abide all the battering from the land and so be a defense of the *Minion* until night. We determined to take such victuals and necessaries from the *Jesus* as the time would suffer us, and to leave her.

"As we were thus determining, and had placed the *Minion* from the shot of the land, suddenly the Spaniards fired two great ships which came directly upon us. Having no means to avoid the fire, it bred a marvellous fear in our men, so that some said, let us depart with the *Minion,* others said, let us see whether the wind will carry the fire from us. But the *Minion's* men which had always their sails in a readiness, thought to make sure work of it and so without consent of either the Captain or their Master cut loose their sails so that only barely was I able to be taken on the *Minion.*

"The most part of the men left alive in the *Jesus* made shift and followed the *Minion* in a small boat. The rest of them which the little boat was not able to take on, were inforced to abide the mercy of the Spaniards (which I doubt not was very little). So with the *Minion* only and the *Judith* (a small bark of 50 tuns) we escaped; which bark the same night forsook us in our great misery. We were now removed away with the *Minion* two bow-shots from the Spanish ships. There we rode all night. The next morning we gained an Iland a mile from the Spaniards, and there a North wind took us, being left with only two ankers and three cables. We thought always upon death which was ever present, but God preserved us to a longer time."

Not without further trouble, however, were some of the English seamen preserved. The damaged vessel could not carry the number of men crowded on her; food lacked, and many of the survivors voted to take their chance on land with the natives. One hundred fourteen were put ashore. Of these sixty-eight reached Spanish settlements, where three were burned and the rest transported to the galleys. Other castaways apparently started to walk north across the continent. Where they actually went remains a question. But some of them, at least, joined that unrecorded fellowship of refugees who seemed to endure well enough with the Indians. Years later three of them were picked up by French fishermen at Cape Breton.

Hawkins wandered the Spanish sea with a famishing crew. Ruefully he relates that monkeys and parrots in the cargo, bought at high prices, were deemed beyond price in providing a meal. A second time the laboring *Minion* was blown back from the Bahama Channel, within reach of the open sea. Hunger drove the Englishmen to shore again, where some died from overeating meat; before they could be tracked down, they took to the sea again, and this time gained the path of the westerly trades, falling in with English vessels that gave *Minion* supplies and twelve able-bodied seamen to work the ship home.

On January 25, 1569, they put in to the coast of Cornwall. *Judith* had reached England long before in little better state. Her young master, Francis Drake, was blamed for sailing away from his captain and consort at the shambles of San Juan de Ulúa. Hurt by the censure and bitterly angered by the attack in the Spanish port, Drake was to devote the rest of his life to warfare against all Spaniards.

The incidents at the River of May and San Juan de Ulúa quickened the undeclared war of Protestant seamen against the flag of the great empire. Until then it had been a matter of contraband traders wringing their pence from the riches flowing out of the New World to Portuguese and Spanish ports; now began the raids on ports and cutting out of the treasure ships. For seventeen years this would increase.

The conflict over the seas went on, as it were, under a mask, with Protestant captains of La Rochelle and Dieppe joining the Elizabethans, with masters sailing under assumed names, with orders given in secret, and destinations changed at sea. To join these phantom raiders, penniless Dutch masters came, the "beggars of the seas," putting out from Amsterdam and Leyden, where the army of the Duke of Alva had entered to enforce the tax and law of Spain and the judgment of the Inquisition.

For years only the raiders opposed the passage of the Spanish flag across the oceans. The embryo navy of France succumbed to weakness after the blood purge of St. Bartholomew's Eve decimated the Huguenot factions. It put an end to Coligny and any plan of migration to the New World, while joining briefly in policy the crowns of Valois and Hapsburg. Weakness of another nature was ending the rivalry of the kindred Iberian power. Portugal, drained of manpower by the century-long effort to hold the sea lanes and markets of the far east, was yielding her mastery to Madrid and would presently yield her throne to Philip.

On the other side of the earth Philip's viceroy ruled the Philippines, the islands named for him. And one of his veteran explorers, Friar Andreas Urdaneta, solved the mystery of the uncharted Pacific. For nearly half a century, since Magellan's first crossing, no vessel had been able to beat its way back from the shores of Asia to the ports of New Spain. The unseen equatorial current and the steady easterly trade winds barred the return to the New World. Urdaneta swung far north—as Columbus had done in the Atlantic—to enter the Japan Current and a zone of favoring winds, to gain Cape Mendocino, and coast down to Acapulco. Now Spanish fleets could ply back and forth from Peru to the Moluccas. The western trade route to Asia had been opened, but the voyage was a lengthy one. Naturally Urdaneta's route was kept secret from other nations.

In the embattled Mediterranean there would be a moment of triumph when the impetuous Don Juan of Austria decimated the Turkish battle fleet at Lepanto. It seemed then as if the flag of the Hapsburgs might dominate the Mediterranean as it ruled the Caribbean, now becoming a focus of world trade. It seemed in the 1570s as if the bullion of the New World would carry the fleets of Spain to conquest of all the seas. Francis Drake was well aware of "this Spanish harvest which they get out of the earth to trouble all the earth."

But Turkish resistance continued unreasonably; Islamic folk kept their grip on the African coast; in Europe the merciless conflict of religions took greater toll of the treasure in Madrid and the lives of Spaniards. Until Lord Bacon would wonder "how they clasp and contain so large dominions with so few natural Spaniards."

At that time of trouble, in the beginning of the 1570s, Francis Bacon was a boy poring over Latin schoolbooks in York House upon the Strand, heedless of the loss of the English wool trade to the Netherlands, or the end of the slave traffic to the Indies, or the failure of ivory to arrive from the African Guinea. There was little gold in England and no prospect of more to come in from the seas. There was poverty in the streets of London Town, and hunger by the docks of Plymouth.

The boy Francis did not know, but a few resolute men did, that England must find a way of her own over the seas in spite of the monopoly of Spain, and that way must lead somehow to Asia. The men who tried to find this way out of despair for England were very few.

Francis Drake sailed first, alone as a captain of privateers, back to the Caribbean. That sea was the source of Spanish power, and the halfway point to Asia. No one that year wasted thought on the shadowy coast lying between St. Augustine and Cape Breton of the French.

VI. The English Take to the Sea

The Pioneers of an Enterprise

THE English had not been a seafaring people. They had fared to Iceland for fish, and sometimes across to the far Newfoundland banks of the Bretons and Basques; otherwise they had coasted in small vessels along their own narrow seas. Even there, around the Baltic, Hansa merchantmen had carried and controlled the trade; Venetians fetched goods from the Mediterranean to the Thames.

John Rut of *Mary Guildford* had been taken to the New Land by an Italian pilot, and even Hawkins, son of an African trader, had been piloted to the Indies by a navigator of Dieppe. The truth is that for the first half of the century Tudor England had been strangely ignorant of the discovery of the outer world, let alone its charting and navigation. There had been only nostalgic memories of voyages of King Arthur's time to northern shores, of the good St. Brendan finding his blessed isle, joined to the wisdom of Bede the Venerable and the medieval science of Roger Bacon. That and the setting out of the Bristol fishermen by their own dead reckoning. The Tudors themselves had been preoccupied with the continent beyond Calais.

In the halls of Oxford geography remained a teaching of the Roman Pliny, with some new lore of learned Italians; Elizabeth herself had been tutored by Italians. Then, too, while stray Italian *cognoscenti* were willing enough to tutor ignorant English boys for good silver coin paid into hand, the Spaniards and Portuguese— who made the actual voyages—were not willing so to do. Maps of the new discoveries and the unfolding shape of the unknown quarter of the world remained closely guarded in Seville and Lisbon. When the tutors of Oxford turned their attention to geography after the stimulating visit of Erasmus, they turned to Ptolemy, who had died some thirteen centuries before Columbus.

The voyages of John Cabot were pretty well forgotten. Worthy merchants of London understood that codfish and sealskins came from a coast beyond Iceland; a few scholarly gentlemen who could afford to buy manuscripts read the *Decades* of Peter Martyr, who told tall tales of simple naked savages; a physician or two may have wondered about the drug called *guaiacum,* which physicians in Seville used to cure venereal disease. It came from a place called *America.* So there were islands across the sea, barring the way to Cathay!

There was a new book from the printing presses, very popular indeed, about the follies of mankind. This *Ship of Fools* made merry at the many foolish descriptions of the "new fonde londe." There was also (after 1516) a volume of fantasy in excellent Latin written by Sir Thomas More entitled *Utopia,* telling of a better land of self-governing folk beyond the sea, beyond *Brazil.* Undoubtedly fantastic—although Sir Thomas might have read one of *The four voyages of Amerigo Vespucci. . . .*

A few young exiles attacked the inertia of England with their pleas. These were sons of London or Bristol merchants marooned in Seville, where they felt the contagion of the discoveries. Roger Barlow wangled a place for himself in the fleet of Sebastian Cabot, bound for the Freshwater Sea of the New World. On that long voyage Barlow apprenticed himself to the navigators, and learned much of the mystery of shooting the stars, and testing ocean currents by slinging overboard a bellying sail. More than that, he wrote out a manuscript of *A Brief Summe of Geographie,* mostly about the river Plate, joined to a translation of the Spanish *Suma de Geografía* of

Enciso (who had shared the misfortunes of Nicuesa on the coast of Golden Castile).

With eagerness and labored spelling Barlow tried to call attention to "the new founde lande which was fyrst discovered by marchantes of brystowe [Bristol] where now the bretons do trat thider everie yere a fyshing, and it is called the bacaliaus. . . . What comoditie is within this lande as yet is not knowen, but it is to be presupposed that ther is no riches of gold, spyces nor preciose stones, for it standeth farre apart from the equinoctiall [zone] where the influens of the sonne doth norishe and bryng forth gold, spices and perles."

Barlow hastened to add that if the English merchants of Bristol had gone on, toward the south and the wealth-breeding equator, they would doubtless have found great riches "as other nations hath done sence that tyme."

As to those other nations the would-be geographer pointed out that the Spaniards sail all the routes to the west, and the Portuguese the way to the east "so there resteth this waie of the northe only for to discover. . . . And for such an enterprise no man should thinke upon the cost in comparison to the grete profyt that may thereby follow, nor thinke the labour grete where so moche profyt honor and glory maye folow unto this, our naturall realme and king."

Now these labored words of Roger Barlow reveal a new and important impulse. He wants nothing for himself except a hearing; the advantage he seeks is for his realm and king. The merchants—and noblemen—of England are to come to the aid of the nation by outfitting voyages to the northern point of America. And in the event they did exactly that, although not in the manner or with the results imagined by Roger Barlow. The devotion of a few men would link England irrevocably to the northern coast of America.

But why to the inhospitable north? These pioneer propagandists at Seville saw no other alternative. Only too well they realized how Spanish and Portuguese sea power had preëmpted the more attractive southern routes. Besides, as Barlow pointed out, the coast of Cabot's discovery (Newfoundland) lay closest to England. It was just across from Bristol. It could be as livable, accordingly, as their own island. Since the Barlow group understood nothing of the Gulf Stream and the warmth it brought to the Bay of Biscay, to Scotland, and all of Scandinavia, it seemed to them that the shores of the opposite land must be as temperate, which is not at all the case.

Moreover, having learned to use globes by then, the circle of English enthusiasts at Seville soon appreciated how much shorter distances were in the northern latitudes—diminishing temptingly toward the Pole itself. Barlow had learned to steer a great circle course. Robert Thorne, his friend, also a scion of Bristol, could not banish the thought that an English vessel might find the shortest way to Cathay, over the Pole itself. "God knoweth . . . I yet have no little mind to this business. If I had the faculty, it should be the first thing I would undertake, even to attempt if our seas be navigable to the Pole or no."

And almost as he imagined it, that search would be attempted, although not by Robert Thorne. He wrote his plea for the discovery of the unknown land lying within the uncharted seas in *The Book of Robert Thorne*. The manuscript was meant for his king, Henry VIII, but it passed through many hands. Robert Thorne also drew a map for his king. It showed what he imagined the world to be like. It was a blend of the ancient Ptolemy world map and odds and ends of the new discoveries that Thorne picked up in Seville. But it came to a focus, as it were, upon the projecting point of the New Found Land, drawn temptingly close to Ireland, with the legend: "Here the lands were first discovered by the English."

A childish mistake? As ridiculous as the thought of sailing a ship over the polar ice? Yes, to our minds. But these pioneers of English seafaring had never seen a realistic map of the world; they had no concept of the future of their island. They were looking into the unknown with courage.

"I judge," Robert Thorne wrote in his book, "there is no land unhabitable, nor sea innavigable."

The awakening spirit of the English was like that of the fellowship of Prince Henry the Navigator at Sagres, and their eagerness like that of the folk of Ferdinand and Isabella on the eve of the discoveries. But Thorne's countrymen were three generations behind other seafaring nations in the science of voyaging. Their fallacies would lead to failure after failure; their courage would not let them admit failure.

Voyage of Master Hore of London

In the year of the publication of Robert Thorne's book and his map, 1527, John Rut lost his way in the Atlantic and sorely disturbed the peace of mind of Spanish officialdom in the Indies.

After that the English borrowed awkwardly from foreign science of the sea. They printed *The Rutter* (Routier, or Courses) *of the Sea,* translated from a work of the French pilots. They unearthed the *Imago Mundi* of D'Ailly, which had fascinated Columbus, along with a route for pilgrims to Jerusalem. Somebody translated bits of Ptolemy from the French as *The Compost of Ptholomeus.*

Much of all this was studied by the gentlemen merchants in their curiosity about the unknown west. One of them, a Master Robert Hore, was stirred by news of the first voyages of Jacques Cartier to search himself with his boon companions for the missing passage through the western lands to Asia. He had plenty of volunteers to go with him, but no experienced navigators. His mariners had the skill of the Tudor age afloat, but lacked provisions for a long voyage.

Years later one of the survivors told the story of this blind voyage, and his fragmentary account has been preserved.

"One Master Hore of London, of good stature and courage, given to a studie of Cosmographie in the 28 yere of King Henry the 8, the yere of our Lord 1536 encouraged divers Gentlemen of the Innes of Court to accompany him on a voyage of discoverie upon the Northwest parts of America. Desirous to see the strange things of the world many gentlemen of good worship very willingly entered into the action with him . . . in two tall ships, to wit the *Trinitie* and the *Minion*—about six score persons. After the receiving of the Sacrament, they embarked themselves in the end of April.

"They were very long at sea, to wit, above two months, until they came to part of the West Indies above Cape Briton [Breton]. Thence they shaped their course Northeastwards untill they came to the Island of Penguin, whereon they went and found it full of great foules as big as geese. They dressed and eate them and found them to be very nourishing meat. They saw also bears both black and white, of whome they killed some, and tooke them for no bad foode.

"M. Oliver Dawbeny, which was in the *Minion,* the same Dawbeny walking one day on the hatches spied a boate with Savages of those parts. He called to such as were under the hatches, and willed them to come up if they would see the natural people of the countrey that they had so long desired to see. Whereupon they came up and tooke view of the Savages. They manned out a ship-boat to meet them and to take them. But they [the Indians] fled into an Island that lay up in the bay or river there, and our men pursued them into the Island, and the Savages fled; but our men found a fire and the side of a beare on a wooden spit left at the same by the Savages that were fled.

"In this journey they went so farre Northwards that they saw mighty Islands of yce [drifting icebergs] in the summer season on which were haukes and other foules to rest themselves.

"And further the said M. Dawbeny told that lying there they grew into great want of victuals. They found small relief [on the shore] more than they had from the nest of an Osprey that brought hourely to her yong great plenty of divers sorts of fishes. Such was their famine that they sought raw herbes and rootes to relieve themselves. The herbes being little to satisfie their insatiable hunger, here and there, seeking in the fields, a fellow killed his mate while he stooped to take up a roote. Cutting out pieces of the body whom he had murthered, he broiled the same on the coles of a fire and greedily devoured them.

"By this meane the company decreased. The officers knew not what was become of them. And then it fortuned that one of the company, driven with hunger to seek ashore for reliefe, came in the fields to the savour of broyled flesh. He fell out with the one [broil-ing the flesh] for that he would suffer his fellowes to starve while enjoying plentie—as he thought. This matter grew to cruell speeches. He that had the broyled meate burst out into these wordes: If thou wouldest needes know, the broyled meate that I had was a piece of such a man's buttocke.

"The report of this being brought to the ship, the Captaine found out what became of those that were missing, and was per-swaded that they were neither devoured by wilde beasts nor yet destroyed by savages. And hereupon he stood up and made a notable oration, including; Howe much these dealings offended the Al-mightie.

"The famine increasing, they agreed amongst themselves rather than all should perish, to cast lots who should be killed. Such was the mercie of God that in the same night there arrived a French ship in that bay, well furnished with victual. Such was the policy of the English that they became masters of the same, and changing ships and victualling them, they set sayle to come into England. They arrived in S. Ives in Cornewall about the ende of October. M. Buts was so changed in the voyage with hunger and miserie that Sir William his father and my Lady his mother knew him not to be their sonne, untill they found a secret marke which was a warte upon one of his knees.

"Certaine months after, those Frenchmen came into England and made complaint to King Henry the 8."

These "Gentlemen of the Innes of Court," who robbed an osprey's nest of fish and pirated a French fishing vessel, seemed to remember the New Found Land only as desolate earth overgrown with pine trees. Their ludicrous tragedy of a voyage ended desire to explore the mysterious America for many years. Venturesome English shipmasters did break out of their narrow seas, but to the northeast, toward the lean pickings of the Baltic, and south-south-west around the hump of Africa where William Hawkins, eldest of his house, found some ivory. Other searchers island-hopped past hostile fleets to the markets of the Levant where the Grand Turk, Suleiman, ruled.

They learned new ways over the seas, but brought back little profit. The pioneers of English expansion realized more clearly each year that the ships must reach Asia.

The Merchants-Adventurers Try the East

There were only four possible routes over the oceans to far Asia. Magellan's route around the south of America was out of the question, being Spanish-held; Da Gama's route around the south of Africa was the property of the Portuguese. That left to the English the possibility of rounding the north of America, and the possibility of circling Europe to the northeast.

It so happened at the mid-century that the "cosmographical friends" of English expansion turned their eyes longingly toward the northeast.

This group of the generation after Barlow and Thorne also happened to include some brilliant minds subject to illusions. John Dudley, Duke of Northumberland, aided it with the influence of the Court. Dudley reasoned simply enough that English shipmasters must carry the few products of the island, the wool, tin, rabbitskins, and leather, to the markets of Cathay, a civilized country. Surely the naked savages of the new America would not clothe themselves in English wool! No, the first need was to find "a vent for wool."

Around the same court circulated a personage more remarkable than the straightforward Dudley. John Dee, a brilliant Welshman—who fancied that Owen Madoc of Wales might have been the first discoverer of America—had crossed the Channel to study the new sciences with men like Gemma-Frisius and Gerard Mercator. John Dee, pallid, bearded, and engrossed, brought back to untaught England a mastery of mathematics, a dream of finding the philosopher's stone, and a conviction that a ship could reach China by sailing northeast by skirting the edge of the arctic ice. Some folk thereafter thought Dee to be mad or dealing with the powers of darkness. But he probably got his idea of the sea route from Mercator.

It came to this: open water extended northeast (actually owing to the warm Gulf Stream) around the North Cape of Norway; beyond lay the great Cape Tabin. And beyond Tabin the unknown coast fell away to the south, to Cathay. Arab geographers said so; even Mercator believed so. Therefore, it followed that if a ship could round Tabin it would have an ice-free course in warmer water to Marco Polo's port of Quinsay and the markets of Cathay.

Nothing could have been more mistaken.

Then, to carry out Dee's daydream, the aged Sebastian Cabot was bought out of his office as Pilot Major of Spain. It cost 100 pounds sterling to smuggle the last of the mariner Italians across to England, where he hinted to the ignorant islanders of vast secrets he could reveal. It cost a deal of trouble also, because the unworthy son of John Cabot had neglected to resign as Pilot Major of Spain when he left for England on plea of personal business. It seemed to the men of London that a Cabot and a master of the secrets of Spanish voyaging could launch them toward Cathay, and Sebastian Cabot did not disillusion them. His price was a lifetime pension of 166 pounds, 13 shillings, 4 pence—an enormous amount in Tudor times. (John Cabot had been given 20 pounds a year for discovering North America.) Sebastian was called Grand Pilot and his first act of record was to send secretly to his former paymaster, Charles V, the false information that the Duke of Northumberland planned to join with the French in outfitting a fleet to conquer Peru. Perhaps he hoped the Emperor would pay more to fetch him back, but Charles did no such thing.

Now Cabot once had fared badly enough in his solitary voyage of exploration to the river Plate. He also claimed falsely that he had once searched the northwest, along the coasts of Greenland and Labrador, only to be turned back by ice on the verge of finding a passage to Asia. Readily enough he agreed that the alternate route through "the north east frostie seas" might succeed. Skillfully enough he supervised the outfitting of three vessels to attempt it, with three Englishmen as captains.

These preparations were closely watched by the Spanish ambassador in London. He reported to Madrid, "They will follow a
northerly course by the Frozen Sea toward the country of the great
Cham of China. The English believe the route to be a short one and
very convenient for the distribution of kerseys [sale of coarse cloth
of long wool] in those far countries, bringing back spices and other
rich merchandise in exchange. . . . Cabot came to see me recently:
I asked him if the said voyage was as certain as it seemed. He
replied, Yes, it was."

They sailed in 1553, with Sir Hugh Willoughby, a naval officer,
commanding, aided by Richard Chancellor, a skilled navigator who
had brought a vessel safely through the gamut of the Mediterranean.
As John Dee had dreamed, they rounded the North Cape. In faring
eastward Willoughby's two vessels were iced in, and all but one
of the band frozen when they tried to outlive the arctic winter.
By luck or instinct young Chancellor found his way into the White
Sea and open water at the port of the Archangel—the future route
of convoys. Discovering that he was not in the legendary Tartary
but in Russia, he journeyed south to Moscow and the Court of
Ivan IV, called "the Terrible." There the wandering Englishman
and the isolated Tsar struck up an odd friendship, and made the
beginning of a trade agreement.

When Chancellor got back safely to London, Cabot and Dee
and the Merchants Adventurers, who backed the voyage, could
point to the discovery of a route to Russia even if the way to China
had not been found. Brilliant Richard Chancellor perished soon
after at sea, attempting to bring back the first Russian Ambassador
to England, but the "Muscovy" trade was secured.

Even as "the incomparable Richard Chancellor" died, a less
noted seaman was undertaking an impossible feat. Stephen Borough
set out with nine men in a pinnace, *Searchthrift,* to probe for the
northeast passage. Aged Sebastian Cabot danced gaily with the
young men at the festival of their sailing. In this open boat Stephen
Borough passed the Archangel channel, crossed the Frozen Sea,
felt his way around arctic Novaya Zemlya to enter the unknown
Kara Sea beyond. He found no mythical Cape Tabin, or warm coast

to lead him south; *Searchthrift* forged her way through deepening
mist and thickening ice floes until the way was closed. Somehow
Borough got out of the dread Kara Sea and raced the winter to
clear water and a village that sheltered him against the winter.

He returned to England to report the truth, that the northeast
passage to China did not exist. The Merchants Adventurers then
turned to exploring inland through Russia to try to tap the trade
of the caravans of Persia. If not by sea, they might reach the luxuries
of Cathay by land.

Sebastian Cabot died, the last personage of the dawn discoverers. On his deathbed this remarkable pretender whispered to
Richard Eden that he carried with him the greatest of secrets, the
art of finding longitude at sea. "I thinke that the goode old man
somewhat doted," remarked young Eden, "and had not utterly
shaken off all worldly vayne glorie."

A new generation shouldered the task of finding new sea routes
for England. Eden himself was translating Martín Cortes's *Breve
compendio de la spera y de la arte de navegar*—Stephen Borough
found a copy of it at Seville. Young John Hawkins was learning the
route from Africa to the Caribbean. In Devonshire a single-minded
squire, Sir Humphrey Gilbert, was listening to the wisdom of John
Dee, and at Windsor, after so many years of foreboding, a young
queen who was "merely English" reigned.

And if there were no passage to the northeast, the way out
might lie in the northwest, around America.

The Invisible Empire of the Seas

It seems to us of the wealthy and materialized twentieth century as if the Elizabethan seamen of the ten years from 1570–80
must have gone mad. Their small vessels like the *Golden Hind*
appeared suddenly in the remote seas. They quested toward each
pole—while other Englishmen on camels sought the golden road to
Samarkand.

To account for this seeming madness, we conclude that it was romanticism. We think of a carefree age of Drake, during the spacious days of Elizabeth—of happy sea dogs roving the Spanish Main for loot and glory. It was not like that.

These voyagers went out to bring relief to their small island. No port beyond Land's End was open to them. In the year 1570 the resources of the seas known to them were failing. The enveloping power of Spain was growing too great to be challenged. Within it the English people lived by cultivating their parishes and profited by selling their coarse wool. Those who had no such work for their hands begged for their food.

A poet, Christopher Marlowe, would write wistfully of phantom spirits that might fly beyond this drab reality: *I'll have them fly to India for gold— Ransack the Ocean for orient pearl— And search all corners of the new-found world.*

The English voyages were planned with anxious care. Men carried them out at risk of their lives, learning to navigate with new instruments as they went, in the hope of finding a new market or a people beyond Spanish dominion inclined to amicable trade with England. The Russians were not too rewarding as customers.

There had been a new prospect opened up when Jean Ribault had taken refuge in England when he was still enthusiastic about his first landing of Huguenots in Florida. Was there an opening here for an English trading colony? Would the experienced Ribault pilot ships of the Queen's Majesty to his fertile coast, to "Floriday"? Ribault would not. When he slipped away from the island, John Hawkins went to spy out the land. But Menendez's swordsmen ended that possibility. . . .

Then Francis Drake came back from his solitary cruise as a privateering captain. He had captured no treasure of silver. He had searched the jungles of Balboa's isthmus, with escaped slaves and friendly Indians. He knew now how the treasure of Peru was portaged over the isthmus to Nombre de Dios. There, he declared in his anger, the Spaniards could be struck at their most vulnerable point. This isthmus was the arterial of their treasure, the treasure, the lifeblood of their power. Few councilors of the young, irresolute

queen agreed with him. To risk war with Philip over a mule-train
load of silver would be a wanton risk. Their caution held Drake in
leash at home.

They heard rumors of great Spanish discoveries in the far
South Sea, of the ancient gold mines of Solomon found in islands
named after him, the Solomon Islands. Where did they lie? And
where lay the last undiscovered continent of the earth, *Terra
Australis,* the long-sought South Land? Might not this be the actual
Ophir of Solomon? Ancient writers believed so. With so much
continental land enclosing the north of the great South Sea, there
must be a vast land undiscovered in the deep south, or the sphere of
the earth would not be in balance. The antarctic must balance the
arctic.

Richard Grenville and merchants of Devon urged Elizabeth to
allow them to voyage through Magellan's strait to search for the
Terra Australis, where a civilized people with untold riches might
be revealed. Elizabeth approved, and then refused. The South Sea
was becoming a Spanish lake. Intrusion there would surely bring
on the conflict her wisest councilors dreaded.

The visionary John Dee urged the search of America—while
he labored at an improved marine compass. America he held to
be nothing less than the lost Atlantis of Plato. If so, it must be an
island, and accordingly a passage could be found around it. Elizabeth held the Welsh prophet in some awe.

His pupil, the stubborn Sir Humphrey Gilbert, became the
most outspoken advocate of this search for a passage to the northwest.

"When I gave myself to the studie of Geographie, I came in
the end to the fourth part of the world, commonly called America,
which I found to be an island . . . through which Northern Seas
the Passage lyeth."

While Dee seemed to rely on occult perceptions, the honest
Gilbert had gathered proof of his belief, proof positive, to his mind.
If America was not an island, it must be joined to Asia. And if so,
surely the people of Cathay and the port of Quinsay would have
made their roads into it to trade. But no trace of them had been

found among the savages of the Unknown Land. Moreover the animals observed in America were unlike the animals of Asia.

Also, Marco Polo had certainly sailed for 1500 miles along the coast of *Anian* in Cathay and had found the sea open before him as far as he could see. (Marco Polo had voyaged south, not north.)

Also, Coronado, on reaching the country of Quivira, and the Sierra Nevada, had come to "a great sea where were certaine ships laden with Merchandise, bearing on their prows certaine birds called Alcatraz, made part of gold and part of silver . . . they were thirty dayes comming thither from Cataia." (Gilbert must have read in Dee's books a fantastic account of the river and great canoes described by the Pawnee called "the Turk" to Coronado on the plains of Kansas.)

Also, Jacques Cartier when he reached Hochelaga in New France heard how "there was a great Sea at Saguinay whereof the end was not knowen: which they presupposed to be the passage to Cataia." (An echo of Cartier at the Lachine Rapids.)

Furthermore and lastly Sebastian Cabot had in person found his way to a strait at 67°30′ north "and finding the Seas still open, sayd that he might and would have gone to Cataia if the mutiny of the Mariners had not bene." (The false claim of the intriguing Cabot that he had reached the northwest passage.)

As Christopher Columbus had once gathered together all ancient lore and contemporary misinformation that would bear out his thesis that Asia lay where Florida was found, so the single-minded Gilbert collected everything from Plato to Sebastian Cabot that would bear out his belief that a passage by sea led around North America to Asia. Hastily he wrote it all down in his *Discourse of a Discoverie for a New Passage to Cataia*. It made an impressive argument.

The Grenville group, determined to search for the missing South Land, opposed it, objecting that ice closed the ocean channels of the arctic. From his communion with spirits John Dee roused to retort "The salt sea never freezes."

Anthony Jenkinson, returning the worse for wear from the caravan route to Bokhara, argued with Humphrey Gilbert for a renewal of the northeast search. Jenkinson had found the overland route to China to be beyond the reach of Englishmen; agents of the Muscovy Company were trying, instead, to reach the court of the Persian Shah. Gilbert offered the northwest passage as the only solution for England. They held their debate before the Queen's Majesty. Elizabeth listened to both and gave her approval to neither. Her practical mind sensed the need of a land across the seas that could be discovered and *occupied*. Perhaps the missing *Terra Australis* would prove to be that land. . . .

The practical thing to do was to go and look for it.

Already Elizabeth had declared her mind to the Portuguese—that only "effective occupation" would give title to a newly discovered land.

Gilbert won her approval by slow degrees. Probably John Dee's great influence helped. The rumor about Urdaneta's passage certainly helped.

That elderly explorer had actually found the northern route from the Philippines back to Acapulco in the Pacific, and after that had returned to Spain prosaically enough by crossing the Panama isthmus and embarking on an Atlantic convoy. But rumor insisted that Urdaneta had sailed his vessel triumphantly through the north of America, passing by wealthy Quivira. If so, he had found the strait of the legendary Dutchman, and discovered the northwest passage for Spain. And the Spaniards were undoubtedly concealing the discovery because it might profit Englishmen more than themselves.

If so, Gilbert argued, Englishmen must sail at once to discover the passage and hold it by building Christian habitations upon it.

Perhaps the maps decided the matter for him and in so doing began the long quest for a New England across the Atlantic.

Maps, especially when printed, carry an illusion of reality. You see an island on a map, neatly colored, with mountains showing, and you can hardly help believing it exists. If a cape projects from a coast, why, someone must have seen it there. Nothing appears to us as dependable as a modern atlas. In the Tudor age of discovery the English maps in manuscript and print showed primarily what the makers imagined might be there.

And in the minds of European cartographers the northern mystery of America was still unsolved. The old notion that the end of Asia extended to the north of America persisted. Were not the Eskimo folk of Labrador-way—"clad in skins, and barely four feet tall"—exactly like the men of northern Asia seen by the English voyagers about the great river Ob, on the way to Cathay?

This fact linked with the mistaken notion that Marco Polo had cruised along the coast of Anian, far to the north. But if this were the case, then firm and continent land must stretch unbroken from Cathay to Labrador. And no English ships could round Labrador to break south into the great South Sea. Some of the cosmographers in Europe held this to be true. Urdaneta might have enlightened them, but he said nothing for publication. The Casa kept its secrets well.

Now there was a solution of the riddle of the Asia-America juncture that occurred to many minds just at this time. Granting the eastward extension of Asia, the missing coast of Anian might stretch up toward the pole, above Labrador and Cartier's Canada. There might be an open strait between America and this far point of Asia. That would account for the hide-clad dwarfish natives being alike on both sides. In their skin boats they could easily pass back and forth across a *strait*.

In the Netherlands the imaginative young Ortels (Ortelius) drew this pattern in his world map of 1564, showing the last provinces of Cathay ending in Anian toward the pole, with a vast strait beneath, and below this open water the coast of the "Region of Quivira." The wandering island of *"Giapan"* (the long-sought Cipangu) occupied the western end of the strait. The methodical Gerard Mercator followed (1569) this schematic method of his countryman; the very popular *Cosmographia* of devout Sebastian Münster showed open water above America.

So when Sir Humphrey Gilbert came to draw a world map for the eyes of his queen, he had noted authority to support his "Northwest Passage." He made the most of it—boldly depicting

Labrador as an island within a brief sail of England. By following his map a ship of Plymouth could round Labrador, sail on above Canada and Quivira, put in to Anian on the north shore of the convenient channel, and then proceed on a thousand miles or so to trade at Giapan. Thence, on the Gilbert map, by crossing perhaps 1500 miles more of open Pacific, the ship could gain the Moluccas and take on a lading of spices. (Had not Cabrillo fared near the Moluccas before he died?)

Now these geographers were working with globes, not with the out-of-date flat maps. Even Gilbert was attempting a cordiform projection. Behind their errors lay the truth that a voyage from England by the north of America would be the shortest way to Japan and the Pacific islands. The route around the globe by Magellan's strait was impossibly long and hazardous. Even the Spaniards who controlled it preferred to portage between the oceans, across the narrow neck of Panama.

The only question was: did the Northwest Passage exist? And the only way to be certain of that was to go and look for it.

So the wish of John Dee and Sir Humphrey Gilbert was granted, although the search was given to another man.

The Iron Will of Martin Frobisher

He was a giant of a Yorkshireman, with a gift for holding his tongue and a knack of getting what he was after at sea. His portraits show a hard-fleshed head, heavy, intent eyes, and a flowing Viking mustache. His record reveals successful privateering trade with Africa, but makes no mention of very capable pirating in the narrow northern seas. Martin Frobisher was not given to explanations.

A writing friend, George Best, claims that Frobisher longed for fifteen years to make the voyage around America to the backside. Probably he did no such thing. Being in shady repute, he wanted to make a good name for himself. They scraped up little enough for him to go on—two small barks and a pinnace, with thirty-five venturesome men and provisions for a year. Departing down the Thames, they saw the Queen wave from her window, and that cheered them greatly.

For guidance they had the lying tale told by the still-revered Sebastian Cabot, of how he had rounded Labrador and sighted the open strait to the west. The strait that would tend south to the backside of the continent and the great South Sea. It lay beyond 62°—between that and 70°. That was the one hard fact unimaginative Martin Frobisher had to go on, the need to turn west after 62°. This took him far to the north of the great river of New France.

His three small craft head west from the Shetlands in the cold, windy June of 1576. They pass beyond waters familiar to Elizabethan seamen and sight the first land rising "like pinnacles of steeples and all covered with snow." This tip of Greenland they imagine to be an island of *Friseland,* which does not exist. They cannot disembark on the ice-barred coast. Their pinnace vanishes in a gale, and one of the barks heads back for home. *Gabriel,* with Martin Frobisher, keeps on to a coast they take to be Labrador.

Beating north through drifting ice, they pass 62° but cannot round a jutting, wind-buffeted point in the damaged *Gabriel.* But to the west the ice parts, and there they behold "a great gut, bay, or passage dividing, as it were, two continents asunder." Into this obscure passage they sail, calling it hopefully Frobisher's Strait. The signs on either hand appear to be right. "That land upon his right hand, he judged to be the continent of Asia, divided from the firm of America which lieth upon the left hand."

So much the learned gentlemen of London had told Martin Frobisher he would find. There remained for him to prove the inhabitants on the right to be Asiatics. Frobisher notices traces of fires made by human hands and sights immense deer almost human in their behavior. A seaman fetches him a specimen of hard black rock. The proof appears after fifty leagues of sailing, when small dark objects resembling seals coming toward him turn out to be men in small boats (kayaks) of leather.

These brown-skinned inhabitants of the *Meta Incognita* (Unknown Destination), as Frobisher christens the northern shore, claiming it for his queen, have brown faces, and are small and hideous as Tartars. Nimbly they perform antics in the shrouds of *Gabriel,* imitating the sailors; they trade garments of sealskin for bells and daggers. And then, when five Englishmen take one Asiatic back in their small boat to his fellows on the shore, the boat and the English sailors are carried off by the Eskimos.

The giant Frobisher manages to capture one of the "Asiatics" in return. By ringing a trade bell close to the water he entices a native in a skin boat close to the bark and hoists him over the rail, boat and all. After that the shore is deserted, and *Gabriel* calls for the missing crewmen with trumpet and signal gun in vain. Without a ship's boat Frobisher cannot land again. He heads back to England to escape the autumn storms and to collect other vessels to return to search for his men.

In London, according to his friend George Best, he is commended "for the great hope he brought of the passage to Cataya."

Frobisher's specimen of black stone, however, caused the real excitement.

Very carefully George Best—the Boswell of the Frobisher voyages—explained that his hero had not meant to cause such a fever of speculation. Not because of "the piece of black stone much like to a sea coal in color, which by its weight seemed to be some kind of metall or minerall. This was a thing of no account in the judgement of the captain at first sight; yet it was kept for its novelty.

"After his arrival in London, being demanded of sundry of his friends what thing he had brought them home out of that countrey, he had nothing left to present them withall but a piece of this black stone. And it fortuned that a gentlewoman, one of the adventurers' [sponsors'] wives, having a piece thereof, she threw it by chance into a fire and burned it so long that, being taken forth and quenched in a little vinegar it glistered with a bright trace of golde. Whereupon, the matter being called in some question, it was brought to certain Goldfiners in London to make assay thereof, who gave out that it held golde, and that very richly for the quantity."

Now every word of this may be truth. Yet on the voyage home, another witness relates, the thirteen seamen remaining on *Gabriel* had been gossiping about finding gold in the black stone, and surely the anonymous noblewoman, wife of a backer, had been trying an experiment of her own in metallurgy. Frobisher himself said neither yea nor nay. He had been sent out to find a strait leading west with open water between Asia and America; he brought back evidence of such a strait, including a still-living specimen of an "Asiatic." When some critics like Grenville (believers in the great South Land) protested this was little to show, why, there was the specimen of gold.

In any case Frobisher was not responsible for the emotional frenzy that seized upon Court and commoners alike. The planners in London Town yielded to the twofold intoxication of successful discovery and prospect of gold without limit. Just across the Atlantic in *Meta Incognita*—this cryptic name, Unknown Destination, was bestowed on the ore-bearing coast, in reality the south of Baffin Land—gold lay on the beaches, beyond the claims of Spain, Portugal, or France. The eager George Best wrote how easily New World timber could feed New World ore smelters, and how the climate over there would be more pleasant than that of Paris for humans who clad themselves in furs, as nature had clad the animals of Meta Incognita. Frobisher's observations of latitude and longitude were carefully deleted from written reports. The great secret must be kept until Meta Incognita, the new Queen's Land, could be occupied.

To accomplish that, a new trading company was formed hastily, the Company of Cathay, backed by the merchant house of Lok, with Michael Lok its prime mover and Martin Frobisher its admiral. The Navy furnished a tall ship of 200 tons to bring back a cargo of gold ore. Even the practical Elizabeth subscribed to a small share in the new company. This meant little in money but much in prestige. It also meant that the greatest of the councilors, Burghley and Walsingham, favored this second attempt.

Two pinnaces were shipped in sections, to be launched off Meta Incognita to explore farther to the west. Enthusiasm ran high.

A colorful *Portraiture* of the kidnaped Eskimo, who happened to die just then, was published for all to read, along with an alluring account of *The Five Ways to Cathay*.

We can smile at the naïve English, knowing as we do that the black stone was no more than fool's gold, and Frobisher's strait in reality an inlet ending a little beyond the point where he encountered the Eskimos. (Perhaps the silent Frobisher realized as much; perhaps he wanted above all to go back with force enough to search for his missing crewmen.)

What happened in that second voyage almost defies explanation. Three vessels set out for Meta Incognita in May of the next year, 1577; they returned safely in October after searching in vain for the five seamen, all of them laden with ore gathered at random along the shore. Why did not Frobisher attempt to explore to the end of his waterway? If the intoxication of loading ships with gold ore seized the entire Company of Cathay, why was not the ore properly tested as soon as the hurrying vessels returned to the docks at Bristol?

They lay at the docks for weeks while "gold finders" argued about the ore, and John Dee came and went like an alchemist among his retorts. Michael Lok, who had most at stake, held the ore to be good; rumor proclaimed it worthless; Frobisher had nothing to say. Something was being covered up by influences of no little power, and evidently something more important than a few tons of ore was in the minds of the leaders of England.

What kept the ships waiting and the ore unassayed may never be established. But one conjecture can be made.

In December of that year Francis Drake put to sea on a southerly course with secret orders.

The Attempt to Circumnavigate America

The written orders Drake carried were clear enough to be misleading, as they were meant to be, to other eyes. His unwritten

orders have never been revealed, although in his speech to the
assembled crews at San Julián he mentioned something of them at
great hazard to himself.

This voyage of 1577 we know now to be the most daring ever
to be attempted by Europeans, with the odds against its success
immeasurably great.

But a new horizon was opening to English eyes beyond
America. There was a sense of urgency, of time running out before
the dreaded conflict with Spanish power would begin. John Dee,
that champion of discovery, was no longer alone in demanding that
the ships penetrate to the "far corners of the earth." He was alone,
however, or at least the first, to prophesy that there could be, even
in this dark time, a "British Impire" beyond the seas. Being Welsh
to the core, Dee could not bring himself to speak of an English
empire.

Now Captain Francis Drake at that time was noted only for
his poor education, his ability to handle a vessel at sea, and his
determination to attack the Spaniards. After his scouting of Nombre
de Dios he had been released once to try a commando-type raid on
the treasure portage of the Panama isthmus—failing narrowly to
capture the port of Nombre de Dios, and, wounded, failing by
mischance to seize a silver train entire on the portage. Allying
himself to the *cimarrones* of the forest, he had eventually carried
off silver enough to make the voyage pay—with the aid of a wandering Huguenot privateer. But with John Oxenham he had had a
glimpse of the far Pacific from the heights of the portage.

Oxenham—not Drake—had gone back with a small com-
mandolike force, inexpensive to send out and possibly very profitable. While Drake was kept in hiding, as Gourgues had been after
the Florida raid, Oxenham was working his way across the Panama
isthmus to build small vessels with the aid of the escaped slaves on
the Pacific coast, where no English ship had been seen as yet.

If Oxenham's small craft could be joined by English ships of
fighting power, they might hold a port on the far South Sea and
collect treasure from the galleons that arrived, unsuspecting, from
Peru. There was that very dangerous possibility. And there was

also the project of Richard Grenville of searching for the missing *Terra Australis* beyond Magellan's strait. . . .

To do this, they called on Captain Francis Drake, not Grenville. They were a few men looking to the far seas, Lords of the Privy Council, the two Winters, the Lord Admiral, among others, and John Hawkins, who had survived San Juan de Ulúa to take in hand the building of an armed navy, a single fighting fleet. That fleet was not yet in being. Behind closed doors these leaders who looked to the future told Drake he could have three ships and some supply vessels, and 130 men. With God's blessing he could take his ships through Magellan's strait, and up the far coasts of the Americas to bring succor to Oxenham. He could supply himself and pay his way thenceforward by capturing Spanish vessels in the South Sea, and then press on to the north.

There, in the north of America, he should search for the other strait, the Strait of Anian, where Frobisher would be trying to come through from the eastern end. The danger would be great there in the colder, unknown sea, and he must preserve his ships if possible.

Those orders were never written down and, after nearly four centuries, can only be conjectured. John Hawkins wrote out for Drake false sailing directions to Alexandria. His crews must think they were bound for trade or raid in the Mediterranean. Officials of Her Majesty's Government must think that Captain Francis Drake would go in search of the South Land along the rim of the great South Sea, or even the mines of Ophir in the Solomon Islands. Her Majesty herself must know no more than that. Drake himself must find his way back to England as best he could, by the north of America or the far Spice Islands and the way of the Portuguese around Africa.

Elizabeth heard of this, and intervened. She summoned Drake to talk with her, and what they said between them has never been repeated. But the wisest scholars believe that Elizabeth agreed he might raid the treasure ports and ships of the Pacific. She could not give open consent to an act of war against the Spanish flag; the risk would be his, and the profit would be England's.

So Drake sailed on his only voyage of discovery, hoping to fill

his holds with Spanish silver. Perhaps he hoped, as well, to circum-
navigate the American continent and return by the northern passage
around the Labrador to England.

Drake met with delay and then trouble. Lagging through the
doldrums off Brazil, he purloined a Portuguese pilot to guide him.
Beyond the river Plate, he entered waters unknown to English seamen. By the time he felt his way down to the haven of Port San
Julián in Patagonia the antarctic winter had set in, necessitating a
wait of weeks on the bleak, dark coast.

The trouble was not simple mutiny, as had befallen that other
superb navigator, Magellan, at this same spot. Drake's seamen had
expected to cruise the thoroughfare of the Mediterranean; they
found themselves marooned under a strange sky in uncanny cold,
bound for a destination known only to their captain. Drake let it be
rumored around that they would raid Spanish shipping in the
South Sea. But this in turn angered a clique of the gentlemen companions, who by the custom of the time expected to share his command and counsel. Drake's orders, as the gentlemen officers understood them, required him to pass Magellan's strait, to find, trade
with, and colonize a new land for England, the undiscovered South
Land. Instead of doing so it seemed as if Drake were turning to his
old fancy for pirating Spanish shipping. *On what authority was he
acting?*

That was the one thing Drake could not tell them. Instead he
called to trial and executed Mr. Thomas Doughty, foremost among
the angered officers, who had made an attempt to set the crews
against him. Then after long days of anxious thought Captain
Francis Drake made his famous Sunday speech instead of a sermon
to the assembled ships' companies. In it he risked revealing a little
of the Queen's secret instructions to him for action in the unknown
South Sea.

"My masters, I am a very bad orator, for my bringing up hath
not been in learning. But whatsoever I shall here speak . . . I will
answer for it in England, yea, and before her Majesty, and *I have it
here already set down.*

"Thus it is, my masters, that we are very far from our country and friends, we are compassed in on every side by our enemies . . . wherefore we must have these discords that are grown among us redressed, for by the life of God it doth even take my wits from me to think of it . . . my masters, I must have the gentleman to haul and draw with the mariner, and the mariner with the gentleman . . . as gentlemen are very necessary for government's sake in the voyage so have I shipped them for that, *and for some further intent*.

"Also, if there be any here willing to return home, here is the *Marigold,* a ship I will furnish to such as will return with the most credit I can give them by my letters . . . I must needs be plain with you. *I have taken that in hand that I know not in the world how to go through withal; it passeth my capacity; it hath even bereaved me of my wits to think on it.*"

So challenged, no man of the listening companies demanded passage back to England. With brutal decision Drake then relieved all his ships' captains of their commands. The startled officers asked by what cause he displaced them. He asked them to give a reason why he should not do so. And he showed them what was probably the only writing he had in Elizabeth's hand—a bill of a thousand crowns she had given to the voyage. He added that she had pledged the death of any man of her realm who revealed her share in the enterprise to the King of Spain.

"And now, my masters, let us consider what we have done. We have now set together by the ears three mighty princes, as first her Majesty, then the Kings of Spain and Portugal. For if this voyage shall not have good success, we shall not only be a scoffing-stock unto our enemies but also a great blot on our whole country for ever. And never again will the like [voyage] be attempted. . . .

"And if it so be that I never come home, yet will her Majesty pay every man his wages . . . for it is only her Majesty that you serve, and this voyage is only her setting forth."

By invoking Elizabeth's name and hinting in this fashion at written orders which he did not have Drake put an edge to the enterprise, and put his own head in a noose. He gave no clue to their destination, yet won the obedience of all in the ships' companies.

Whereupon he restored his captains to their commands, as serving the Queen herself through the single person of Captain General Francis Drake.

Having assumed sole command, Drake proceeded to scupper the supply vessels, going on from San Julián with the three fighting craft, his own *Pelican,* and the smaller *Elizabeth* and *Marigold*. By some whim, or perhaps to make the break with the past more complete, he rechristened his flagship, *Golden Hind*.

Golden Hind and the skill of her captain would have measurable effect on the destiny of North America.

When the belated Drake entered Magellan Strait, Martin Frobisher was already putting back, much battered, from his third attempt to find the northern passage around the continent. Drake's three vessels negotiated the 300 miles of the wind-swept southern strait in the remarkable time of sixteen days. They emerged into the stunning blast of northwesterly gales that scattered them, sinking *Marigold*. *Elizabeth,* with John Winter commanding, was blown back into the mouth of the strait and took shelter there.

The advent of Englishmen into the Pacific could not have been more unfortunate. For a month *Elizabeth* clung to her shelter, unable to emerge into the battering winds. Then, losing hope of finding Drake, John Winter turned back. He did not desert his captain, as Gomez deserted Magellan; he believed if he voyaged east to the Moluccas he might chance upon Drake thither bound from the South Sea. It was a long way to such a rendezvous, and a long chance that the two vessels would ever meet. But Winter never reached the rendezvous; his crew forced him to head back to England. In London the master of *Elizabeth* reported his last sight of Drake, driven south in the great storm toward the dark antarctic region.

For a month *Golden Hind* was forced south by the winds of a strength beyond the imagination of her seamen. Driven past what we know to be Cape Horn, she fought for life at 57° south. Drake and his men probably expected to end up on the rocks of *Terra Australis*. They had no charts of this ocean, and at least two of the published maps in the captain's locker, those of Ortelius and Mercator, showed the mighty south continent extending out on either side of Tierra del Fuego, as Magellan had named the land below the strait. *Golden Hind* passed through the shore line on the maps, yet sighted no land.

The region of Cape Horn is inhuman, removed from any familiar sight. The waste of gray water, the sweep of wind from the low broken sky, with the faint sun low in the north, bewilder the human observer. When the sky clears, great winged things, circling albatross and tern, come from nowhere, not drawn toward men, but to the apparition of a ship moving on the water.

In this lost region of the world *Golden Hind* found some shelter in an isle of rock that Drake named the Queen's Land for Elizabeth.

After two months the ship came back, passing the entrance of Magellan Strait. Drake had orders to search for the South Land, but in the ordeal of those two months he had sighted no firm and continent land. He had been among islands where the great oceans merged. Nor was it possible to search farther to the west, in the teeth of the westerly winds. So, with his larders filled with penguin meat, Drake sailed north to look for John Oxenham and the English raiders of the isthmus. Before long he learned from captured Spaniards that Oxenham and his small band were no longer afloat, having been taken prisoner and most of them hanged. In a desperate effort to save Oxenham, Drake released his own captives with messages to the authorities at Lima urging that the Englishmen be spared. The messages had no effect. The raiders were executed as pirates.

If Drake had had his three ships and crews intact, he might still have attempted to seize the bridgehead near Panama that he and Oxenham had planned. But he could not hope to accomplish that with the battered *Golden Hind*. Putting in to a sheltered bay, he beached his vessel for a refit and tallowing. He also pieced together the parts of a pinnace that had been stowed aboard, and hoisted more cannon from the hold to mount on the main deck. This was January of 1579, when *Golden Hind* took to sea as a raider.

The only treasure hunting Drake did was on this leg of his northern cruise, off Peru. He could not have anticipated that it would bring such rich reward, that he would come upon a cargo of silver waiting at the docks of a port, or the galleon *Cacafuego* loitering unsuspecting at sea. Word of the appearance of the English ship had not yet been passed along the coast, and Drake did not linger for a welcome.

With, incredibly, a full shipload of pure silver, gold coins, and jewels he sped north far out from Panama, where he suspected the Spanish forces would be gathering to meet him—as, in fact, they were. He was hurrying to carry out the third part of his mission, to search for the western end of Frobisher's strait.

Francis Drake Visits California

On April 16, 1579, after taking on water and some food at the Guatemala coast, the Devonshire explorer headed his vessel to sea on a westerly bearing, and in so doing sailed out of the historical record. We have only fragmentary English remarks about this long voyage north. These did not come into print for years, until the great Spanish war ended. When *Golden Hind* reached England, the seal of secrecy was laid upon her navigators. On the other hand Spanish captives released by Drake testified as to what he had told them of his plans. But quite clearly the anxious Englishman told the prisoners the opposite of what he really intended to do.

Clearly he had no intention of taking *Golden Hind* back into the tempests of the roaring forties or where vengeful, hostile squadrons would be waiting for him off Peru. Yet why did he make his famous, seemingly futile, cast for more than 3500 miles up to the northwest coast of America? Why, if his real purpose was to head across the Pacific to the East Indies?

Some modern writers explain that Drake had no belief in the existence of a Strait of Anian, and made a token voyage to the north merely to be able to report that he had carried out his orders to search for it. That explanation fits the circumstances, yet it fits the character of a Martin Frobisher more than a Francis Drake.

Probably Drake had no plan at all when he left the coast that April. The man who had told his assembled crews at San Julián, *"I have taken that in hand that I know not in the world how to go through with"* was not following out a route fixed in his mind. He was dealing with circumstances as he met them—as he dealt with the storms off Cape Horn, and the news of a treasure ship, *Cacafuego,* loitering up the coast ahead of him. Now he had no certainty what he might find in the north of America.

By that April he had learned quite a bit about the prevailing winds in this unknown South Sea. By heading out from the isthmus he could escape the northwest winds that came down the coast, and could work into the northeasterly trades. Off Nicaragua he had captured a pair of Spanish pilots who happened to be bound for Panama on their way to take a galleon across the ocean to Manila. The two had refused to pilot Drake, but he had their sailing directions and excellent charts, which would serve him almost as well. Yet if these charts were the usual ones issued to Spanish ships, they showed the outline of the northern coast only as far as Cape Mendocino. Up there in northern California his enemies the Spaniards had no outpost or interest—a fact of which Drake took immediate note.

Beyond that cape, at about 40°, lay only an unexplored void, whether of land or sea. There the end of Asia might appear, as some believed, or the missing Strait of Anian, as Drake had been told. (For map makers in England conjectured that Frobisher's strait ran southerly from the icebound east to the warm South Sea, at about 40°.) Up there Martin Frobisher *might* be waiting for him with English ships.

Now Drake had lost his own consorts; Oxenham was removed from the scene. The man of Devon was alone, facing a terrifying responsibility. His first duty now was to get *Golden Hind* back to England with her twenty-five tons of bullion—a godsend for the lean treasury of England. And if the missing strait should by some chance appear in the coast ahead of him, it would open up the quickest escape route to England, far removed from Spanish pursuit. The alternate route of the South Sea charts, west to Africa, would be three times as long and certainly more hazardous. Must not *Golden Hind* make a quick, sure search for the passage before turning to the escape route across the far oceans?

Above all, if by any chance the passage existed, it would solve England's problem; it would furnish an English route, not only to the spices of the East Indies, but to the treasure portage at Panama that Oxenham and Drake himself had tried to seize. On that narrow neck of land, which he had just passed by, Drake's whole yearning centered. No, he must make certain what lay beyond the horizon on the northern coast, even if the odds were ten to one against the strait's existing, and a hundred to one against Frobisher awaiting him there. On this voyage Francis Drake left no chance untried. Not long before he had ventured to write a letter to the missing John Winter and had entrusted it to—of all persons—the master of the captured *Cacafuego*. "Master Winter, if it pleaseth God you should chance to meet with this ship of Sant Juan Anton . . . although I am in doubt this letter will never come to your hands . . . you will not despair of God's mercy, for he will preserve you and bring us to our desired haven."

By the first of June, Drake was hardly bearing northeast toward an unknown coast merely to carry out a portion of his orders, nor was he making a casual cast to the north during a spectacular predetermined circumnavigation of the earth. He must have been watching, torn with anxiety, on the overage and leaking *Golden Hind,* to see what the coast would disclose. He had headed far west to catch a wind; he had left the route of the charts, to Manila, far astern, and now he had turned in, to close the coast. Suddenly the air had turned bitter cold—or so it seemed after the tropical heat of the last months—and his ship drove through mist into sleety rain.

His men were discouraged and ill after the long sea leg; it took six of them to do the work of three on the sleeted ropes—in spite of his cheering and driving them. And then unexpectedly a dark shore line showed through the mist.

"The land in that part of America," a companion wrote long afterward, "bearing farther out into the West than we imagined, we were nearer on it than we were aware." So Drake had underestimated the width of the continent that he had no means of judging in this northern latitude. Then by so much was the chance of a navigable strait existing across it diminished. (Probably *Golden Hind* made her landfall well up in the modern Oregon.)

They must have put in to the first shelving cove for urgently needed water and wood. Then for a little they kept north along the coast, struggling against head winds, seeking a good anchorage in which repairs could be made. The crew grumbled at the "most vile, thicke and stinking fogges." Until they were forced by the head winds "to cast anchor in a bad bay, the best roade we could for the present meete with." This bay obviously would not serve to careen and refit the leaking *Golden Hind*. They waited there enveloped in fog. The wind that cleared the air at times penned the ship in her anchorage.

By their reckoning they had sighted the coast at 42° and had turned north for a space. Then or later some of them claimed sight of snow on the hills, and one report gives 48° as their turning point; this would have taken them past the great estuary of the Columbia River, of which no mention is made. At that point snow might have been visible on the inland peaks, while in clear weather the snow peak of Shasta could have been seen south of 42°. But the tale of the snow may have been the invention of disgruntled men. The crew had experienced such winds and wintry cold the year before off Magellan's strait, when it was summer by their calendar. Now in the north of the unknown America they met with the same ominous chill in the early days of June—a sign, by their reckoning, that they were nearing the arctic.

What Drake thought of it is not recorded. At the "bad bay" he was north of his objective, the conjectured entrance to the Strait of Anian. Probably the captured Spanish charts did not show this coast so far north. And if he took stock of the published maps of Ortelius and Mercator—he must have been dubious about those after failing to find their *Terra Australis* in the far south—he would have found the legendary Quivira, and a large river marked on this coast at 40°—well to the south of his anchorage.

His first need was to careen and repair the 120-ton hull of his ship. And he had scant time left to do that, and find and negotiate any passage leading northerly to Frobisher's realm of ice. In both voyages the experienced Frobisher had been careful to get clear of his strait before the end of summer.

Whatever his reasoning, Drake wasted no more time, but headed south before the wind from his "bad bay." This could hardly have been as far up as the Columbia entrance. (Possibly there is a clue to its position, little noticed. After Drake's return to England, John Dee completed a map of America for the Queen, and on it the Pacific coast is drawn with surprising accuracy, perhaps the result of Drake's observations and the captured Spanish charts. In any case Dee's remarkable effort shows the California coast with Cape Mendocino, and ends abruptly midway through modern Oregon, just short of 44°.)

For some ten days *Golden Hind* followed the coast down, past her landfall, past the given latitude of Anian—and the "Quivira" of the maps—sighting only low hills turning from green to a strange brown, and no sign of a strait, river, or port. Then the weary Englishmen, wondering why the summer should be chill and the grass brown in this strange world, sighted white cliffs that reminded them of the cherished cliffs of Dover. There at last they entered "a convenient and fit harborough." (This was not, apparently, San Francisco Bay; it appears to have been a small bay near Point Reyes more than twenty-five miles north of San Francisco; by Drake's reckoning it was at 38°30'.)

Drake made thrifty use of the two weeks he spent at the haven in California. The hard beach served to careen *Golden Hind* for calking her timbers. Her cargo, unloaded, was tented against storms that did not eventuate, and the camp was guarded by a trench and stone wall against an attack that did not come. He added mussels, seal meat, and native root meal to his larder. Exploring parties went inland, finding the ground plagued with gophers, which the Eng-

lishmen called conies, and thick with deer. "The inland we found
to be farre different from the shoare, a goodly country and fruitfull
soyle, stored with many blessings fit for the use of man."

The summer weather in this northern California never ceased
to puzzle the interested Englishmen, accustomed as they were to
the moist warmth and bloom of June in their homeland. Fogs
rolled in, preventing taking observations of the sun; afternoon sea
winds chilled them until they longed for winter clothing or their
beds. Among themselves the men arrived at an explanation of this
phenomenon, which may not have been their captain's idea. A little
north of them, they conjectured, the continents of America and
Asia merged or leaned toward each other. They had seen snow on
the summits up the coast. Well, there must be ranges of snow
mountains up where the continents came together, and so the northwest wind, blowing thence, carried the cold of the snow. They did
not think the strait existed.

More than the gophers, the native Californians troubled the
seamen of Devon. In greater numbers each day the native people
thronged down from the hills, to admire and watch the supermen
from the house on the sea; each day they brought gifts—even the
children carrying some feathers or down or tobacco herbs, which
meant nothing to the Englishmen, ignorant as yet of pipes and
smoking. Their obvious worship of the white men (which showed
that they had met no others) disturbed Drake's company, especially
when the women took to tearing their faces and beating their bodies
on the ground as a sign of humiliation before the godlike strangers.

The Englishmen discovered very quickly that psalm singing
interested the Californians, and put a stop to the tedious ritual of
greeting, women "sacrifice," and gift giving. "In the time of singing
of Psalmes, they sat very attentively; observing the end of every
pause they cried with one voice, *Oh,* greatly rejoicing in our exer-
cises. Yea, they took such pleasure in our singing that whensoever
they resorted to us, their first request was commonly *Gnaah,* by
which they intreated that we would sing."

Not only that, the sailors had to bandage sores, and give out
medicine for native ailments. Drake was very patient in cultivating

the good-will of the Californians, although he took precautions
against attack—having been wounded in the face himself by two
Indian arrows on an island off Peru. He made the visitors leave their
bows outside the palisade. Even when the natives were unarmed,
the Englishmen judged the tall men of the country to be a match
in strength for two seamen.

Drake had made good use of the *cimarrones* on the isthmus; he
would make alliance with the sultan of Ternate in the far Indies.
It was important, at that time, to gain the friendship of the strange
people of the New World who might aid English voyagers in the
future.

When he discovered that the Californians kept some rude political order—sending "ambassadors" in advance with gifts, clothing a
"king's" bodyguard with feathers and conie-skin cowls—he paraded
himself rather ostentatiously, accepting their greeting as homage.
"In the name of her most excellent Majesty, he tooke the crowne
and dignity of the sayd countrie into his hand, as it was now her
proper owne . . . and the riches thereof might be attained there."

He had a reason for this showman's act of taking the fealty of
"so tractable and loving a people." The country he named *Nova
Albion*. In some way he was convinced that "the Spaniards never
so much as set foot in this country, the utmost of their discoveries
reaching only to many degrees Southward of this place." That was
true enough, although how the English knew it is hard to say.

Before now Francis Drake had made use of hidden harbors to
refit his vessels and serve as a base for raids against enemy shipping.
Did he believe his small bay in New Albion would serve as a hidden
Pacific base? Or did he think of it as an English post not far from
the missing Strait of Anian—if that should be found to exist? Then,
too, China might not be so far away. In any case, not having found
the passage, he could say that he had found a friendly country at
New Albion.

"Before we went from thence our General caused to be set up
a monument of our being there, as also of her Majesties right to that
kingdom; namely a plate of brasse fast nailed to a great post,
whereon is engraved her grace's name, and the day and yeare of
our arrival there."

And this plate may have been found today. Near the Laguna River by Drake's bay a battered plaque came to light, bearing such an inscription, with the patina of age upon it. When tested by metallurgists, it proved to be an alloy of earlier centuries, hammered out by hand, not rolled by machinery. This is either Drake's "monument" or the work of a jester of genius who has kept silence for twenty-odd years about his share in the find. It is cherished as genuine at the University of California, overlooking the San Francisco Bay that Drake seemingly never entered.

When *Golden Hind* was afloat again, with treasure and cargo shipped, Drake found that his friends of the shore grieved at his departure. So the Timucuas of Florida had bewailed the departure of Dominique de Gourgues. Drake, however, gave no promise to return. Instead the English visitors staged a last "exercise" of prayer and psalm singing that served to distract the Indians.

"They tooke a sorrowfull farewell of us. But being loath to leave us, they presently ranne to the tope of the hills to keepe us in their sight as long as they could, making fires as sacrifices (as we supposed) at our departure."

Whether fog hid the entrance to San Francisco Bay, or whether Drake was not willing to put back to explore another haven, *Golden Hind* bore away to the Farallones, pausing there to take aboard more seal and bird meat. Then she set out on her long voyage home.

No other English ship was to follow Drake's course to the northwest of America for two centuries. His appearance in the Pacific, however, caused some searching of the California coast by Spanish men-of-war. Five years later a naval officer, Francisco de Gali, bringing in the yearly galleon from Manila, bore to the north to Cape Mendocino. Thence he ran the California coast south, looking for a good harbor where a Spanish guard post might be set up. Like the other explorers, he failed to notice San Francisco Bay, and picked on Monterey Bay as suitable for an anchorage, supplying fresh water, fish, and timber. But nothing was done about that at the time.

When Thomas Cavendish came around on Drake's track in

1586–87, he was bent on raiding for profit, not exploring. This Elizabethan visitor found the coast of Peru guarded against Englishmen; keeping to the Spanish shipping lanes in the south, he picked up a Manila galleon with Chinese goods by chance, and went on to complete the fastest circumnavigation of the earth. But when Cavendish tried to repeat his feat after the war years, his fleet was decimated by the guns of his enemies and by storms off *Tierra del Fuego.* Cavendish never got back to England.

The last of the Elizabethan Englishmen to follow Drake's track was Richard Hawkins, the only son of Sir John (for these early voyagers had been knighted by their queen after the time of the Armada). Richard was brought to bay in his ship, *Dainty,* by Spanish patrol fleets. For in the trade winds of the broad Pacific the Spanish galleons could outsail the smaller English craft. Young Hawkins had hoped to explore the south Pacific route to the Moluccas, paying his way, as Drake had done, with captured silver. But that could no longer be done. Cornered off the coast of Peru, the son of Sir John fought his ship for three days, stirring the admiration of the chivalrous Spanish officers when he answered their demand to surrender after two days: "Came we into the Pacific to raise a flag of truce?" When taken alive, he was held captive, because they would not release a navigator who had learned so much of the Pacific routes.

This route by Magellan's strait proved to be too long and hazardous for the English. No Strait of Anian appeared, and "Quivira" faded into a myth of the maps. Drake's Nova Albion became no more than a name.

The Pacific itself remained in the grip of Spanish sea power, to be invaded at length by the Dutch, not the English, and in the far Indies, not upon the American coast.

California was destined to be explored by missionaries of later generations instead of the conquistadors and voyagers.

While the western coast of North America was left in this peaceful isolation, the conflict of the sea powers in the Atlantic drew closer to the eastern coast.

Then Golden Hind *Came Home*

The half-taught Elizabethan voyagers were learning their sea-craft only by hard experience. They had, however, one peculiarity. They never learned that they had failed in their "search and discovery of the most unknown quarters of the world."

Their stubborn effort did not gain the results they hoped for. But it did gain unexpected results. To the end of the century the Elizabethan voyagers failed to master any one of the four ways to Cathay; instead they found the way to Christian habitation on New England. *Meta Incognita* remained a name, an unknown destination in the frozen seas, and never became the hoped-for new Queen's Land; that would be in the south, and would be named after her, Virginia. Nor did the English capture the strategic Panama isthmus, key to the Spanish world trade route. Instead they made the sea route to North America, above the Spanish zone, their own.

To begin the two years of disaster, stout Martin Frobisher met with complete check in his third try for the northwest passage. This was the most costly effort of the Elizabethans. Fifteen assorted vessels carried mixed companies of soldiers, miners, "goldfiners," and housebuilders. Frobisher himself carried sadly mixed orders, to fetch ore in all vessels, to explore his strait further, and to set up a fortified colony if habitable land could be found on a shore of the strait. But he knew very well that his Company of Cathay wanted nothing but a fortune in gold. The naïve folk in London had succumbed to gold fever.

This gold-mining flotilla got lost in miserable weather. Frobisher's compass gyrated wildly, close to the Magnetic Pole, and mist veiled the low sun. If the sky cleared at night, the ever-present sun dimmed the Pointers of the North Star. Frobisher lost his bearings, and wandered into a wide waterway he named the "Mistaken Strait" (actually Hudson Strait).

But he had with him Captain Edward Fenton. And Fenton

took a pinnace—ignoring the warning of the carpenters who put it together that its hull was only "held by nails"—for 200 miles up the new waterway. It seemed to offer more promise than Frobisher's old waterway. However, they abandoned this search to return to Frobisher's strait and load the laboring vessels haphazard with rock along its shore. While doing this the great ship carrying all equipment for the insanely planned colony was lost in crushing ice. Snow drifted down on the vessels and ice formed around them at night. Although Fenton volunteered to attempt a settlement with sixty men for the winter, Frobisher wisely overruled him. A test building was erected hastily, to determine what the winter cold of *Meta Incognita* would do to it—when the expedition should return the next year. Frobisher still had hopes of the new passage they had probed. But he never came back.

Before his fleet regained England, the bubble of the gold speculation had burst. The ore was admitted to be worthless, bankrupting the Company of Cathay, and impoverishing its chief backer, Michael Lok, who had spent his fortune and pledged his credit to pay for the outfitting of the fleet.

With the ending of this search to the northwest a desperate try was made for the old route to the northeast. Naval officers planned it this time—William Borough drawing the charts. News came in that Francis Drake was in the Pacific. With luck and the providence of the Lord two vessels might find the way around the north of Cathay and join Drake in the East Indies, to aid him home to England. (The old illusion persisted that the warmth of the Gulf current around Norway would be found to the eastward.)

One of the masters, Pett, brought his vessel home after battering without avail at the arctic ice. The other, Jackman, had turned back for a second try and vanished without trace. "Winds we have at will," Pett's journal of the northern voyage explained laconically, "but ice and fog too much against our wills." Beyond any doubt the northeastern way to Cathay was closed. As if to expel the stubborn Englishmen from Asia entire, the land route failed as well at this time. A thin network of Muscovy Company traders had been gleaning some silk and jade and oddments from China by way of the caravan routes—the ancient Silk Road—to Persia. To do that, they had sailed the inland sea, the Caspian, and strained to reach Bokhara amid "sundry dangers." Now outbreak of war between the mighty Turkish Empire and Persia ended that traffic. The Muscovy Company stagnated, and out of its remains was formed a new Turkish joint-stock company, to drive with armed merchantmen straight through the Mediterranean to the markets of Constantinople, for the Turks were active enemies of the great antagonist of England, Philip II.

In this crisis of 1578–80 some amateur strategists among the Elizabethans longed to try their strength against the Spanish plate fleets. What exploring of unknown routes, they argued, could equal the profit of capturing a single treasure ship? But the Queen's ministers—especially Burghley—would allow no such act of war on the high seas. By the concepts of that time a skirmish between ships in the far-off Americas was outside the sphere of sovereignty, but an attack in Spanish waters would be an insult to His Catholic Majesty of Spain. Had not Philip himself explained to the French Crown that the Huguenots at the River of May had been punished, not as vassals of France, but as robbers? Elizabeth herself saw in peace the only safeguard for England.

Two zealous soldiers from battlefields in Ireland and the Netherlands, Sir Humphrey Gilbert and his half brother Walter Ralegh, pooled their money to outfit raiders, while Sir Humphrey wrote an appeal to Elizabeth—*A Discourse how Her Majesty may annoy the King of Spain*. His naïve plan was to capture the Spanish, Portuguese, and Catholic French fishermen off the Newfoundland bank, and with this profit of a year's supply of fish, to raid Spanish convoys on his own responsibility. This served only to annoy Elizabeth, although she had a fondness for both the impetuous Sir Humphrey and the charming Walter Ralegh. The project of raiding Newfoundland died—yet lingered in Gilbert's mind—and the two soldier-seamen sailed into the Atlantic in silence and on their own responsibility. Their ships returned empty, badly battered, and without explanation.

It seems that the Gilbert-Ralegh squadron had found a plate

fleet escorted by galleons of the new Indies Guard. Then, too, the more experienced Spaniards were sending a new type of vessel to sea, the *gallizabras*—frigates swift enough to escape from hostile galleons, yet powerful enough to beat off piratical small craft. The Spanish hold on the Atlantic was tightening; the English were being penned again into their own narrow seas. The "British Impire" of visionary Dr. Dee appeared more than ever to be a fantastic dream.

Just then Walsingham, supporter of Drake and well-wisher of Gilbert, sent a Portuguese pilot, Simon Fernandes, to make a hurried survey of the American coast around Newfoundland. What lay behind Fernandes's mission was not revealed.

After that, in mid-1580, ominous news arrested the attention of all English seafarers. A Spanish army had entered Lisbon, and Philip was proclaimed King of Portugal as well as of Spain. This meant the unification of the Iberian sea powers, and the end of the old papal Line of Demarcation of the oceans. It gave to Madrid mastery of all the outer seas.

Then, in September, *Golden Hind* came home to Plymouth. Two years and ten months she had been away, circling the world, and she brought an undreamed-of cargo of tons of bullion and other tons of precious cloves from the East Indies. She brought new hope to England. Characteristically Elizabeth rewarded Drake with inexpensive knighthood, while she contrived to keep the Spanish silver and peace with Spain as well.

The tale of the fortunate survivors of *Golden Hind* echoed through the taverns and dockyards of England. How they had found the great South Sea, how they had made their claim to a New Albion and, beyond all, how they had hoisted the silver bars out of *Cacafuego* became the tale of the new hope.

Characteristically the Elizabethan strategists of enterprise reacted to the new Spanish monopoly of the seas by sending forth new fleets. Steadfast Edward Fenton, who had offered to wait out the winter on Frobisher's strait, was dispatched with a large force to venture back on Drake's track along the—now hostile—Portuguese route to the East Indies. He did not get far. The attraction of American treasure for his crews and officers overcame any will-

ingness to open a new trade route. Most of Fenton's squadron disappeared into the west. In fact he himself was taken west by his
officers to raid Brazil. John Drake, nephew of Sir Francis, disappeared into the Plate River, and failed to return to England.

Two skilled seamen, John Hawkins and a kinsman, crossed
with their ships to Drake's isthmus. John Hawkins was at home in
the Caribbean. The pair returned with a rich lading of American
products, pearls, sugar, dyewood. These, the Hawkinses explained,
were got in the way of trade, and as for the pearls, their sailors had
learned to dive like the natives for the shellfish. Perhaps it was all
true.

Young Richard Hakluyt, who had taken Eden's place as chronicler of the voyages to the New World, pleaded for a garrison
colony to be planted in Magellan's strait, to hold open Drake's route
to the South Sea. But the Queen's ministers forbade that. The route
by the south of America could not be tried again, with the menace
of war drawing closer to home. The way by the south of Africa
was closed, because the Portuguese, while disliking Philip's rule,
adhered to Spain against England. The third route, around Russia,
did not exist. And search for the northern passage around America
had brought only loss.

Then Sir Humphrey Gilbert brought forth his patent, to "discover and inhabit at his choice all remote and heathen lands not in
actual possession of any Christian prince." That is, not in the possession of Philip II of Spain.

He was allowed to start, and proceeded with all his impetuosity to do so.

VII. Utopia and the New Land

Sir Humphrey Gilbert's Reason Why

THE patent he had from the hand of Queen Elizabeth was not, as it is often said to be, the first charter of the British Empire. Other Tudors had handed such grants to other voyagers, John Cabot being one. Those pieces of parchment had come to nothing. Gilbert's cherished document was rather the first charter of an English America.

It contained two words, *"to inhabit."* Until then the incentive of the English seafarers had been to take some position across the western road to Asia. Now appeared the incentive to occupy a new land across the Atlantic. Master Edward Hayes, owner and captain of Gilbert's flagship, put it in these words. This would be a voyage, he believed, to accomplish what others had neglected to carry out— "exact discovery into the bowels of those maine, ample and vast countreys . . . neither hath a right way bene taken of planting a Christian habitation and regiment upon the same."

The French, in the opinion of honest Master Hayes, who relied chiefly on the Bible for his authority, had been prevented from settling the American coast by their "garboils" at home, while the efforts of the Spaniards to do so north of 30° had been brought to nothing by the manifest providence of God.

Moreover his hero and commander, Sir Humphrey, argued that

the rogues and beggars of English villages could be carried over to do useful work on this new soil of England. "Also we might settle there such needy people of our countrey which now trouble the common wealth and through want here at home are inforced to commit outrageous offenses whereby they are dayly consumed with the gallowes . . . also, we shall set poor mens children to learne handie craftes and thereby to make trifles and such like which the Indians and those people do much esteeme: by reason whereof there should be none occasion to have our countrey cumberd with loiterers, vagabonds and such like idle persons."

For the first time little is said about finding gold or other treasure—although Sir Humphrey had ideas of his own about that. Though the riches of the new country were few, he argued, still timber and turpentine, resin and tar could be had, to build new ships for England. That argument carried weight in 1583. It drew to Gilbert's aid such strong personalities as Walsingham and Ralegh.

An Elizabethan voyage such as this was no happenstance exploit of the dynamic sea rovers so often found in modern fiction. It was paid for by shillings from private purses and launched to meet a nation's need. To pay for this voyage, Sir Humphrey "had taken the clothes off his wife's back."

His backers pondered the vital question, where should Sir Humphrey plant his people? Surely above the Spanish possessions, but where?

By now they had accounts of the Verrazano voyage, and Cartier's; young Hakluyt had just published his research on the new continents—*Divers voyages touching the discoverie of America and the Ilands adjacent . . . And certaine notes . . . for such as shall heereafter make the like attempt*. They had new maps, the pioneer work of English hands, and these reveal to us a little of the reasoning of the Elizabeth strategists of enterprise.

For one thing, Asia no longer extends across to the New World. The mythical *Terra Australis* no longer waits below Magellan's strait. (Drake, and possibly Frobisher as well, may be responsible for that.) The two great continents stand apart from the others in English eyes. Broken islands fill the arctic and antarctic regions. The northern continent, sea-girt on every side, would be a proper habitation for a maritime people like the English.

More than that, the three newest maps—of Dr. Dee and Michael Lok and Gilbert himself—reveal a notable and startling attraction to seafarers. The nebulous North America is a country of great waterways. Of the three John Dee's map is the most accurate. It almost seems as if this remarkable alchemist of discovery had looked into the future when he made it. Yet his map has the St. Lawrence offering a navigable waterway far inland, as far as the actual Rocky Mountains! Gilbert's sketch makes Newfoundland comfortably secure as an island, adjacent to a vast St. Lawrence which runs conveniently into a broad strait which quite severs the north from Spanish Mexico and Florida.

Michael Lok's map, finished in his debtors' prison, follows Gilbert's in scheme, with many wistful details added. It keeps the sanctuary of St. Brendan's Isle, with the Demons' Isle in the Atlantic —may they not still be found?—and it christens the shores of Frobisher's strait with the names of Elizabeth and Lok. It ends in the northwest with the Sierra Nevada (seen by Drake) and, to banish all doubt, shows a ship sailing by, with the inscription "hence it is 50 days to the Moluccas." Lok adds a flourish with the note that here went the voyages of the Portuguese, 1520, the Spaniards, 1540, and the English, 1580. This leaves the impression that the future belongs to the English. And he was not so wide of the mark, at that.

The map was Lok's last contribution to the great enterprise, and Dee's as well, for the enigmatic Welsh philosopher took his books and himself to Bohemia, to indulge in his mathematical dreams. Gilbert and Ralegh took up the tasks they laid down.

Now these wish-fulfillment maps appear ludicrous compared to the splendid Padrón Real at Seville. Yet they reflect the reality, unknown to the Europeans, of the great lakes far inland. Gilbert's fanciful river system leading from Newfoundland to the Gulf of California may be a reflection of Indian tales, but is more probably his answer to the argument of the Russia-minded explorers, that if the northeastern salt-water route did not exist, the rivers of Russia might lead to Cathay. So the rivers on Gilbert's map of America lead to the South Sea.

Certainly Spanish observers did not find the efforts of the stubborn English to be ludicrous. Already Don Bernardino de Mendoza, ambassador, had written to his king: "I have men watching this shipmaster . . . to know what is Onpegilberto's [Humphrey Gilbert's] aim . . . and I have plans well advanced for getting hold of Jorvirger's [Frobisher's] sailing chart."

The promoters of Gilbert's enterprise did their best to get first-hand information of the American coast. They unearthed David Ingram, one of the three survivors of the seamen who had been left ashore long since by John Hawkins and who had taken their chances with the Indians. David Ingram insisted he had walked 2000 miles of the continent, to be picked up by the French vessel of the fishing grounds. Yes, he maintained, he had seen plenty of turquoises, and elephants, too; he had walked by a mighty inland sea for two days; he had visited the court of a native king who sat on a silver throne shining with jewels. Yes, Hochelaga was a great town . . .

Of those who listened to Ingram young Hakluyt later rejected his story as incredible; Gilbert seemed to hope that the silver and riches might be found. (It may well be that Ingram's tale of his walk through the unknown continent had grown in the telling during his dozen years at home thereafter; his neighbors in England would expect to hear of at least a few wonders—of elephants rather than bison. But the inexperienced Elizabethans were making the mistake of so many Europeans in believing that all the desirable products of the American coast could be found in one place. Moreover they assumed that since food seemed to be plentiful among the Indians, it could be had in the way of trade at all times, which was not the case. The Indian communities seldom had a reserve laid by for winter.)

These searchers for a new England took the testimony of one visitor to America who relished a jest. Anthony Parkhurst, a gentleman of Kent, had commuted thither some years with the fishing fleets, to make his own proof of all that he had read and heard tell. The seeds he planted there all grew and flourished, said Anthony

Parkhurst; he found the firs straight and tall enough to make masts for ships; as for fish, why he could sweep them up with a broom where they tumbled out of the surf, without wetting his feet. Even his mastiff dog hauled them away from the water. Why, with such plenty of flounder, cod, smelt, and lobster he could feed a regiment —not to mention the wild cherries and pears, or the oysters that grew on the trees! And every oyster had its pearl.

"The Squid I say—when I please to be merry with my old companions—have a nature that comes by night—so I tell them I set him a candle to see his way, with which he is much delighted. . . . There are Duckes, wild Geese and many other kind of birde, especially at one Island named Penguin, where we may drive them on a plank into our ship, as many as shall lade her."

While Anthony Parkhurst may be the pioneer of Yankee fish yarns, he had some facts behind his disarming fiction. His oysters and mussels clung to tree branches and roots that were under water; his penguins *may* have been herded up a gangplank into the ship's larder. "Now to let these merrie tales pass, and to come to earnest matters"—the icy cold of the coast he believed to be caused by the drifting ice; inland regions were warmer. There was a fine harbor in the Bay of the Castles. There were iron and copper as well in the Newfoundland hills. In warmer regions he believed that salt could be made by the sun's heat, and more precious metals found. Belle Isle could be settled and fortified, and "we shall be lordes of the whole fishing in small time—if it do so please the Queene's Majestie."

It did please Sir Humphrey's imagination. Yet there was hard common sense in the argument of his sponsors to the practical merchants of Bristol (whence vessels had sought the western lands for a century). All the shipbuilding materials they traded from the Russians at Archangel could be found near Newfoundland. All the products of the Mediterranean could be grown on the American coast to the south. If not on the coast, then in the "hindmost parts." And did not the French carry on a paying trade in furs at their river of Canada?

It can be seen that the backers of the new enterprise were drawn to favor the north rather than the southern coast. The "trade way," as Master Hayes calls it, to Newfoundland was shortest; its advantages were known. "We ought to shape a course most likely to minister to [our] supply. At that time of year a multitude of ships repairing thither for fish, we should be relieved abundantly with many necessaries."

In a soft gale of wind five ships with 260 men departed from Causet Bay June 11, 1583. "Our voyage undertaken with Sir Humfrey Gilbert," Master Hayes added regretfully, "began, continued, and ended adversely."

The Port of the Fishermen

Master Hayes sensed the beginning of the trouble in this enterprise of the English nation. While its commander, Sir Humphrey, was both "vertuous and heroycal," he could not keep discipline among his people. Most of them were strangers to salt water, being ex-soldiers and miners. Some Channel pirates had been released from jail to make the voyage. Almost at the start the largest ship, supplied by Walter Ralegh, deserted. Of the two small craft, *Squirrel* proved to be unhandy, being overloaded topside with cannon. *Swallow* parted company in a fog to plunder fishing craft. (The pillagers from the Channel were little disposed to labor at a settlement.)

The chief trouble was caused by the length of the voyage. Owing to their late start, the voyagers missed the favoring winds after the equinox; for seven weeks the vessels ranged north and south to escape head winds. The three remaining vessels limped in to the rendezvous at St. John's with their people sick and wearied. One ran aground in the narrow entrance of the sheltered harbor.

There, however, they found a strange community of fishermen at home. Thirty-six sail, Portuguese, Spanish, French, and English filled the bay. Huts and frames for drying fish lined the shore. In fact these armed fisherfolk would not suffer the discovery fleet to

enter until Sir Humphrey sent in a boat with his letters of authority
from the Queen.

Luckily the English fishing crews were "admirals" or rulers of
this maritime summer colony. They received the letters with good-
will—fired a salvo of welcome, and sent out small craft to tow the
stranded vessel from the rocks. As Parkhurst had predicted and as
Sir Humphrey had hoped, the mariners from Bristol, St. Malo, and
Viana had organized the harbor base and supplied themselves well.
Straightaway Sir Humphrey commandeered supplies for his ailing
expedition. Each day the fishermen sent over the choicest things,
wines and marmalade, fresh salmon and lobsters. And fat partridges
and raspberries from the shore.

Even the methodical Master Hayes was struck by the singu-
larity of this country; for beyond the comfortable village there was
only wild animal life and wild growth untouched by the hand of
husbandman. The fishers took him to view their Garden, as they
called it, but he found there only brambleberries and the natural
flowers of the place. It cheered him greatly to hear that the Portugals had filled an island, Sable Island, with swine to breed and
peas to harvest.

Sir Humphrey's sanguine spirit rose to the occasion; he set
forth claim in the name of the Queen's Majesty to all land within
200 leagues around; he set surveyors and plan makers to work, and
he set his mineral finder, a German named Daniel, to search for
ores. One act of discipline he carried out, sending home the lawless
Swallow (which had rejoined the fleet) with the sick and disaffected of his people. In the frigate *Squirrel* he inspected the
forested coast of his Newfoundland. Meanwhile to his joy the in-
dustrious Daniel brought him discoveries of ore, both copper and
silver. Or so Daniel said.

Master Hayes, who was ill at the time, did not feel so sanguine
about the finds of metal. The copper seemed to him to be iron, and
he doubted the silver. He asked the opinion of his "General."

"Content yourself," Sir Humphrey assured him, "I have seen
enough. Touching the ore, I have sent it aboard [*Delight*] whereof
I would have no speech to be made so long as we remain within

harbor—here being Portugals, Biscains [Biscayans] and Frenchmen not farre off, from whom must be kept any muttering of such matter."

Odd that in this same spot forty-one years before Jacques Cartier and Roberval had argued so hotly over the ore found on the St. Lawrence.

With Daniel's specimens of silver hidden away on *Delight* and the storms of autumn at hand, Sir Humphrey had to decide what the discoverers would do next, and he evolved a plan to meet all his needs. The malcontents among his people—who were slipping away to the fishing craft now departing for England—he would allow to go back with the Bristol vessels. This Newfoundland he had surveyed and claimed; now he would avoid the storms and lay claim to other unknown lands by turning south with his three remaining vessels. Once at sea, safe from taletelling, he would have tests made of the ores. If the silver proved to be fine, as he hoped, then they would head for England with the news. (And perhaps raid Spanish shipping on the way.)

Neither Drake nor Cartier would have indulged in such wishful thinking. Master Hayes, who thought only of the handling of ships, was well content to leave the hazardous coast. They commandeered supplies for the winter from the departing fishing fleet, and put to sea on a southern course. They left Cape Race behind, and they were off Cape Breton Island when Master Hayes sensed the storm coming from the north.

It was a fair and pleasant evening, he recalls, and on his ship, *Golden Hind* (named after Drake's famous ship), the crew had harpooned a porpoise. On the larger *Delight* the would-be colonists had amused themselves by sounding off trumpets, fifes, and drums.

That night the helmsmen fancied they heard voices crying at them from the dark sky. Master Hayes told them it was no more than the wind. It came on the ships with rain and mist; it drove them on into shoals where white spray flung up until the lookouts cried that it was land ahead. Visibility dimmed to a cable's length and Hayes, keeping his lead line sounding, bore away and tried to signal the heavier *Delight* to come into the wind.

Golden Hind fought away from the shoals in the heavy sea, and *Squirrel* followed. They saw *Delight* strike, and her stern break in.

With the large transport most of the colonists were lost with all the plans of Newfoundland, supplies of food, and the trove of silver ore. A dozen seamen got away from the wreck in the pinnace, and found their way back to St. John's, thence to voyage safely in a fishing bark to France.

With the two surviving crews pinched by hunger Sir Humphrey gave in to their beseeching and headed home for England. "I will set you forth royally next Spring, if God send us safe home," he promised Master Hayes. For the first time the captain of the *Hind* doubted the wisdom of his hero. It seemed to Hayes that they should keep on toward the southern coast of America. The ebullient Sir Humphrey pledged him that next year they would outfit two fleets, one to seek the southern coast, one to settle Newfoundland. Master Hayes doubted they could find the money for that. "Leave that to me—I will ask a pennie of no man. I will bring good tidings unto her Majesty, who will be so gracious to lend me ten thousand pounds."

Troubled by this wild assurance, Master Hayes judged that his commander counted upon the discovery of silver ore to win such a loan from the penurious queen. But the ore itself was lost, with Daniel, who had found it. Master Hayes mistrusted Sir Humphrey's fervency of mind, but left the issue to be decided by God's will.

Again, in mid-ocean with the Azores south of them, he saw signs of a storm gathering. Some of his crew said they beheld on the main yard an apparition of a small fire in the darkness. He spoke the *Squirrel,* urging his general to come aboard the *Hind.* But Sir Humphrey would not have it said that he feared the sea. "I will not forsake my little company going homeward, with whom I have passed so many storms."

The seas ran heavy, breaking short and high, Master Hayes relates. "Munday the ninth of September, in the afternoon the Frigat [*Squirrel*] was neere cast away, oppressed by waves, yet at that time recovered. And, giving forth signes of joy, the General sitting abaft with a booke in his hand, cried out to us in the *Hind* so often as we did approach within hearing—'We are as near to heaven by sea as by land' . . . the same Monday night about twelve of the clocke or not long after, the Frigat being ahead of us, suddenly her lights were out, and withall our watch cried, the General was cast away, which was too true. For in that moment the Frigat was swallowed up of the sea. Yet still we looked out all that night, and ever after, untill we arrived upon the coast of England."

As soon as the death of Sir Humphrey was known, his half brother, Walter Ralegh, stepped into his place. With a clearer mind and greater means—as well as influence at Court—Ralegh took over the patent to "discover and inhabit" the eastern coast of North America.

Before the next summer two exploring vessels were at sea. They had an experienced Portuguese pilot and two skilled captains with clear orders to search, not the familiar shores of Newfoundland, but the warmer coast to the south.

Masters Amadas and Barlowe Select an Island

Sixty years before, Verrazano had noticed the odd islands. They stretched out into the ocean like a natural breakwater. The cape at the outermost point where the Hatorask (Hatteras) people dwelt rose like a lighthouse battered by winds and spray.

This chain of islands sheltered the shallow sounds lying between them and the mainland. Over them waterfowl swarmed. On their sandy soil red cedars screened the people from the winds; a tangle of flower growth and wild grapes added scent to the fragrant cedars. The Algonkian families who had taken refuge upon the islands in a forgotten time possessed food in plenty. They planted maize and some beans, gathering in harvests from July to September. Pumpkins and gourds grew rank, and the hunters killed only what they needed of the swarming geese and ducks—or the animals between harvests. The shallow waters yielded fish and shellfish at all times.

It was seldom necessary for the weapon-bearing men of the islands to raid the larger harvests of the forested mainland. There in the forests the hunting people were dangerous enemies as far as the blue mountains. On the other hand the forest folk, who dreaded the sudden storms of the sea, could make only clumsy attempts to invade the islands. From the Bending Island (*Wakakan*) to Shell Island (*Roanoac*) the people lived quietly in scattered houses, having no desire for change. On one hand they had the barrier of the dark coast with its river trails, on the other hand the mystery of the great water, home of the unseen Mantoak gods.

They held memories, often discussed, of the clothed men who had passed by in floating houses on the great water. One house had been blown ashore, in the memory of older men. For a part of one moon the clothed men cast on the shore had lived among the families of Roanoac, and then they had tried to go back to the sea in a pair of tree boats of the village. Something had happened to them out on the sea because their two tree canoes had been found on the shore, empty. The visitors from the sea must have returned to the abode of the Mantoak; they could not have died, being spirit men of the Mantoak, who do not die . . . and there had been a priest, clothed in black, who landed and went away again.

Then one man of Wakakan, seeking fish before the first harvest of a year, sighted two of the dwellings of the men of the sea coming in. They came into the bay where he waited expectantly.

Far out at sea the Englishmen on the two small vessels had sniffed the fragrance of the forest. "The second of July," reported Master Arthur Barlowe, "we found shole water, where we smelt so sweet a smell as if we had been in the midst of some garden, by which we were assured that the land could not be farre distant."

They were skilled seamen—Simon Fernandes, the pilot who had made that swift survey of Newfoundland, Philip Amadas, master, Arthur Barlowe, master, and John Winter, who had sailed with Drake. Ralegh was not with them, being held at the Queen's side. Fernandes had brought them across the track of the southern trades and up the Gulf current, keeping away from Spanish ports. He knew they were drawing into the façade of the unknown continent that stretched 500 leagues from St. Augustine to the shoals where *Delight* had broken up.

Closing the coast and slackening sail, they headed north until a cape rose upon the horizon, and they turned into the first inlet, to find themselves anchored in the lee of Wakakan Island near Hatteras. Cramped by the weeks on shipboard, they took delight in the luxuriant growth where grapevines spread into the sand of the beach and climbed the high cedars. They went through the usual act of claiming it for their Queen's Most Excellent Majesty, and fired a volley from their arquebuses that startled the waterfowl into flight "with such a cry as if an armie of men had shouted all together."

They searched for a trace of inhabitants, anxious to arrive at a truce with any dwellers on this American shore, now the land of the Queen. (Master Hayes of the *Hind* had told them how the savage folk of Newfoundland had forsaken the bay of St. John's after the Christians built their huts.) They had orders, as well, to find a secure haven where people could be planted and fed within a short sail of the homeward route of the Spanish treasure fleets. It was important above all to keep the friendship and gain the products of the native folk.

The first native who paddled up in a canoe seemed to be an omen of good relations. He showed no fear of the Englishmen and they gave him wine and meat, with a shirt and hat to take away. The man of Wakakan then viewed their two vessels attentively and returned to his own canoe, pushing offshore a little way to fish. "In less than half an houre, he had laden his boat as deep as it could float, with which he came again to the lande, and there divided his fish into two parts, pointing one part to the ship, the other to the pinnesse. After he had as much as he might requited his benefits received, he departed out of our sight."

This good omen marked the days of exploration and meeting. The chieftain of the island chain gladly exchanged his coral and deerskins for English tin plates and copper kettles; the giant cedars yielded trunks that could be squared to four feet (being trees of the

primitive American forest before the advent of destructive tools).
Fragrant sassafras seemed as precious to Elizabeth's seamen as incense of Araby (had not Drake loaded his *Golden Hind* with
cloves?). They feasted on fruit and grape juice and the fish of their
joyful Indian hosts (who were generous with the first harvest). The
great oaks of the mainland forest were stout as English oak.

Having no interpreter to explain their good-will, Messrs.
Amadas and Barlowe could only use signs and make gifts. They
understood the name of the country to be *Wingandacoa,* when the
Algonkin uttering it had merely meant to observe courteously,
"You have fine clothes to wear." They believed the name of the
king, their new ally, to be *Wingina.* (And when this was repeated
at Court upon their return, Elizabeth herself was prompted by
Ralegh to call the land *Virginia*—he claiming it should bear the
name, in honor of the Virgin Queen.)

At the end of the first sound they came to a desirable island,
having a village with nine dwellings belonging to the brother of
the king. This island the Indians called *Roanoac.* The king's brother
was not there that day to welcome them, but his wife came running
out "very cheerfully and friendly." The surf beat heavily on the
shore, and the lady of Roanoke Island commanded some of her
people to draw the boat of the clothed men through the surf, while
others carried the visitors to the dry beach. She led them then to her
house, into the last of five rooms.

"She caused us to sit down by a great fire, and tooke off our
clothes and washed them, and dryed them again. Some of the
women plucked off our stockings, some washed our feet in warm
water. She her self set on the board for us to eate some wheate like
furmentie, sodden [pounded] Venison, and fish boiled, and Melons
raw, rootes of divers kindes and divers fruites . . . their drink is
water with Ginger in it and sometimes Sassafras . . . we were en-
tertained with all love and kindness, and with as much bountie
(after their maner) as they could possibly devise. We found the
people most gentle, loving and faithfull, void of all guile and
treason, and such as live after the maner of the golden age."

It may be that the appearance of the hunters while the Englishmen sat at meat led them to bestow such high praise. The hunters happened to carry in their bows and weapons, and this caused the watchful seamen to exchange glances and reach for their own weapons. Noticing this, their hostess was moved to quick anger against her heedless warriors, ordering their bows to be broken, and themselves to be beaten out of the gate again.

Nor was the lady of Roanoke at all willing to suffer the visitors to sleep the night in their boats, as they resolved to do. "She was very sorry, and gave us our supper, pots and all . . . and sent us five mats to cover us from the raine and divers men and thirty women to sit all night on the banke side by us." The women were assurance that no attack would be made on the honored visitors while they slept.

So it happened that after their survey of the sounds inside Cape Hatteras, Messrs. Amadas and Barlowe selected Roanoke Island as a most promising site for a settlement. It did not occur to them that the people of the islands had beheld them only as guests for a month, with gifts in their hands, or that the outer coast offered no safe anchorage in winter storms.

Master Arthur Barlowe added a postscript to his report: "We brought home also two of the Savages, being lustie men, whose names were Wanchese and Manteo."

Sir Richard Grenville Burns a Village

England rejoiced in that winter of 1584–85 at the safe return of the explorers with two lusty native Americans and a glowing report of Roanoke. It was a little like the exultation in Spain ninety years before at the safe return of the Genoese Columbus with his Indians from the new-found islands. To be sure, Masters Amadas and Barlowe brought back only some chamois furs, coral, and white pearls in the way of trade. But, as with Drake in 1580, they brought a new hope.

The shadow of war was deepening over England. With Spanish

forces stirring conflict in Ireland, and the invincible armies of the
Duke of Parma closing in upon the Channel ports of the Netherlands—with William of Orange assassinated, and Guise and the
League triumphant in France, this undeclared war had entered at
last the narrow seas around England. It seemed then that the English must fight as Harold Godwinson had fought at Hastings on
their own Channel shore.

Now the sea captains who had explored the American coasts
were drawn into the war council of those who planned and plotted
to strike back at Spain by sea. As Admiral of the Queen, careful
John Hawkins would have gathered the small craft of the exiled
Dutch, of Huguenots and Protestant Scots, to aid the English to
harry the sea routes of the Spanish Empire. Such an offshore
blockade, Hawkins held, could cripple Spain—at slight cost to Her
Majesty's treasury. But Burghley and the Queen put their trust in
compromise that would keep the peace.

Sir Francis Drake was all for striking at Cádiz, the great port
of Spain, and at the Panama isthmus, the arterial of Spanish treasure.
Yet the aging Elizabeth would not suffer the Queen's ships to leave
the Channel. The sea captains, watching their ships rotting in port,
tasted the dregs of defeat.

There remained the unpredictable Ralegh, high in favor after
his captains had brought home good tidings of the new Queen's
Land. Sir Walter Ralegh now, gleaming in gold-chased armor and
jeweled shoes, taking great Durham House for his home, wealthy
with the monopolies bestowed on him by Elizabeth, was friend to
all. The poet Marlowe, writing of *Tamburlaine,* called for the conquest of the seas by the ships of his hero—"Keeping in awe the bay
of Portingale, And all the ocean by the British shore; And by this
means I'll win the world at last."

For the dream of the far sea routes and the "British Impire"
still lingered in stubborn English minds. Marlowe was speaking for
his own people, not for a legend of Asia. Merchants of London and
voyagers of Devon put their heads together over the new maps, now
that failure stared them in the face. The "colleagues of the fellowship for the discovery of the northwest passage" opened their purses

again to send John Davis back to search for the passage Frobisher had failed to find. A way might be found to reach even the Sultan of Ternate, the ally of Drake. Was not Nova Albion waiting, on the backside of America?

Such plans verged on the fantastic, but Ralegh helped them all. Richard Hakluyt, called back from searching for maps and voyagers' reports in Paris, wrote out a plea for Ralegh at white heat. While he listened to the latest tidings of Arthur Barlowe and burned candles to finish his *Particular Discourse on the Western Planting* (settlement), unnamed personalities looked over his shoulder. Hakluyt, the scholar of the voyages, hardly framed himself the words he wrote of the Spaniard—"If you touche him in the Indies you touch the apple of his eye; for, take away his treasure . . . his bandes of soldiers will soon be dissolved, his purpose defeated."

Every page of the *Discourse* harped on the one thought that an English settlement in the west could thrive on the resources of the American forest and end the Spanish monopoly of the western seas. Shrewdly Hakluyt—or his prompters—argued, for Elizabeth's benefit, the cheapness of it. In the western planting the fur and food would grow themselves; the tall timber to be felled would cost not a penny. Hakluyt knew his voyages; he could quote from Verrazano and Friar Marcos how wine, drugs, spices, metals—even the drug *tobacco*—could be gleaned from the west. Every product England imported from Europe or through Europe could be shipped from America in time in vessels built from the trees of that far coast.

Now in so arguing the zealous Hakluyt proved himself a good prophet. However, when it came to planning an actual colony, he showed his ignorance. This being a novel undertaking for Englishmen, Hakluyt and his sponsors could draw only on the experience of the Spaniards in a different climate with a very different purpose. Therefore the *Discourse* urged the launching of a sort of Noah's Ark stuffed with all imaginable cattle, fowls, seed, and tools for the urgently required "western planting." Jacques Cartier would have smiled at such equipment.

Unwritten, there remained the hope of a rich traffic in pearls, and the chance of exploring for the northwest passage. (John Davis, the first scientifically trained English sea captain, was sailing to seek it.) Had not Verrazano sighted open water beyond this very cape of Hatteras? Might not the rivers of America offer a way through to Drake's port in Nova Albion?

Swiftly, by Ralegh's legerdemain, the ships were outfitted. They had the approval of Elizabeth because the voyage cost her nothing, and Burghley's consent because it seemed to be no overt act against Spanish power.

In May 1585 the seven good ships sailed. They carried back Amadas, and the lusty Wanchese and Manteo, with a mathematical man, Thomas Hariot, friend of Marlowe. Skilled Simon Fernandes piloted them again down to the track of the trade winds.

They sailed, however, to defend the realm of England by planting the first garrison and opening the first port of England beyond the sea.

Once at sea, the sea captain held full command. In this case he was Sir Richard Grenville, cousin to Ralegh, harsh disciplinarian and self-avowed enemy of Spain. Sir Richard remembered only too well the affair of San Juan de Ulúa, and perhaps his truculent mind dwelt upon the plans of the new fighting ship, *Revenge,* streamlined, deep-keeled to balance the weight of her forty cannon. Certainly he had not forgotten how he had been passed over for command of Drake's exploring fleet eight years before. He was not a man to forget, or forgive, a slight.

Being in command, Sir Richard detoured south to the islands in the heart of the Caribbean, the closed sea of His Catholic Majesty of Spain. Off the islands he picked up prizes; landing on Puerto Rico and Santo Domingo for wood, water, and any food within reach, he held courteous but armed parleys with wary governors of the Spanish Crown. He dug trenches around his encampments, built new pinnaces, and doubtless hoped that his hostile hosts who "gave him the looking and gazing on" would attempt another Ulúa onset. Nothing like that happening, he seized a group of noblemen in the Florida channel, allowed them to ransom themselves, and duly set them ashore at the Spanish forts whence Ribault's garrison had been evicted.

In other words Grenville, with young Cavendish at his side, used his colonizing fleet to carry out a thorough armed reconnaissance of the Caribbean. Briefly he reported as much, adding that if the Englishmen had not presented such a vigilant armed front "we might have looked for no better curtesie at their hands than Master John Haukins received at Saint John de Ulloa, or John Oxnam [Oxenham] near the streights of Darien, and divers others of our Countrymen in other places."

By this delay he angered Master Ralph Lane, Governor of the Roanoke settlement-to-be. Sir Richard retorted that by "playing the Merchant" in trucking and trading through the Caribbean he had acquired for the expedition "divers commodities, as horses, mares, kine, bulls, goates, swine, sheep, bull-hides, sugar, ginger, pearles, tabacco." Apparently also the downright Sir Richard managed to set against him the silent Portuguese pilot. Simon Fernandes came from the breeding ground of Atlantic navigators, Terceira in the Azores, which never took kindly to Spanish rule. Until then he seemed to have served the English faithfully. But after the Caribbean raid Fernandes caused mischief, nearly wrecking Sir Richard's vessel on one isle where he claimed they would find seals, and then running the flagship of Amadas on a reef off Wakakan. Grenville reported that the pilot was "deserving of a halter for hire."

Because of the long delay in the Caribbean, Grenville did not land the settlers on their island home until July—too late for spring planting. Then, while exploring the inner sounds, he gave the "loving" natives a taste of his discipline. Finding a silver goblet missing after a visit to a mainland village, Grenville rowed back in a small boat with Amadas and an escort to demand his property. "Not receiving it, we burnt and spoiled their Towne and corne— all the people being fled."

By the ethics of an Elizabethan sea commander this was a mild chastisement to inflict on "Savages" who had stolen a valuable article. But it gave the Algonkins a new impression of the clothed men of the sea who had come back to stay among them.

Promptly after that Sir Richard sailed for England with the fleet. He promised to be back the next April with supplies and reinforcements. Again he made an inexplicably long voyage, and brought a richly laden galleon as prize into Plymouth.

The Exploration from Roanoke

Master Ralph Lane, the General of the settlement, had more ability than René de Laudonnière. He had been summoned hastily from governing in strife-torn Ireland. At Roanoke Island he had Amadas to aid him, and loyal Manteo, who had been learning much about the English. The neighboring Algonkins, especially those of Delaware strain, were straightforward and friendly people.

Lane blamed Grenville's domineering—the buccaneering voyage out and the burning of the Indian village—for the failure of the Roanoke settlement. More justly he should have blamed himself and his hundred would-be settlers. These were mostly ex-soldiers and Irish Protestant exiles; they had been sent out to garrison a post. Like soldiers in any post, they proceeded to eat up their rations as long as the rations lasted; they put up shelter cabins; they felt no need of fortifying such a quiet island, and made no real effort to cultivate the strange ground. They had no women. Willingly enough they turned to exploring the mainland coast for exciting savage girls, better pearls, and—after supplies failed—Indian harvests.

Even zealous Thomas Hariot craved to go inland to find more specimens of the plants and animals of these immense forests. And anxious Master Lane cherished the hope of discovering a passage leading west. Inevitably they listened eagerly to the tales of older Algonkins, who wished to please their Christian friends. One called Menatonon told of a river rushing from rocky mountains, "near unto a Sea." The old father of Wingina described a great river flowing from the west. This promised much. Thomas Hariot thought from its description that it might have its source "from the bay of Mexico, or else from very near unto the same, that openeth out into the South Sea."

There being an abundance of rivers flowing into Albemarle

and Pamlico sounds, good Master Lane and his company spent
months in examining them and following as well the elusive trail
of the valuable white pearls which always seemed to come from
the native kingdom farther on. They discovered quickly enough
that the shallow, wind-swept sounds were treacherous waters for
small craft, and that the harbor of Roanoke offered no shelter
in a storm. That harbor, Lane decided, "was naught." Still, they
surveyed the northern coast for 130 miles, hearing of but not reaching the broad waters of Chesapeake Bay, "the lands of the Chesapians."

In so doing they heard of a far-off mine. It was a tale that the
ghosts of De Soto's cavaliers could have told them. The mine in the
mountains of *Chawnis Temoatan* yielded a soft, pale metal, "one of
the richest metals in the world." Lane did not call it gold, although
he believed the ore to be so rich that when melted one part in three
would be the precious metal.

They did not try to track down the *Chawnis Temoatan* that
year. Master Lane became aware of dangers that he had not sensed
at first. He feared, if they ventured farther, the uprising of "their
own Savages." He feared starvation.

When winter came, the English sustained themselves on bears,
oysters, and roots. In vain they tried to bargain for more food from
Wingina's people, who were living also on oysters and roots. Then
as so often happened, the parasitic Europeans took to raiding for
food—the Algonkins to withdrawing from the now-detested island
of Roanoke. Lane complained that the Indians, by refusing to sow
their fields, were bringing the English company to starvation. Nor
would the Indians repair the fish weirs in the streams, and the
English seemed unable to do so.

By mid-April the tension grew acute. Grenville had not appeared. The well-disposed father of Wingina died, and that young
chief, for reasons purely Algonkian, changed his name to Pemisapan
—perhaps because he had changed his feelings toward his unbidden
guests. "All our fear was of the two months in which space if the
Savages should not help us with Cassavi and *Chyni* and our weirs
should faile us (as often they did) we might very well starve, not-

withstanding the growing corn." In other words the settlers might starve before the Indian corn ripened for harvest in July.

It is clear that Master Lane and the Roanoke garrison suffered less from fear of the Indians than from dread of famine. Hunger sapped the spirit of the stalwart Englishmen more than it weakened the mentally resolved Spaniards. The officers and men at Roanoke had no misgivings about defending their post; they had to scatter, however, to attempt to fish, or grope for shellfish, or row over to the mainland for "Cassava and roots." Then Pemisapan's hostile folk destroyed the fishing weirs in the hope of driving out the invaders. Lane ordered his foraging parties to seize all the canoes of the natives, and this led to resistance and killing.

Except in the mind of Master Lane the English were secure enough. As always happened when armed Europeans quartered themselves on the natives, the Indians held to their own inner feuds, failing to combine against the invaders. Manteo's folk rallied to the Englishmen, and old Menatonon offered them the protection of his village. Through Menatonon's son (held hostage in the stocks by Lane) the garrison was warned that Pemisapan's people planned to burn the Roanoke encampment by a surprise raid. Lane dallied with the thought of abandoning his island and moving to a site on the coast among his native friends. Uncertainty and near-famine had disillusioned him about the desirability of the Virginia settlement. "For the discovery of a good Mine or a passage to the South sea, or some way to it, and *nothing else* can bring this Countrey in request to be inhabited by our nation."

On the first of June the famishing English broke the armed tension, and unwittingly decided the fate of the Roanoke colony. Supported by their Algonkian friends, they opened fire on Pemisapan and his people. It was a case of ambushing the Indians, who may or may not have come to burn the settlement. Wounded, Pemisapan tried to escape; he was followed and killed by an Irishman named Nugent, who brought back his head.

To alarm his antagonists, Master Lane spread the rumor that the relief fleet of the stern Sir Richard Grenville had been sighted off the coast. A week later he was startled himself by word from the outpost on Croatoan Island that they had sighted twenty-three sail bearing in. An armada of that size, Lane fancied, must be Spanish and hostile. It proved to be Francis Drake on his way home from his great raid on the Caribbean.

The arrival of the unpredictable Drake should have preserved the settlement on Roanoke.

Drake was in a mood to do his utmost for it. Had he not planned for such an English way-post as this in Nova Albion, on his route to the eastern Indies? Had not his courteous patron, Sir Philip Sidney, hoped to send him presently to plant another settlement on this American coast? Moreover the confident, practical Drake brought in with him spoils from the very coast of Spain, cannon and ransom from the Spanish officials of Santo Domingo, silver and furnishings from looted Cartagena, and artillery stripped from St. Augustine. Behind him—except for the Nombre de Dios-Panama arterial—he left the Caribbean terminals stricken. He had prizes and victuals to spare, although not too many men left alive.

But Sir Francis brought disturbing news as well. There would be war. An English expeditionary force had landed in Flanders to aid the Dutch. He had put to sea this time, not as a privateer, but as General and Admiral of the Queen, and he was bound to sail for England as speedily as he might leave worthy Master Lane.

This news disquieted Lane and his officers. Otherwise they had little to fear. With ample supplies being put ashore on Roanoke, with the harvests ripening in a month, and Grenville pledged to bring in his relief—Laudonnière would have held his post with such prospects.

While Drake anchored his fleet off the harbor—being wary of entering a bay exposed to the north winds—Lane and his people held council. They asked for much. For ships to ferry them home at need, for victuals to serve them through August, new weapons, lead, clothing, and tools—their own sick to be transported home by the Queen's fleet, while two masters and crews were to be left to man their new shipping.

All this Drake granted them readily. He made over to Lane

the *Francis* of seventy tons, with supplies for one hundred men for four months, as well as smaller vessels.

The relief stores were being landed when the storm struck Hatteras. It beat upon the barrier islands for four days. Drake's fleet wore away to gain sea room. *Francis* was lost with the shipmasters and crews allotted to the settlement.

When his surviving vessels returned to the anchorage, Drake came ashore, apparently undismayed. He offered the settlement this time a larger vessel, fully manned, and asked for Master Lane's other requests to be put in writing. He would fulfill them most willingly. The one thing he would not do was to enter that harbor or delay one day beyond need off that coast.

The storm had affected Lane and his garrison more than the seamen. One account describes how "for fear they should be left behind, they left all things confusedly—as if they had been chased from thence by a mighty army."

Lane himself reported that he summoned his captains and gentlemen to decide whether to accept Drake's second offer. And, although he was their commander, he shifted the responsibility to them. "Their whole request to me," he excused himself, "was that considering the case we stood in, the weaknesse of our company, the carying away of our first barke [*Francis*] with those two Masters and our provisions, by the very hand of God to take us from thence —considering that his [Drake's] second offer, though most honorable, yet not to be taken . . . seeing furthermore our hope for supply with Sir Richard Grenville, promised us before Easter, not yet come neither likely to come this yeare, considering the doings in England for Flanders and also for America . . ."

So Lane reported that his people bade him request Drake for immediate passage home. "Which request of ours by my self delivered, he most readily assented unto."

The embarking of these first settlers at Roanoke, in heavy weather and at the hands of sailors exasperated by the wait off the dangerous shore, was inglorious. "The weather was so boisterous, and the pinnaces so often on ground, that the most of all we had, with all our Cards [charts] Books and writings were cast overboard by the Sailers, they being much aggrieved with their long and dangerous abode in that miserable road."

If Master Lane had been more determined to carry out his mission the Roanoke settlement might have endured. Drake's fleet had hardly cleared the coast when an emergency vessel sent by the anxious Ralegh came in. This bark carried some supplies and the message that Grenville was on the way. Its master, finding the island deserted in apparent haste, searched the sounds without finding a trace of the settlers. Then, sorely puzzled, he put back to England with his cargo unbroken.

Hakluyt gives a brief picture of the arrival of testy Sir Richard with three vessels two weeks later, to discover the messenger craft missing as well as the colony. What that indomitable seaman of Cornwall thought is not in the record, but he made a prompt search. No natives appeared to enlighten him in the familiar, deserted waters.

"Sir Richard Grinvile, Generall of Virginia, not finding the aforesayd shippe according to his expectation, nor hearing any newes of our English Colony seated and left there by him anno 1585, travelled up into divers places of the countrey, as well to heare any newes of the Colony under the charge of Master Lane, as to discover the places of the countrey. But he found the places they inhabited desolate."

After deliberating the mystery Grenville decided that it would never do to lose possession of the country that had been held by Englishmen. Accordingly he put ashore on Roanoke a token force of fifteen armed men with supplies for two years, and returned to England to discover what might have happened in America.

On the way back he relieved his feelings and helped pay the cost of the voyage by raiding the Azores.

Thomas Hariot Tells the Truth

The ensuing winter of 1586–87 brought deep discouragement to the English explorers of North America.

Ironically, at the moment when they had mastered the difficulties of the passage across the seas, the struggle for possession of the seas frustrated their efforts. Wild Tom Cavendish had sailed with the faint hope of forcing Magellan Strait and proving Drake's route to the South Sea to be practical; no word had come back from him. Patient John Davis had returned from his second try at finding the northern passage between Greenland and America; he brought only surveys of icebound coasts where the Norsemen had left ruined churches; his Dartmouth backers lost heart, although Davis did not.

Bad news came from the army in Flanders, where the beloved Sir Philip Sidney was numbered among the dead; with him died his dream of reaching America. The clairvoyant Drake, who would have piloted Sidney to the New World, lost all interest in a western colony. Rumors told of an invasion fleet, preparing at command of Philip of Spain to descend upon the English coast. Drake prayed again for the Queen's ships, to strike at this armada gathering in Cádiz—careful William Burrough called it madness to take a squadron into a fortified harbor, against Spanish naval power.

Sir Richard Grenville, who had never forgiven the younger captain of Devon for supplanting him in command of the South Land search, accused Drake of uprooting his Roanoke colony—an unjust accusation. But the fiasco at Roanoke set heads to wagging at Court. Gentlemen who had never ventured to sea found it mystifying and amusing to wonder what one fleet was doing, carrying all the colonists home, while the other fleet searched for them in vain. Ralegh's enemies, who dared not jest at the Queen's favorite, the bejeweled Captain of the Guard, made his "Virginian conspiracy" their laughingstock. What had this promoter of the "new paradise of the world" to show for his efforts? His Master Lane burned incense in a stone pipe and blew out the smoke of this Spanish *tabacco! Virginia tabacco!*

Master Lane's own excuses did him no good. So he had been driven out by hunger and fierce Savages? The courtiers could laugh, with much reason. What then, they wondered, had become of those loving people of Master Barlowe's golden age? Who, then, was lying? Master Lane had charts, journals, and ore—but all, unfortunately, cast overboard in the haste of his departure? A most great pity, said the courtiers, and laughed. Truly his mine of *Chawnis Temoatan* yielded, instead of plates of most precious metal, naught but Turkey cocks and turpentine.

Worst of all, many of the captains, gentlemen, and soldiers of Virginia, anxious now to excuse their hurried departure, made much of their misery in the New World. Even Ralegh, worried by the failure and vexed by the ridicule, protested later that he had lost all of 40,000 pounds in the voyages. This was not true.

In these anxious months no man grieved more than Richard Hakluyt at the fate of his western planting. That untiring clergyman hurried into print *A Notable Historie* of the experience of René de Laudonnière in Florida as an antidote to the ridicule of America.

Thomas Hariot did more. The scientist of the expedition had kept his head through its alarms and excursions. Now he wrote out an honest evaluation of what he had seen—*A briefe and true report of the New found land of Virginia.*

In it he castigated the talebearers of the party. Most of them who professed to know so much about the new land, said Hariot, had hardly left the island. After they failed to find gold or silver, they thought only of pampering their bellies. Shrewdly he pointed out the effect of the wilderness on Englishmen brought up in towns: "Because they found not any English cities, nor any of their accustomed dainty food, nor soft beds of downe, the countrey was to them miserable, and their reports thereof according."

As to the country Hariot gave a cheering list of its "commodities" either salable or usable. Wine grapes and flax might grow scantily when wild, but could be improved by cultivation. He numbered off the furs, aromatic gums, and mentioned metals with caution. But he was confident of the abundance of foodstuffs when cultivated by the skill of husbandmen. An acre of Virginia soil, he thought, could yield two hundred bushels of corn or beans, whereas an acre in England would yield no more than forty bushels of wheat.

As to the "herb called Tabacco" he fancied it to be medicinal. Lighted and sucked through a clay pipe, the smoke "purgeth superfluous flem and openeth all the pores of the body," thereby preserving health. This effect of the smoke, he added, had been tested by men and women of great calling and learned physicians also in England.

Materials for housebuilding and shipbuilding existed there in a natural state. The natural people Hariot believed to be ingenious, with quick wit. And he came very close to the truth (after studying Cartier's journals) of the Algonkins' estimate of the Christian invaders. Because of the immense superiority of English instruments and tools these "natural inhabitants" believed the white men—who had no women with them—to be spirit folk with souls of the dead. Whenever the Christians stayed long in a village, some of the villagers died of unknown sickness. Since the supernatural visitors showed no evidence of sickness, the Algonkins attributed the ensuing deaths to their "invisible bullets." (This was a case of mild diseases of white invaders proving fatal to Indians exposed to them for the first time.) The religion of the natives Hariot thought to be a general veneration of one supreme God—so they might easily be won to Christianity. He noticed that when drought withered their cornfields, the people begged the Englishmen to have their God preserve the harvest—promising that the strangers could have a share of it in reward.

"Some likewise seemed to prophecie that there were more of our generations yet to come, to kill theirs and take their places."

His conclusion was that if husbandmen and workers, with sufficient cattle, were given a year's supplies they could feed themselves and thrive after that on the Virginia coast. They would have to cultivate the land. But they would have all the vast interior to draw upon, as the Spaniards had done elsewhere.

The Crisis of 1587

In these months Hariot and Hakluyt spoke for the dwindling group who believed in an American settlement. They were learning to face hard realities. The Spaniards in the south had found gold mines and a slave population to work them. No such mines or population existed in Virginia. There was no evidence of a western passage. (Their growing awareness of reality differed from the opinion of Master Lane.) They faced a "want of English means" to make another effort. Sir Humphrey Gilbert and Sir Walter Ralegh had failed. "It is a difficult thing," they realized, "to carry over colonies into remote countries upon private men's purses."

It was a difficult thing. The sea empires of Portugal and Spain had been built by government enterprise and sustained by the bullion of South America and the wealth of Asia. The impecunious treasury of My Lord Burghley could not aid the English explorers. The small Navy laid its demand upon all seaworthy vessels. Howard and Hawkins termed these wooden hulls "the walls of the realm."

Under such difficulties the "well willers of the enterprise for the inhabiting and planting in Virginia"—as Thomas Hariot called them—set to work with makeshifts. They rid themselves of many illusions. They finished a new map in Paris that May. Dr. Dee's manuscript chart served for pattern. In it North America assumes its true shape and size, for the first time under English hands. The mythical Sea of Verrazano has disappeared; the Mississippi is suggested. Nova Albion stands firm in the west, above a diminished Quivira. Virginia appears now on the east coast.

Although stripped of older illusions, this map dedicated to Richard Hakluyt bears marks of at least two stubborn hopes. Through Virginia runs the great river sought by Lane and Grenville, from a vast inland lake. (No European had set eyes on the Great Lakes as yet.) In the far blank spaces of the north appears the hazy outline of a *Mare dulce*—the open sea sought by John Davis.

Even while the map was printed—and Cavendish fought the winds of Magellan Strait—John Davis was at sea again, beating his way toward the northern route. Beyond the Arctic Circle with a handful of men in a twenty-ton pinnace he was on the course that

Robert Thorne had imagined sixty years before. Two barks accompanying him had stayed off the Labrador, to pay his cost by fishing.

Beyond Frobisher's landmarks, leaving the Greenland capes
behind, Davis forced his way above 70° north. Pumping his leaking
pinnace, he beat to and fro against unceasing head winds, edging
to the north and west until his provisions failed. He had to turn
back down the Labrador to the food in the fishing craft. But he
had been nearer the Pole than any European man of record had
ventured. He reported, "With God's great mercy . . . I have bene
in 73 degrees, finding the sea all open, and forty leagues betweene
land and land. The passage is most probable, the execution easie.
. . . Yesterday I landed all weary; therefore I pray you pardon my
shortness."

John Davis did not return to the strait that bears his name.

That spring Sir Francis Drake gained grudging permission to
put to sea. Before he could be recalled, he had his ships, half
victualed as they were, out of port and beyond recall. He took his
fleet straight into the harbor of Cádiz, to strike at the armada assembling there, and to challenge the power of the empire believed to
be invincible. Thereafter he held his famishing crews on patrol off
Cape St. Vincent until he fell in with the treasure-laden carrack
San Felipe, by which he paid the cost of his Cádiz voyage. He also
raided the point of Sagres where Prince Henry of Portugal had
watched the first navigators set out into the Atlantic.

By now the Spaniards told each other that "El Drago"—the
Dragon—must possess a magic mirror in which he could watch the
movements of their ships over all the ocean.

Drake returned in June eager to reëquip his vessels and seek out
more of the Spanish armada gathering for invasion. But he was held
in port again by the Queen's authority. Elizabeth, with many of her
Council, believed that Philip's caution would never risk open war
at sea. They were wrong. The solitary man in the Escorial had
overlooked the raids of the Elizabethan captains and had resisted
the pressure of the Guise faction and militarists of the Counter
Reformation to make an end of peace. Now something in his mystical nature had changed. It was not apparent outside the gray walls

of the Escorial that he believed himself summoned to take the lead of the Counter Reformation, to make an end of heresy once and for all. To do that, he was resolved to invade England with his armies.

Drake's preventive attack at Cádiz made it impossible for the invasion fleet to take the sea that summer. The quiet after June 1587 allowed the Spanish ports time to prepare a larger, apparently invincible armada.

For a dozen years thereafter the work of discovery by all European nations would be at an end.

Growth of an Idea

The legendary isles of refuge had not been found in the Atlantic. Although the new Hakluyt map still showed a *S. Brandan* off the Labrador, no voyager had sighted such a blessed isle along the rocky, spruce-grown shores; the Seven Cities of refuge had vanished into the pueblos of New Mexico. The lost Atlantis remained only in the name of the Antilles chain.

There was, however, the unmistakable reality of the new continent, with its hinterland unexplored. Seventy years before the saintly Thomas More had written his *Utopia*. He had imagined this better land to be beyond the farthest discovery of that time, beyond the river Plate. In a year of dearth and darkness he had pictured his Utopia—his *Nowhere*—as a land apart from warfare, free of the bondage of old laws, with "free liberty of mind, and the garnishing the same."

Then, too, he had imagined his better land as governed, not by princely powers, but by town meetings. Fantastically the inhabitants could educate themselves; burghers of the towns shared work with the farmers of the fields, living quietly without wealth of gold or jewels, adapting themselves to the natural conditions around them. It had seemed quite a fantastic, a Utopian way of life.

Yet there was a new force felt of late in Europe, wasted by

the internecine wars of the religions. Men were gathering into con- gregations; they were following pastors and priests. Merchants of Flanders and adventurers from Estremadura alike no longer hoped for new avenues of trade or treasures of silver; they sought to find again what had been lost. Now in devastated Louvain the book of Thomas More was being printed again and read by common folk. They found, perhaps, new meaning in it.

Not long since Sir Humphrey Gilbert had sought eagerly for a way to Cathay. In failure and in danger he had shouted his last cheerful assurance to Master Hayes that heaven was as near by sea as by land. He had called that from the afterdeck of the doomed *Squirrel,* sitting with a book in his hand. That book may have been Thomas More's, with the words "The way to heaven out of all places is of like length."

It began to enter the thoughts of persecuted congregations and impoverished townsfolk that the way to better things might lie in the Unknown Land itself. The thought had come to others before then. A wearied follower of Coronado had talked of the better land he had not found; swordsmen of De Soto returning to a civilized town had boasted of the great meadows and forests they had left behind them.

This wilderness of America might offer refuge to the defeated and the persecuted.

In France, bleeding from the strife of the religions, the far-off America was assuming a new aspect. With Court torn asunder and beleaguered towns stagnating no voyagers went forth to search for gold or a western passage. Instead the remote land became a dream world of the storytellers. The French fashioned it into a Utopia of their own imagining. Surely in remote times the lords of Babylon and Cathay had found the way into America! From the Indies and Quinsay ships had sailed the Strait of Anian to seek this new world. Why had this happened?

> Soit que le désespoir d'un peuple tourmenté
> De peste, guerre et faim . . .

Such suffering in Asia had driven people across to America, where their descendants survived in Florida and Canada.

The despair of the peoples of Europe, in hunger and in warfare, turned their thoughts to America. There was nothing remarkable in that. Ever since the day of Moses congregations who suffered had left their old homes to search for a better land. The French poets who sang that the Plate was another Nile spoke the truth. It was remarkable only that these people now seeking American soil should become a nation different from all others.

The Journey of Governor John White

When he sailed from Plymouth in May 1587, John White had 150 people with him, including seventeen women and some children. He had farming implements. Many of the new migrants were farmers or craftsmen, and all hoped to cultivate land in Virginia granted them by deeds.

This, then, was to be a colony, not a field force posted by a strategic channel. Master Ralph Lane did not accompany it, nor was any mention made of gold mines. Thirty-two Englishmen, including nineteen merchants of the city of London, helped pay the cost of the new venture to found "The City of Ralegh." Sir Walter himself, of course, did not go; nor did he allow Grenville to take the three makeshift vessels—the overage *Lion* and the fly-boat and pinnace, none of them armed for combat. Cannon and fighting craft, as well as experienced English shipmasters, were all required at home in the crisis of that spring. Still, it is strange that the three vessels were entrusted to Simon Fernandes, the Portuguese of doubtful leanings, as master. He was the last of the Portuguese to guide vessels to North America. By hard experience the English were learning to pilot themselves.

Whatever his abilities or failings may have been as a navigator, Fernandes proved that he could act the tyrant in command at sea. He sailed away from the small flyboat, leaving it to shift for itself; he prevented the colonists from landing at islands on the way to get salt, fruit, and sheep; finally he made his landfall far from

Roanoke, at Cape Fear—so named, apparently, by Grenville, who had endured a storm there.

As Governor of the venture, John White had planned to pick up the fifteen men of the garrison at Roanoke and then seek a site for settlement in the inviting bay of the "Chesapians" to the north. Fernandes refused point-blank to take the vessels on to Chesapeake Bay, and anchored instead off the familiar and dangerous Roanoke shore. And there they found only the skeleton of one of the garrison.

As if in warning the earth ramparts of the fort built by Lane's company had been overturned, but the cabins were still standing. Over them twined the vines of melons, planted with the last year's seed. On these grazed a herd of deer.

John White must have stepped ashore with pride. He had been an inconspicuous member of Lane's expedition; now he was Governor of Virginia, the Queen's new territory, with broad acres of forest and good riverbank to his name, and twelve assistants to aid his government, not to mention Manteo, loyal as an Englishman after making this second voyage with them. And White showed understanding of his greatest need—as Laudonnière had realized it. He must hold the friendship of the native people. Then he must move his colony of inexperienced workers away from the ill-fated Roanoke to a safe site inland, perhaps by old Menatonon's lodges. He must keep his distance from Spanish posts. Did he not have all the length of the coast to the Newfoundland fishing grounds to choose from?

The melons of Roanoke were ripe, the deer in throngs, the harvests ripening. While his craftsmen repaired the cabins and unloaded supplies, John White took Manteo to the Algonkin's home on Croatoan and learned from the friendly folk on that island what had happened to the garrison. Some of them had been killed by raiders from the mainland, in revenge for the slaying of Pemisapan by Lane's soldiers; others had fled in a boat toward Hatteras and had disappeared. Perhaps White took warning from this, and from the pleas of the Croatoan families for him to leave them their corn and to give them tokens to wear so that his people would not shoot them down by mistake with bullets visible or invisible. Such tokens proved to be necessary, because White himself, leading an armed party to take vengeance on Pemisapan's village, fired in darkness there on Indians before he discovered them to be Menatonon's families, who had come over to gather the fruit and grain of the village, abandoned by the enemy.

Then, too, John White had misgivings because the neighboring chieftains, summoned to council by him through Manteo, failed to appear. But by mid-August he was cheerfully inclined, writing as he did: "Our Savage Manteo was christened in Roanoak, and called Lord thereof, and of *Dasamonguepeuk* [the village on the mainland opposite] in reward of his faithfull services . . . Elenor, daughter to the Governour [White himself] and wife to Ananias Dare, one of the Assistants, was delivered of a daughter in Roanoak, and the same was christened there the Sunday following, and because this child was the first Christian borne in Virginia, she was named Virginia. By this time our ships had unladen the goods and victuals of the planters, and began to take in wood and fresh water . . . for England."

To add to this good cheer, the missing flyboat had come in with the remaining colonists, after finding her way somehow alone to the settlement on the unknown coast.

There were, however, two problems to be solved. After a storm almost wrecked the largest vessel, *Lion,* White realized that the colony had to move to a safe anchorage. And it must have more supplies from England in the lean months before the next harvest could come in. (Possibly Fernandes's action in preventing the collection of sheep and salt at the southern islands made this more necessary.) The assistants and all the colonists urged him to return in *Lion* for the relief shipment. White himself was determined to remain, to manage the move to the mainland. In the end he had to sail, at the signed request of all the settlers.

No doubt John White left reluctantly because it meant parting from his daughter and young grandchild, Virginia Dare. His memories of Roanoke were not encouraging. And it seems that after his departure the assistant commanders delayed in making the move to the river. Probably the Croatoans refused to leave their home, and the settlers depended for much upon Manteo's people. Then, too, it could not have been easy to make the inexperienced settlers leave their comfortable quarters. Exactly what happened at Roanoke in the next years will never be known, because no survivor was found to tell of it.

White had a hard voyage home, because Fernandes went by the Azores and lingered with *Lion* in his old home, Terceira. Going on in the flyboat, the anxious Governor wandered the sea, battered by storms, with his crew dying from thirst and injuries until they reached a coast unknown to them, which they found to be Ireland. Not until November 5 did he land on Cornwall.

He found England in a state of siege. The armada of Spain was manned for sea. In the invasion ports of the Netherlands the host of Parma waited to cross the Channel. All English vessels in the home ports were commandeered for the war.

Ralegh, kept at the Queen's side—she and the Council still put their hope in a last negotiation—could do little for the anxious John White, yet that little he did. A pinnace was readied for the voyage to Virginia, and Grenville agreed to take it across. Then he was ordered not to sail. Left to his own endeavors, White managed to release two small vessels and took command of them himself late in April.

But he could not keep the crews in hand. The English seamen detoured to look for prizes near Madeira; they fell in with Spanish or French armed vessels and took such a battering that they turned back to port.

There was time for nothing more. The great armada of Medina-Sidonia was sighted off the Lizard. The fighting fleet of Howard, Hawkins, and Drake beat out from shore to meet it, and from every port armed merchantmen followed. All the captains of the discoveries were in the Channel that July day—Frobisher and Fenton, John Davis and Grenville.

The battle for the mastery of the seas was not ended in a day, or a year.

Ralegh seemed to lose all thought of aiding his colony, yielding his rights to John White, Richard Hakluyt, and others, while keeping, with characteristic egotism, his patent and title as Governor of Virginia. Two years passed before White managed to find passage to the western continent. Then, in spite of Ralegh's name and his own payment for the voyage, he was taken as sole passenger by one of three vessels of a London merchant, which carried him on a long raid through the Caribbean before they consented to head north toward his colony. It was August before they sighted the sandy gleam of Hatteras, and three years had passed since John White had left the beach at Roanoke.

Watching the familiar cedar fringe of the islands, he had a moment of high hope when the smoke of a signal fire rose over the trees. The master of his small fleet allowed two guns to be fired in answering signal. The weather was bad, with a heavy surf running, and the seamen made much ado about landing except for water. Once on the beach, White left his oarsmen to dig for water. In the sand he noticed fresh tracks of Indian feet.

Strangely, this time he found the houses gone and a new strong palisade of logs standing around the settlement site. One log at the entrance had the bark cut away and the word "CROATOAN" carved on it. Again White was hopeful, because no cross had been cut near the word, and he had agreed with his people that if they moved elsewhere they would make a sign with the name of the place, with a cross added if they were in distress.

"We entered into the paliside where we found many bars of iron and suchlike heavie things thrown here and there, almost overgrown with grasse and weedes. From thence we went along by the water to see if we could find any of their botes, but we could perceive no signe of them, nor of the small Ordinance which were left with them."

The seamen showed White where heavy chests had been buried and dug up again. Around the broken chests White found his old belongings, books, maps, and armor spoiled by the rain. There was no other message.

"This could be but the deed of the Savages our enemies who had watched the departure of our men to Croatoan; and as soon as they were departed, digged up every place where they suspected any thing to be buried. Although it grieved me to see such spoyle of my goods yet I greatly joyed that I had found a certaine token of their safe being at Croatoan, which is the place of Manteo and the Savages our friends."

Croatoan's tip was within sight, out toward the sea. But the weather was thickening and the captain of the ships ordered the boats to put off without delay. They reached their vessels, but could not take off the heavy water casks. That night the vessels dragged their anchors, and White's ship lost all but one anchor. The sea rose under the wind. The captain worked his ship off the shore and barely cleared the point at Hatteras.

Once safe in deep water, they refused to put back to search another of the dangerous shores, arguing that they had little water or victuals. They would go south, the captain said, to supply themselves at St. John's in Florida, to seek prizes in the Florida channel. Under White's urging he promised to return to the Virginia settlement.

But the small fleet scattered in search of loot. White was taken back, not to Croatoan Island, but to the Azores, where he found the battle fleet of Sir John Hawkins waiting to intercept Spanish convoys. He never learned the secret of Croatoan. His daughter and the settlers might have survived somewhere with the people of Manteo and Menatonon, or they might have been slain like the fifteen of the guard by the enemies of the English.

There is a tradition, heard long afterward, that they were taken into villages of the interior, and that their descendants merged with the people there. But the tradition is doubtful, and no evidence of their survival was found after John White saw the word "CROATOAN."

The Captains and the Kings Depart

Sir Walter Ralegh said of his Virginia, "I shall yet live to see it an English nation." However much he may have hoped to restore the colony at Roanoke, this paradoxical man never willingly endangered his career at Court, with the wealth of his monopolies and the favor of the aging Queen. Even in later disgrace he retained his title as Captain of the Guard. When he did venture to sea, it was to gain new success, not to redeem an old failure. He sailed to the Caribbean, to charm the Indians of the Orinoco with his personality in a search for the mythical gold of El Dorado.

The Adventurers, as they called themselves, who sought to reach Roanoke had no means of doing so. John White had no more strength or money. Richard Hakluyt, "preacher and sometimes student of Christ-Church in Oxford," never lost his belief in America—although he hated to call it that because the detested Spaniards held fast to the southern continent that bore the name of America. Yet as he labored, collecting the narratives of the "warrelike and other shipping of this realme of England," he was filled with the wonder of what he chronicled. The obscure realm of England had become a sea power. A little more and it would be a sea empire. A little more . . .

Ten years passed between the defeat of the great armada and the death of Philip. For ten years even Philip's fanatical determination could not succeed in reaching England's coast with an invasion fleet, nor could the Elizabethan sea captains succeeded in preventing the bulk of the western treasure from reaching Spain through their blockade. This unremitting conflict filled all the areas of the discoveries of a century before.

It took its toll of lives from the coast of the French fishermen in Europe, where Frobisher perished, to the Gold Coast of Africa and the mid-station of the Azores, where Sir Richard Grenville was lost with *Revenge,* to Balboa's isthmus, off which John Hawkins sickened to his end, and Francis Drake did not long survive his last failure to capture the treasure portage of Nombre de Dios-Panama.

The struggle came to focus here in the Great Gulf of Christopher Columbus and the little discoverers. Because this was the source of the New World treasure, which alone sustained Philip's fleets. The silver of New Spain was like the blood infusion that kept life in a wounded man. The Elizabethan captains could not stop the flow of it. The coast of North America lay outside this critical area; as in Cortes's day, it remained unvisited.

No Elizabethan ship put in again to Nova Albion. The finest of the navigators, John Davis, was sent with the erratic Tom Cavendish and an ill-found fleet to try the transworld route of Magellan Strait again. Cavendish, starving off Brazil, seemed to go mad, and disappeared into the Atlantic. Davis, searching for him, fought the winds of the continent's end, feeding his crew on penguins and then on mussels until his rotten sails gave way. He brought his ship back to Ireland without sails, himself and the cabin boy being the only two able to keep their feet of the seventeen who still lived after two years.

The next year, 1594, John Davis put all his skill in navigation into a book, *The Seaman's Secrets,* in which he said nothing of himself. He invented an improved quadrant, a century after Martin Behaim devised the astrolabe of the first discoveries. Edward Wright devised a working method for the use of Mercator's map projection. The English had at long last mastered the "sea causes" that had enabled the Portuguese and Spaniards to chart and travel the seas.

By then, as the century drew to its end, the Elizabethan captains had rendered their country secure from attack, although their anxious queen was not aware of that. They had also made the North Atlantic an English sea, to be traversed at will to the American coast, although no one had the means or thought to do that.

There were four ways to Cathay. One, by the northeast passage, had been found closed. Dutch seamen released at last from the Spanish blockade of their ports went up to that Frozen Sea for whales. One, to the northwest, had not been found—although Davis had tried to reach the western end of that passage of Anian in the last years. One, by the southwest through Magellan Strait, the English abandoned reluctantly after the loss of Richard Hawkins and the failure of Davis and Cavendish to open it. A ship could not be victualed for the long ocean traverses while Spanish forces held the South America coasts.

Only the fourth way remained, the route of the Portuguese around Africa. And to this route the English now turned.

The war had opened it to them. Even while the wrecks of the great armada were breaking up along the Irish coast, Cavendish had sailed home from Asia after his swift circumnavigation, with his sails made of Chinese silk, and chains of Indian gold on the necks of his seamen. Wild Tom Cavendish had brought home charts of Malaya, maps of China, and tales of the riches of Goa and Calcutta. . . . English traders had got through to incredible India by land.

A veteran of the armada's day, James Lancaster, was sent with a survey fleet the way of the cape to India. The English ships could not supply themselves; their crews sickened in the strange tropics; Lancaster got to Ceylon, to the Malacca Straits, to Drake's rendezvous of the Spice Islands. He got back to England with twelve survivors, picked up by a bark of Dieppe in the Atlantic. The way was open to the unimaginable Court of the Great Mogul—if English ships could be supplied, as were the Portuguese by their chain of coastal bases.

The way was open indeed, for Portuguese power had become a shell, a semblance. No longer did they hold the gorgeous east in fee. Many of them, exiled, in revolt against Philip's domination, became friends of Lancaster; some exiles told their secrets to the eager Hakluyt in Paris. Certain fortresses of the way of the cape would be opened to the red cross of St. George—others could be taken. The great navigator, John Davis, surveyed the route in Dutch vessels, and the free merchants of London and other towns joined together, as their fathers had done in the Company of Cathay, to form the Honorable East India Company, in the year 1600.

America was not needed now as a way station. With the death of Philip passed the desire for a fortified point near Florida "to annoy the King of Spain." The old myths had been cleared away. Cipangu was no other than Japan at the far end of the East India Company's route; Cathay, it seemed, did not exist, except for the truly remarkable China.

In September of 1600 Richard Hakluyt ended his great chronicle of the conquest of the seas with *The Third and Last Volume of the Voyages, Navigations, Traffiques and Discoveries of the English Nation . . . to all parts of the Newfound world of America.* Yet the northern continent of this new world remained almost unknown, even to him. The names bounding it in his work read like a ghostly roll call of landmarks of the century's voyages. *Meta Incognita, Tierra de Labrador—up the grand bay, and the River of Canada, to Hochelaga and Saguenay, along the coast of Arambec* ["Norumbega"] *to the shores of Virginia and Florida.* On the west, or backside of the continent, stand Cibola, Quivira, and—defiantly— Nova Albion.

How could he know more than this? As the century ended, there was not a single Englishman or Frenchman who made his home upon northern America.

The west of the continent, however, Hakluyt in his last writing bounded with a new legend—*the 15 provinces of the kingdome of New Mexico.* This was not a kingdom. It was the incoming of Spanish Dominicans and Jesuits and settlers with families and cattle.

For Spain herself had suffered a change. After Philip's death the Hapsburg effort to maintain the vast hegemony of the Holy Roman Empire had faltered and ceased, although the structure of that empire remained. The wars of religion were drawing to an end. Spanish manhood, spent upon the far seas, in Flanders and Italy, reverted to its medieval dream, to the appearance without the reality of grandeur.

In Spanish America the Casa de Contratación still kept its records, but no conquistadors searched for new frontiers. The Spaniards of the haciendas merged insensibly with the native families. Life centered around the schools, cloisters, and cathedrals. This was not the hopeful social state imagined by the early sovereigns, Ferdinand and Isabella. It was the work of individuals, book in hand, carrying out a tradition of service. Out of it came the first blooming of the splendid Latin-American culture. So, in the end, the teaching of Bartolomé de las Casas prevailed over the demands of the emperors.

The war at sea ended with Elizabeth's death in 1603. Although Ralegh wrote of them and William Shakespeare mused upon them, no one was found to carry on the exploits of the Elizabethan captains in the far quarters of the world.

There was a weariness and inertia in those first years under James Stuart. In troubled Europe there was hunger and questioning, a gathering of the folk around pastors and priests. The new idea of migration to far lands filled the minds of men who seldom had titles or wealth. The thought of profit might be there as well, but after the experience of the last century men distrusted any venturing for gold or precious things. It seemed more possible that those who were idle at home could work and gain for themselves in a colony.

Three years after Elizabeth's death, little-known merchants of Bristol and London joined together for such a venture in the "Old Dominion" of Virginia. And toward Christmas, three ships sailed down the Thames. As in the vessels of John White colonists filled them. They were bound to seek the bay of the Chesapians. Although this might lack pearls or gold, it would be theirs to hold. They had heard it was like to a paradise, for growing things.

Instead of a City of Ralegh somebody said their new town should be named for the King, Jamestown.

Without attracting much public notice the three ships went down with the tide, into the mists of the sea.

AFTER WORD. The French Turn North to Canada

THE English colonists who left the Thames in 1606 bound for Chesapeake Bay might have found the French *fleur-de-lis* planted at their destination on the strange coast if it had not been for some rather unusual circumstances.

More than two years before their sailing three determined gentlemen of France swept into a deep bay north of the Chesapeake on a rushing tide. The three bore the Biblical names of Peter, John, and Samuel, and they liked all they saw on the nearest shore. The virgin land of *Acadia,* touched with the magic of early summer, appealed to the three in different ways. Samuel de Champlain, ex-soldier and sailor devoted to exploration, picked out a broad bay sheltered by an island as "one of the finest harbors I have seen along all these coasts."

He thought that a thousand vessels might lie there in safety. And he named it after his king, Port Royal. Peter—Pierre de Guast, Sieur de Monts, a Huguenot seeking a site for a colony, objected to the rush of the tide, but admitted the abundance of fir and birch for housebuilding. John—Jean de Biencourt, Sieur de Poutrincourt, Baron de St. Just—a passenger with the explorers, quite lost his heart to this bay with its friendly river. He felt at home in such a forest. This spot in Acadia, St. Just maintained, would be ideal for their New France.

With his usual care Samuel de Champlain ascended the river,

and agreed that the place was the best they had seen for a settlement. But he had noticed some dangerous shallows; he was not
certain of the native people hereabouts. "All of New France," another gentleman remarked, "is here upon our ship." It was important to make no mistake in picking the site of the first town of
New France.

They searched north along the mud-tinged tidal bay that they
called as a matter of course French Bay. They held a title to this
virgin coast, from 40° of latitude to 46°. With experienced eyes they
took the measurements of the waiting continent, with its wilderness and meadowland, its streams of unpolluted icy water and its
hidden dangers.

They were actually searching, that summer, at the 45° level,
in the Bay of Fundy, where Canada of today touches the border
of the United States.

"So many voyages," Samuel de Champlain would report to his
king, Henry IV, who had been Henry of Navarre, "and discoveries
without success—so much hardship and expense, have caused us
French to try to make a lasting settlement in those lands we call
New France."

Because they were determined to succeed, they had studied the
record of failure in the past, both French and English. Or at least
Samuel de Champlain had done so. A thoroughgoing worker, without means of his own, Champlain in particular had conned the
narratives of the voyages, from the quest of the Cabots to the last
arctic thrust of John Davis. At that time he was no more than a
young employee of De Monts—who held the title—and Pontgravé,
the merchant prince. He carried out the field exploring, and charted
the geography of their domain beyond the sea. He had no least
thought then of becoming the founder of that first town of *Quebec*
on the far St. Lawrence River, or of a French Canada.

Perhaps De Monts envisioned a new feudal domain of unlimited seigniories, and probably the Rabelaisian Pontgravé saw in the
venture a new fur empire. Being devout men, both Catholic and
Huguenot, they anticipated fraternizing with and converting the
Indian peoples—under military overlordship.

But at this point Samuel de Champlain—seignior only in name —was gripped by the mystery of the north. He saw in De Monts's settlement a means of finding the way through the north of the continent to China.

Such voyaging had been his inheritance, at the harbor of Brouage in the province of Saintonge, where the great pilot Alphonse had told tall tales of discoveries, where the vessels of Huguenot La Rochelle and the brown-sailed Basque whalers passed by. At the death of Philip and the end of the wars in France his uncle, Pilot Major of Spain, had got him command of a ship with the rare privilege of going with the yearly fleet to the closed sea of Spain, the Caribbean. There the thirty-year-old Champlain had observed the wealth and weakness of the Spanish terminals; he had sketched and mapped what he saw. And, sighting the Pacific, like Drake, from the Panama portage, he had worked out the plan of a canal to sever the link of the continents at this point, "to shorten the voyage to the South Sea by more than fifteen hundred leagues."

Whatever Henry IV may have thought of this project of a Panama canal, he realized Champlain's value as an observer. He had made proof of the loyalty of the Catholic from Brouage during the wars. He promoted Samuel de Champlain by a meaningless brevet nobility and the vague title of Geographer Royal, and gave him the hard duty of seeing what he could make of the St. Lawrence waterway, which still bore the name of New France on the maps, sixty years after Francis I had sent Jacques Cartier thither. In that year, 1603, Elizabeth of England died and peace returned to the seas.

Champlain sailed with a simple order to carry out—to bring back to Henry "a true report of what happened."

He found Cartier's landmarks much changed by time. Stadacona had vanished with its people. He wondered what had become of the town of Hochelaga—now only a cluster of bark huts. The truth was that compelling forces had changed this entry of the continent.

Elsewhere, above the Spanish zone, the visitation of the Europeans had made no change in the native peoples. The intruders had left behind them only scattered trinkets, and a few weapons, swine, and horses. Here at the mouth of the St. Lawrence the summer fishing fleets had maintained their contact; by degrees even the unruly Basque whalers had turned to the more profitable trading in furs. Marten pelts and especially beaver skins—since the beaver hat was coming into vogue—commanded higher prices in European markets than the earlier gleaning of wolf, bear, and fox skins. Indian hunters who had habitually assembled around the gulf in the summer brought their winter's catch down to tidewater at Tadoussac. With the years the flow of European implements into the tribes of Cartier's day—the strong Huron and Iroquois—had altered their way of living. Steel hatchets could break into beaver dams; brass kettles made a difference in cooking; steel traps caught fur-bearing animals that escaped the hunters. Apparently the Huron folk moved to other ground, or were driven thither by the stronger Iroquois coming in from the lakes.

So it happened that the Algonkian people now on the north bank of the river became partially Europeanized. They fell into conflict with the Iroquois nations, who in their turn sought the trading terminals to gain the European implements. And, as Hariot had noticed around Roanoke, the European mastery of the magic of steel, forge, and weapon making endowed them with great powers in Indian eyes. Gunpowder had little to do with it; a French seaman who could find his way around by a tiny metal compass, or start a fire with a fragment of glass, was unquestionably a superior being, akin to the tutelary spirits of the forest and fire. The Micmacs—"Allies"—in particular held to the French as protection against the Iroquois.

On their part the summer traders from Dieppe, St. Malo, and Rouen pressed farther up the great river to reach new areas of furs and the inland hunters. They were penetrating beyond the façade of the shore, following what would be called the "beaver frontier." François Gravé, Sieur du Pont—Pontgravé—the most ambitious of the fur entrepreneurs, sought to build a permanent trading post as far up the river as the Three Rivers. (Champlain came with the ships of this Rabelais of the frontier, with De Monts a guest of the exploration.)

Champlain did not, then, create the French-Algonkian accord, which he found awaiting him, nor did he at first seek a settlement "by way of trade." His mission was to determine what the river offered to his country, France, not to the fur traders, who wanted no interference from him or colonists. The traders sought only three things—beaver, whale oil, and cod.

In that first summer on the St. Lawrence, Champlain realized the importance of reaching the stronger settled people (the Iroquois nations) inland, beyond the scattered "barbarous tribes" of the coastal belt. He saw at once that European vessels were useless on the river routes of the hinterland, where the French must travel with the Indians in canoes that could be portaged around the falls. At the Lachine he marveled at the rush of water from the unknown interior. "I never saw any torrent of water pour over with such force."

He was not the first explorer to be fascinated by the mystery of the north of the continent, but he was the first to penetrate it a little way with the aid of Indian allies. From them he learned the river routes as far as Lake Ontario; beyond they believed he could reach a vast inland sea (actually Lake Huron). Some of them told him the water of this sea was salt (which is true only of the lower reaches of Hudson Bay). Giving only cautious belief to what he heard, Champlain realized that if the inland body of water proved to be salt, it might be an arm of the nebulous South Sea.

He so reported to Henry, on "the feasibility of discovering the passage to China without the inconveniences of the ice of the north or the heat of the torrid zone." On seeking that passage the young Geographer Royal had set his heart. He thought a station at Three Rivers on the St. Lawrence would yield advantageous trade with the Iroquois, but those powerful nations barred the way to the headwaters. It would be better to quest inland farther south.

De Monts, who took over the project of the royal colony, also favored the south as being free of the bitter winter cold of the Tadoussac-Three Rivers shore. Besides the astute De Monts wanted to seek out a new entry, free of the jealousy and claims alike of the merchant folk who had pioneered the St. Lawrence route.

The King of France desired a colony under military rule that would establish the French claim to the coast above the vague Spanish Florida. The grant given De Monts extended from 46° (at Cape Breton Island, the early landfall of the fishermen) to 40° (the latitude of Philadelphia today). Sully, his minister, believed that the coast above 40° offered them nothing, and observed that the treasury had no money to squander on a colony. To pay for the venture, De Monts was given a monopoly of the fur trade entire.

In this manner the ambition of Henry, the caution of Sully, the desire of De Monts for a warmer climate combined in that mild summer of 1604 to draw the ships bearing "all of New France" south from the area of modern Canada toward the United States of today. Samuel de Champlain merely went along as the trusted technician of the enterprise.

A ghost of an American legend also served to lead De Monts into the first great bay of the coast, Fundy. The year before, on the St. Lawrence, a veteran of the river trade had told them a tale of rich mines to be found there. The Sieur de Prévert, of St. Malo, swore that at the head of the bay they would come upon a "Port of Mines" of copper, iron, and perhaps silver. This exploring *Malouin* had good specimens of copper to show in proof; he had imagination as well, because he described how the precious metals were guarded by a monster *Gougou* twice as tall as the mast of a ship and hungry as well for human flesh, because the *Gougou* carried human victims in a belly pouch, to be eaten at will.

Samuel de Champlain dismissed the *Gougou* as a legend of his friends the Indians, but he had to investigate the story of the metal deposits. With his usual care he traversed the shores of the "Port of Mines" (now the Basin of Mines), finding some vestiges of copper and also learning from the Indians that Prévert had never ventured thither in person, as the man of St. Malo claimed to have done. The ships went on to search the western shore of Fundy.

There in a nest of islands swarming with magpies De Monts

chose his site for a settlement. He called it Ste. Croix (Holy Cross) Island. These war veterans, like Grenville and Ralph Lane, held to the notion that an island in this New World was safer than the mainland because it could be more easily defended against natives or possibly enemy fleets. Here they had a good anchorage, and plenty of brick clay, and timber on the adjacent mainland shore. They had fish and fowl everywhere.

Champlain approved. The warlike Indian people he believed could be managed as neighbors. They dwelt on the river the Frenchmen christened St. John. And this river, Champlain soon discovered, offered a canoe route to the upper St. Lawrence, and toward a lake unknown to him (Lake Champlain). By now he carried in his mind a hazy but fascinating map of the routes leading inland toward the undiscovered sea of fresh or salt water. So while De Monts had his people fell trees and plant wheat—it was lovely June weather—Champlain drew the plans for the first town of New France.

Their enthusiastic guest, St. Just, begged for a grant of the harbor across the great bay, the sheltered spot in Acadia that Champlain called Port Royal. De Monts, who had several hundred miles of virgin coast at his disposal, made no bones about bestowing Port Royal on his friend. They had been enemies during the wars of the religions, for St. Just had been an officer of the Catholic League. But here in Acadia there was a sense of a new beginning.

The patient tolerance of Samuel de Champlain was making itself felt in this undertaking. Aware of the difficulties and the mistaken notions of the past, the explorer of the Caribbean was determined not to fail in New France.

From the construction of the log fort at Ste. Croix he could spare time only for a quick survey down the coast that is Maine today. The Frenchmen knew it as *Norumbegue* ("Norumbega"), a name bestowed during Verrazano's voyage. Since he was careful to report only what he saw, day by day, Champlain gave no evidence of his own impressions. He went with friendly Micmacs, who led him up the *Pentegouet* (Penobscot). He found that and the *Quinibequy* (Kennebec) navigable only by canoes. But he pieced out more of the routes toward the unseen lakes; he learned how the Indians

kept alive and traveled in the deep snow of winter. And he banished
the tales—from the day of Jean Alphonse—of a vast city of wealthy
folk on the river of Norumbega.

When September gales made the outer coast dangerous, he
turned back from his inspection, intending to push farther south
in the next summer.

Champlain rejoined the settlers barely in time. Wintry wind
and snow struck Ste. Croix the first week in October. Before the
first grass and the fresh food of spring thirty-nine men of the
seventy-nine at Ste. Croix died from scurvy.

Such a death rate could not be endured. De Monts prepared
to abandon the ill-chosen Ste. Croix Island to search for a livable
site. At the first fair weather of 1605 he set out with Champlain
and a score of people in their eighteen-ton bark to explore the coast
to the south. They moved slowly, Champlain charting and sounding the way, past the shore of Maine of today, to Massachusetts. As
they did so, Champlain learned of a new route inland, along the
little Chaudière to the narrows of the St. Lawrence that the Indians
called the *quebec.*

They reached Cap Blanc (Cape Cod), white with its sand
dunes, and turned in to quest carefully along the shore, passing
what became Plymouth Rock and lingering long in Boston Bay.
After sounding it Champlain believed this could be a safe anchorage
for the largest vessels. In fact he expressed guarded approval of the
bay area as "a moderate region, very pleasant and agreeable." This
part of Norumbega had fine oak forests and fertile meadows where
Indian corn grew. The Indians themselves, a poorer sort than the
Algonkian and Iroquoian tribes, obviously had not encountered
Europeans at close hand before. They danced for joy at sighting the
Frenchmen.

But here Samuel de Champlain and his companions were at a
disadvantage. They did not know the dialect of the White Cape
people. Champlain and the Massachusetts chiefs resorted to ingenious pantomime. He drew under their eyes a sketch of the bay,
pointing out the landmarks. Where were the habitations of the
people?

The Indians placed pebbles on the sketch to show the situation of their villages. Champlain pantomimed the question—how much snow in winter? The quick-witted natives answered readily, by scattering sand on the ground, pointing to the white collars of the Frenchmen, and gesturing a foot above the ground. So much snow in winter.

De Monts seemed to be skeptical of the climate of this bay. Champlain, who judged native reactions well, believed the winter here would be milder than in their great tidal bay of the north. Where were rivers leading inland? Wide and deep enough for their ship? The Indians of the White Cape knew of no such river.

If the French bark had coasted south for another week it would have reached the mouth of the Connecticut, a little more and Champlain would have found himself in the broad entrance of the tidal Hudson, where Verrazano had found the country so promising. Champlain had Verrazano's journal, which gave no hint of the length of the majestic Hudson; De Monts held title by his patent to the coast well to the south of that river.

But there were clashes with the strange folk of the White Cape. The French had consumed most of the food stored in their vessel—they did not, like the Spaniards and English, attempt to seize the Indian harvests. As the summer waned, De Monts's anxiety for his settlers increased. He ended the probe of the south to make speed back to Ste. Croix.

There they decided to move the settlement over to St. Just's more sheltered site at Port Royal. And Champlain was kept occupied in planning the new habitation with the ground to be cultivated. In some way a remedy had to be found for the "sickness of the country"—the plague of scurvy in winter. From Cartier's journal he knew that a decoction of some evergreen branches served as a cure, but the Indian word for it on the St. Lawrence was unknown to the natives of the Port Royal area.

Held again to settlement building, Champlain prepared to stay out the winter at Port Royal, "hoping for a chance to make a new exploration toward Florida," while De Monts embarked on one of the ships that brought supplies from watchful France.

That winter of 1605–6 at Port Royal proved to be less severe, with beneficial rains that aided green growth. Only twelve died of the band of forty-five.

By the irony of fate Samuel de Champlain, intent on his southern exploration, never got his chance to search down the unknown coast toward Spanish Florida. First the rollicking Pontgravé, who wanted to voyage thither, fell ill; then the French bark, starting off too early in the spring, met storm after storm off the treacherous mouth of the Fundy, to be wrecked in the end. This ended the desire of the ailing Pontgravé to see what the Florida climate might be; his real interest lay in the monopoly of the fur traffic of the northern entry. On his part St. Just swore that he would keep his abode in his cherished Acadia if he had to settle there alone with his family.

Champlain himself helped defeat the scourge of sickness the next winter. The Acadians had their farm producing and a mill built; a witty newcomer, Marc Lescarbot, declared that the mine they needed was "waving wheatfields and grazing cattle." Under Champlain's driving they mobilized for the winter in the *Ordre de bon temps*—with a routine of good cheer, fresh food, and outdoor work each day. No more than seven settlers died, and Port Royal could endure.

That same Christmas the three English ships left the Thames to seek Virginia.

More than that, other English craft were questing along the strange coast of Norumbega. Champlain heard of one of them from his friends the Indians.

He might have returned to the White Cape, where he noted that the Indians were "better disposed than those of the north." Pontgravé might have sent his fur traders up the Kennebec to seek for a way around the Iroquois.

Then circumstances in France ended the prospects of their colony at Port Royal. The hostility of the traders from the French seaports, Dieppe, St. Malo, and Rouen, made much of accusations against the Huguenot De Monts, causing his patent to be revoked.

Merchants and courtiers at home proved in the end to be too strong for the explorers who labored in the New World.

Champlain worked to the last on his chart of the coast he was forced to leave. He never returned. St. Just alone carried out his vow to make a home for his family in Port Royal. After two years the irrepressible Pontgravé sailed back to his fur empire, up the St. Lawrence. Champlain, accompanying him as De Monts's lieutenant, selected a point on the river for their permanent station.

It was beyond Tadoussac, at the narrows where the little Chaudière flows in. He named it by the Indian word for the point below the rocky height, Quebec. From Quebec he believed that they might "penetrate inland as far as the Western Sea, and thence at some future day to reach even to China."

This he failed to do, as Christopher Columbus had failed more than a hundred years before him. But he found the way to the Great Lakes; he allied the French firmly to the Algonkian peoples of the north, in conflict with the Five Nations of the Iroquois, who turned thereafter to alliance with the incoming English.

The coast of Champlain's first survey became a New England, not a New France. Yet Champlain himself at Quebec laid the foundation for a Canada, along the great river of Cartier, still known as "French Canada."

By now the New World had been found, circumnavigated, and mapped—all but the still unknown Northwest.

To it through the coming centuries would migrate hundreds and then millions of men, women, and their children, from the Old World and Asia. They would merge together with the native people of North America to create one nation. That nation would be new, not only in its abode on the earth, but in its political form and realization of personal liberty—in its Utopian quest for such liberty to be shared by other nations.*

*That story beyond the boundaries of this book is told by other authors following the course of the Mainstream of America.

Note on Further Reading

More than twenty years ago I had hoped to write a story of the first discoverers of North America. But for more than twenty years my work had been in Asia, and I wish to thank the editors of the Mainstream of America, especially George Shively, Lee Barker, and Lewis Gannett, who entrusted this first volume of the series to a man who had no visible qualification to do it.

In turning to America I had no theories, prejudices, or any plan. I had one hope. That was to bring out the continuity of the early discoveries, and the exploration that followed to the time of the first successful colonies. For there is a continuity in the story of the discovery of the unknown continent in the limbo of the known world. Those who made the first voyages thither had no awareness of what they would find.

This book attempts to tell in some measure why those discoverers set out, what they expected to find, and what they did find, with what consequences to each other, to the Old World of their day, and to the still-undreamed-of United States of America.

I wish to acknowledge my indebtedness to the many specialists who have worked over the source materials upon which this book is based. Chief among those who have laid bare for us the genesis of America during this last half century I have relied upon Samuel Eliot Morison in all matters relating to Columbus, and upon James A. Williamson in his masterly clarification of the sea activity of the Elizabethan Age. Among the translators I have relied particularly on John and Jeannette Varner for their superb rendering of the main De Soto narrative. The list which follows may suggest books for further reading, mainly in English, which can be found in most good libraries.

GENERAL

Justin Winsor, *Narrative and Critical History of America,* Vols. II and III, Boston, 1884–88, for maps and source material of that day. Diego Luis Molinari, *El Nacimiento del Nuevo Mondo,* 1492–1534, Buenos Aires, 1941—summary and charts of the earlier voyages. Henry Harrisse, *Discovery of North America,* London, 1892—analysis and early maps to 1536, with notes on the pilots.

John Fiske, *Discovery of America* (2 vols.), Boston, 1899—a rounded narrative of the whole until the late 1500s as it appeared to his generation. Few such works have appeared since. John B. Brebner, *The Explorers of North America,* 1492–1806, London, 1933, gives an authentic summary. Arthur P. Newton (editor), *The Great Age of Discovery,* London, 1932—a brilliant discussion, confined in the main to the earlier happenings.

GEOGRAPHICAL BACKGROUND

Sir Raymond Beazley, *The Dawn of Modern Geography* (3 vols.), Oxford, 1897–1906—full, definitive background until the Portuguese voyages. George Kimble, *Geography in the Middle Ages,* London, 1938. E. G. R. Taylor, *Tudor Geography,* 1485–1583, London, 1930. Boies Penrose, *Travel and Discovery in the Renaissance,* 1420–1620, Harvard Press, 1952—one-volume continuation of Beazley's great work, helpful in spite of minor mistakes.

I. THE UNKNOWN LAND

Samuel Eliot Morison, *Admiral of the Ocean Sea,* Boston, 1942—a masterpiece, to be enjoyed. George E. Nunn, *The Geographical Conceptions of Columbus,* American Geographical Society, 1924.

Helen Wormington, *Ancient Man in North America,* Denver, 1949.

E. H. Sellards, *Early Man in America,* University of Texas, 1952.

Diamond Jenness, *American Aborigines,* Toronto, 1933, and *The Indian Background of Canadian History,* Ottawa, 1937.

Kai Donner, *La Sibérie . . . des temps anciens,* Paris, 1946.

William Babcock, *Legendary Islands of the Atlantic,* American Geographical Society, 1922. Edgar Prestage, *The Portuguese Pioneers*, London, 1933.

II. RIDDLE OF THE NEW WORLD

F. A. McNutt, *De Orbe Novo of Peter Martyr*, New York, 1912—translation of the Peter Martyr letters.

H. P. Biggar, *The Precursors of Jacques Cartier*, Canadian Archives No. 5, Ottawa, 1911—valuable records of voyages to the northwest until 1534. James Williamson, *The Voyages of the Cabots*, London, 1929. Harrisse, *Les Corte-Real et leurs voyages au nouveau-monde*, 1883.

The famous works of Las Casas and Oviedo deal primarily with the Caribbean and Central America, but Antonio de Herrara, *Historia general de los hechos de los Castellanos*, 1601(?), has much to say of Juan Ponce de León.

Frederick Pohl, *Amerigo Vespucci*, New York, 1944—good detail, rather enthusiastically presented. The earliest map making is summarized in Molinari, critically scanned by Harrisse in *Discovery*. Lloyd Brown, *The Story of Maps*, Boston, 1949, offers a pleasantly readable account of methods of navigation and charting, and Spanish regimentation of the new maps.

III. THE SEARCH FOR THE MIDDLE PASSAGE

Biggar's *Precursors* gives a vista of the records, while Hakluyt's *Voyages* of 1582 yields an English version of the shadowy voyages of this time toward America. L'Abbé A. Anthiaume, *Cartes marines . . . voyages de découverte chez les Normands*, Paris, 1916—activities of the French, chiefly Normans. Charles Bolton, *Terra Nova: the northeast coast of America before 1602*, Boston, 1935—carefree but fascinating account of real fishermen and legendary isles.

IV. THE QUEST FOR INLAND EMPIRE

F. W. Hodge and T. H. Lewis, *Spanish Explorers in Southern United States* (Original Narratives of Early American History), New York, 1907—translation of narratives of De Vaca, De Soto, and others. Henry Burrage, *Early English and French Voyages*, chiefly from Hakluyt, 1534–1608 (Original Narratives of Early American History), New York, 1906—account of Cartier.

H. P. Biggar, *The Voyages of Jacques Cartier,* Archives of Canada, No. II, Ottawa, 1924—critical examination by the chief archivist. Gustave Lanctot, *Jacques Cartier devant l'histoire,* Montreal, 1947—new material on the man of St. Malo. Ch.-André Julien, *Les voyages de découverte et les premiers établissements* (XV–XVI *siècles*) (*Colonies et Empires*), Paris, 1948—background and consequences of the French undertakings.

John and Jeannette Varner, *The Florida of the Inca,* University of Texas Press, 1951—the best translation of Garcilaso's story of De Soto. A joy to read.

V. THE FIRST FRONTIER

Narratives of Laudonnière, Alarcón, and others are rendered in English in Hakluyt's *Voyages.* Williamson, *Hawkins of Plymouth,* London, 1949—best work on the pioneer Elizabethan sea captain.

George Hammond and Agapito Rey, *Obregon's History,* Los Angeles, 1928 —accounts of the Spaniards after Coronado to 1583. Herbert Bolton, *Spanish Exploration in the Southwest* (Original Narratives of Early American History), New York, 1916. Henry Wagner, *Juan Rodríguez Cabrillo, Discoverer of the Coast of California,* San Francisco, 1941—story of Cabrillo and Ferrer on the West Coast.

For the mapping of the Pacific coast: Henry Wagner, *The Cartography of the Northwest Coast of America,* University of California Press, 1937. Lawrence Wroth, *Early Cartography of the Pacific,* Bibliographical Society of America, New York, 1944.

VI. THE ENGLISH TAKE TO THE SEA
AND
VII. UTOPIA AND THE NEW LAND

Richard Hakluyt, *Third and Last Volume of the Voyages of the English Nation . . . to all parts of the Newfound World of America,* London, 1600. The massive collection of the narratives from Master Hore and the *Mary Guildford* to the end of the conflict with Spain. Available in the reprints of Everyman's Library and the Glasgow University Press, 1905.

George Parks, *Richard Hakluyt and the English Voyages,* American Geographical Society, 1928—life of Hakluyt and lists of his works and English books of geography, 1480–1600.

James Williamson, *The Age of Drake,* London, 1938—concise summary of the motivation and accomplishments of the Elizabethans. Vilhjalmur Stefansson, *The Three Voyages of Martin Frobisher in Search of a Passage to Cathay by the North-West* (2. vols.), London, 1938. David Quinn (editor), *The Voyages and Colonising Enterprises of Sir Humphrey Gilbert* (2 vols.), Hakluyt Society, 1940. Sir Richard Temple (editor), *The World Encompassed by Sir Francis Drake,* London, 1926—reprint of what survived Drake's voyage, in 1628.

Biggar (editor), *The Works of Samuel de Champlain* (7 vols.), Toronto, 1922–36.

Francis Parkman, *Pioneers of France in the New World*—still the finest narrative of the Frenchmen upon our continent.

Index